European Monetary and Fiscal Policy

European Monetary and Fiscal Policy

Professor Sylvester C. W. Eijffinger

Jean Monnet Professor of European Financial and Monetary Integration,
University of Tilburg

Professor Jakob de Haan

Jean Monnet Professor of European Economic Integration,
University of Groningen

OXFORD
UNIVERSITY PRESS

OXFORD
UNIVERSITY PRESS

Great Clarendon Street, Oxford OX2 6DP

Oxford University Press is a department of the University of Oxford.
It furthers the University's objective of excellence in research, scholarship,
and education by publishing worldwide in

Oxford New York

Athens Auckland Bangkok Bogotá Buenos Aires Calcutta
Cape Town Chennai Dar es Salaam Delhi Florence Hong Kong Istanbul
Karachi Kuala Lumpur Madrid Melbourne Mexico City Mumbai
Nairobi Paris São Paulo Singapore Taipei Tokyo Toronto Warsaw

with associated companies in Berlin Ibadan

Oxford is a registered trade mark of Oxford University Press
in the UK and in certain other countries

Published in the United States
by Oxford University Press Inc., New York

© S. C. W. Eijffinger and J. de Haan 2000

The moral rights of the author have been asserted

Database right Oxford University Press (maker)

First published 2000

British Library Cataloguing in Publication Data

Data available

Library of Congress Cataloging in Publication Data

Data available

ISBN 0–19–877616–0

10 9 8 7 6 5 4 3 2 1

Typeset in Swift
by RefineCatch Limited, Bungay, Suffolk
Printed in Great Britain by
The Bath Press, Bath

Contents

List of Figures

List of Tables

List of Boxes

Abbreviations

ACIR	Advisory Commission on Intergovernmental Relations
BBR	Balanced Budget Rule
CAP	Common Agricultural Policy
CEEC	Central and Eastern European countries
CFA	Communauté Financière Africaine
CIP	Covered Interest Parity
CP	Commercial Paper
DG	Directorate-General
EAGGF	European Agricultural Guidance and Guarantee Fund
EBRD	European Bank for Reconstruction and Development
EC	European Community
ECB	European Central Bank
ECJ	European Court of Justice
Ecofin	Council of Economic and Finance ministers
ECSC	European Coal and Steel Community
ECU	European Currency Unit
EDF	European Development Fund
EEC	European Economic Community
EIB	European Investment Bank
EMI	European Monetary Institute
EMU	Economic and Monetary Union
EMS	European Monetary System
EP	European Parliament
EPM	ECB Payment Mechanism
EPU	European Payments Union
ERDF	European Regional Development Fund
ERM	Exchange Rate Mechanism
ESCB	European System of Central Banks
ESF	European Social Fund
EU	European Union
Euratom (EAEC)	European Atomic Energy Community
FDI	Foreign Direct Investment
GATT	General Agreement on Tariffs and Trade

GDP	Gross Domestic Product
GDR	German Democratic Republic
GNP	Gross National Product
HICP	Harmonised Index of Consumer Prices
ISMA	International Securities Market Association
MFI	Monetary Financial Institutions
mln	million
MMF	Money Market Fund
mrd	milliard
NCI	New Community Instrument
NDA	Net Domestic Assets
NFA	Net Foreign Assets
OCA	Optimal Currency Area
OECD	Organisation for Economic Co-operation and Development
OEEC	Organisation for European Economic Co-operation
OTC	Over-the-counter
RTGS	Real-time Gross Settlement
SEA	Single European Act
TARGET	Trans-European Automated Real-time Gross Settlement Express Transfer System
TEU	Treaty on European Union (Maastricht Treaty)
UIP	Uncovered Interest Parity
UK	United Kingdom
VAT	Value Added Tax
VSTF	Very Short Term Facility
WTO	World Trade Organisation

Preface

THIS textbook focuses on European monetary and fiscal policy in the third stage of the Economic and Monetary Union (EMU) as from 1 January 1999. It gives a brief history of European economic and monetary integration until the transition towards EMU. We then analyse the Treaty on European Union and the Statute of the European (System of) Central Bank(s) with respect to central bank independence and accountability and with regard to the policy goal of the E(S)CB. We also discuss the targets and instruments of European monetary policy and the relation between the 'ins' and 'outs'. The book analyses both European fiscal policy and the national fiscal policies within the EMU, including the Stability and Growth Pact and the harmonization of taxes. It also discusses the integration of European financial markets and the competition between financial institutions in Europe. Finally we look at the international role of the euro and the future of international policy co-ordination.

Our aim was to write a completely new and comprehensive textbook on the political economy of European monetary and fiscal policy based on the most recent and relevant literature. We have chosen a forward-looking view of economic, financial, and monetary integration. Throughout the whole book we try to explain to the reader the framework of monetary and fiscal policy in Europe through a blend of institutional characteristics, empirical evidence, and modern theoretical considerations. The last were incorporated in the various chapters with (very) simple, stripped models in order to clarify the economic intuition to the reader. Practitioners may be able to read the book by skipping these stripped models. We have written the book, in the first instance, for second- or third-year undergraduate students of international economics and finance, international business, economic and monetary integration, European economics, and European studies. Whilst writing the book and inviting comments from colleagues we discovered that our work may have a wider potential readership, including central bankers and other policy-makers, bankers and financial analysts, and economists and political scientists interested in the present framework of European monetary and fiscal policy. We hope that the reader will enjoy our book in the same way that we have enjoyed writing it.

In the different stages of preparing this first edition, we have benefited from the support of many of our colleagues. First of all, we acknowledge the comments of the four reviewers, who were as enthusiastic as we were and gave us very useful suggestions. We would also like to thank the Center of Economic Studies of the University of Munich and, in particular, Hans-Werner Sinn and Helge Berger for the generous hospitality offered to us as CES visitors in January 1999 which kick-started the book. We also owe a lot to the criticism of colleagues who commented on versions of the manuscript. We are especially grateful to Ivo Arnold, Helge Berger, Steven Brakman, Marco Hoeberichts, Lex Hoogduin, Harry Huizinga, Flip de Kam, Ger Lanjouw, Jan Lemmen, Günther Opperman, Elmer Sterken, Dirk Strijker, Willem Verhagen, and Els Wester for their comments. We also express our thanks to the students in Groningen, Munich, and Tilburg for their very helpful reactions to a first draft of the book. Finally, we thank our respective partners for being so patient with us.

Oisterwijk/Groningen   S.C.W.E.
1999   J.deH.

Introduction

Aᴛ the stroke of midnight on 1 January 1999 11 European Union (EU) countries launched a single currency, the euro. For the first time since the Roman Empire, a large portion of Europe now shares a common currency.[1] The euro is used for electronic financial and business transactions, but euro coins and banknotes will not be issued until January 2002. Until then, national coins and notes will be used for non-electronic payments. Still, consumers can already have euro-denominated bank accounts.

The launch of the euro has created the world's second largest single currency area in terms of economic size after the Unites States. The euro area accounts for some 15 per cent of global GDP with a total population of 292 million. Not so long ago, the idea of merging the EU's national monetary systems seemed fantastic. Nevertheless, a plan for doing so was drawn up. Then, with the ink of this blueprint hardly dry, the forerunner of the single currency, the Exchange Rate Mechanism (ERM) of the European Monetary System (EMS), almost collapsed, casting doubt on the prospects of the project. Indeed, sometimes EMU was perceived as an ambitious project that would never fly, just like the emu, the large Australian bird. Still, the European governments carried on. With the start of the European Economic and Monetary Union (EMU) in January 1999 their vision became reality.

At the start of EMU the irrevocable conversion rates for the euro were adopted (see Box 1). This implies that the currencies of the participating countries also have a fixed relationship. The various national currencies can be regarded as expressions of the euro. Participating countries no longer have their own monetary policy. Instead, decisions about interest rates will be taken by the European Central Bank (ECB). Together with national central banks, the ECB is part of the European System of Central Banks (ESCB). While the ECB is responsible for policy decisions, national central banks play a role in implementing monetary policy.[2]

At the launch of the euro, predictions about what has been dubbed 'euroland' were mixed. Supporters say the unprecedented switch to a single currency will benefit business and consumers alike. But critics warn that EMU is a giant leap into the unknown. Some observers fear that the currency is arriving without enough popular support. And some critics have pointed out that few examples exist of sovereign countries successfully sharing a single currency that lasts. The purpose of this book is to bring together and to assess the available evidence to date about EMU, focusing on European monetary and fiscal policy.

---

[1] At the time of writing, four EU member states do not (yet) fully participate in EMU: Denmark, Greece, the UK, and Sweden. Still, it is expected that at some time these countries will also use the euro, as will some potential future EU member countries in Central and Eastern Europe.

[2] The central banks of the member states that do not participate in the euro area are members of the ESCB with a special status. They are allowed to conduct their respective monetary policies, but they do not take part in the decision-making for the single monetary policy for the euro area and the implementation of such decisions.

Box 1 Euro Conversion Rates

1 euro equals:

40.3399	Belgian francs	1.95583	German marks
166.386	Spanish pesetas	6.55957	French francs
0.787564	Irish punt	1936.27	Italian lire
40.3399	Luxembourg francs	2.20371	Dutch guilders
13.7603	Austrian schillings	200.482	Portuguese escudos
5.94573	Finnish marka		

Source: ECB, *Monthly Bulletin* (Jan. 1999).

EMU is not like manna from heaven: it has quite a long history. The following chapter highlights the coming into being of the euro. Special attention is paid to EMU's predecessor, the EMS. Chapter 1 also briefly discusses the economic costs and benefits of a monetary union.

Chapters 2 and 3 deal with the ESCB. Chapter 2 analyses its independence and accountability, while in Chapter 3 the monetary policy strategy of the ECB and its instruments are discussed. The following two chapters are about fiscal policy. Chapter 4 deals with national fiscal policy in EMU, while Chapter 5 presents the main issues on the European budget. We will discuss in Chapter 4 whether it is necessary to restrict budgetary policies of member countries in a monetary union through rules like the Stability and Growth Pact. Harmonization of taxes is also taken up. Chapter 5 deals with the need for a European stabilization policy and with (reform of) the European budget.

The final chapters deal with European financial markets and the international role of the euro, respectively. Monetary union in Europe has often been regarded as the inescapable and beneficial consequence of the elimination of capital controls and the development of the EMS to a system of almost fixed exchange rates. It is therefore important in a book like this to analyse the integration of financial markets, notably money markets. Chapter 6 also deals with differences in financial market structure in the EU member states. This is an important issue as differences in financial market structure may lead to asymmetries in monetary transmission. An important question is whether existing differences will disappear due to financial market integration.

Proponents of EMU often argue that the euro may become as important as the US dollar, thereby making the international monetary system more symmetric. Chapter 7 discusses the arguments and evidence to date on this issue. It also addresses the possible consequences of the international position of the euro for international policy co-ordination.

Chapter 1
European Monetary Integration

Introduction

IN December 1991 the member states of the European Union (EU) adopted the Treaty on European Union, usually called the Maastricht Treaty after the city where the summit took place. The Maastricht Treaty arranged for an Economic and Monetary Union in Europe (EMU), which ultimately started in 1999.

EMU has quite a long history (section 1.1). During the initial phase of European integration, the emphasis was on economic integration. It was only at the end of the 1960s that the issue of monetary integration was put high on the political agenda. A detailed proposal for a monetary union by the Werner Committee faltered, however, with the demise of the Bretton Woods system. At the end of the 1970s the European Monetary System (EMS) was created, which was an important step towards monetary integration. The main features of the EMS are sketched in section 1.2.

The founding fathers of European economic integration considered it as a means to avoid new conflicts between the European contenders of the Second World War. Indeed, various observers believe that EMU was also primarily motivated by political considerations as it is thought to further political integration. Apart from political motivations, there may be economic reasons for monetary integration as well. Those who travel a lot know how cumbersome (and costly) it is that various countries have their own currency. After the (full) introduction of a common currency one can pay with the same money throughout the euro area. However, a common currency brings not only benefits: there are costs involved as well. Section 1.3 offers a review of the costs and benefits of monetary integration. The final part of the chapter deals with the transition process towards EMU.

1.1 Origins of European Monetary Integration

THE integration of Europe was proposed as early as the fourteenth century, but it was not until the period of reconstruction following the Second World War that the idea was put into practice. After the war most European countries faced enormous physical destruction. Nevertheless, by the end of 1948 pre-war production levels had been attained. During this relatively short period of reconstruction the foundations were laid for European economic integration. The United States played an important role in this regard. Money provided through the Marshall plan was conditional on the co-operation of the European countries. This resulted in the *Organisation for European Economic Co-operation* (OEEC) in 1948—later to be transformed as the OECD (Organisation for Economic Co-operation and Development)—and the *European Payments Union* (EPU) in 1950. The EPU was designed to multilateralize trade and payments in Western Europe. This was necessary as European trade in the late 1940s was mainly conducted through bilateral trade agreements (Berger and Ritschl 1995).

The next step in the European economic integration process was the Schuman plan of May 1950. It was named after the French foreign minister Robert Schuman, but had in fact been elaborated by Jean Monnet. The plan foresaw the establishment of a *European Coal and Steel Community* (ECSC). It was very much inspired by political considerations as the ECSC was seen as the basis for Franco-German reconciliation. The principal concern of the plan was with ensuring that reconstruction in the western part of Germany should not endanger peace. That is why the ECSC aimed at the integration of two sectors which were at the time considered to be of central importance for the defence industry. The plan was also welcomed by Germany, as it regained at least some control over its heavy industries that had been under allied control after the Second World War (Bulmer 1994). The main objective of the ECSC was the elimination of barriers and the encouragement of competition in the sectors of coal and steel.

The ECSC was in many ways characteristic of the European integration process of the years ahead. First, its membership was limited: Only Belgium, Germany, France, Italy, Luxembourg, and the Netherlands were members of the ECSC. The UK and various other European countries remained outside the organization. It was only in 1973 that Denmark, Ireland, and the UK joined what was then called the European Community (EC), to be followed by Greece (1981), Spain and Portugal (1986). Austria, Finland, and Sweden became members in 1995. Only with the collapse of communism at the end of the 1980s did the possibility of the membership of Eastern and Central-European countries become an issue. Second, although it seemed to be based on free market principles, the ECSC implied much government intervention. Over time, the balance in the EC has swung more in the direction of a free market, but certain policy areas (for example, the Common Agricultural Policy) are still characterized by strong government involvement. Third, much of the organizational structure of the EU as we know it today (see Box 2) goes back to the ECSC. For instance, the High Authority, the ECSC's supranational executive organ, was the predecessor of the European Commission. The first president of the High Authority was Jean Monnet. Other institutions of the ECSC were: the Council of Ministers (representing member governments), the Assembly (composed of sixty-eight delegates from the national parliaments, later transformed in the European Parliament), and the European Court of Justice.

With the ratification of the Treaty of Rome in 1958 the *European Economic Community* (EEC) and the *European Atomic Energy Community* (Euratom) came into being. Of the three communities, the EEC was by far the most important and far reaching in terms of scope and instruments.[1] Although the Treaty aims at the creation of a *common market* (that is, an economic area with free movements of goods, services, labour, and capital), actual policies aimed primarily at the abolition of tariffs and quotas. The Treaty of Rome is distinctly more market-oriented than the Treaty of Paris (1951), which established the ECSC. Still, there were various areas in which government intervention remained very important. The most notable one was agriculture which at the time represented more than one-fifth of the total labour force of the member countries (Tsoukalis 1997). Initially, the Common Agricultural Policy was directed towards establishing minimum prices for a range of agricultural products (see section 5.1 for further details).

As far as monetary issues are concerned, the Rome Treaty described exchange rate policies as a matter of 'common concern', but did not offer substantive contents as to its meaning. It was only at the summit in 1969 in The Hague that the European governments agreed on an economic and monetary union. Pierre Werner, prime minister of Luxembourg, was appointed to chair a committee that was to draw up a plan. The Werner Report was completed in 1970. It called for the completion of a monetary union by 1980. The Werner Committee proposed a three-stage approach towards monetary union, leading eventually to fixed exchange rates and a common monetary policy. The report was rather vague as to how the central monetary authority in charge of the common monetary policy should be constituted.

Although the Council of Ministers adopted the proposals, the turmoil at the currency markets at the time made the plan falter. One of its few elements that survived was the so-called 'snake in the tunnel' arrangement. This reduced bilateral exchange rate fluctuations of the participating currencies to a narrow band (that is, plus or minus 2.25 per cent from the central rate). It was called 'snake in the tunnel' because it made the participating currencies move together within the wider 4.5 per cent band established for the US dollar by the Smithsonian Agreement of 1971. Under the latter agreement, two EC currencies would have been able to move by up to 9 per cent against each other, which was considered incompatible with the functioning of the common market (Gros and Thygesen 1998). However, the 'snake' was not very successful in limiting exchange rate fluctuations.

---

[1] The three communities were merged in 1967. Since then, one often referred to the European Communities, later to be changed into the *European Community* (EC). Since the Maastricht Treaty one generally refers to the European Union.

Box 2 The Institutions of the European Union

The structure of the EU comprises three supranational institutions that are independent of national governments, namely: the European Commission, the European Parliament, and the European Court of Justice. The *European Commission* is the executive body of the European Union. It also initiates legislation by making proposals and recommendations to the Council of Ministers which represents the member countries. The Commission consists of twenty members, appointed by the national governments for five years. However, they are expected to detach themselves from national interests. The five large member countries have two commissioners. The apparatus of the Commission is divided into directorates-general (DGs), which deal with specific policy areas.

The role of the *European Parliament* (EP), which since 1979 is elected by the people of the EU member countries in direct elections every five years, is limited. It has the power to dismiss the Commission. It also has the right to reject the EU Budget. Legislation is routed via the EP, which may go through different procedures. Under the consultation procedure the EP only gives its opinion. Under the co-operation procedure the EP has the right to amend or even reject legislation, but these decisions may be overruled by the Council. Under the co-decision procedure rejection by the EP can kill legislation. Since the Maastricht Treaty the last procedure applies to fifteen areas, but some of these were formerly subject to the co-operation procedure (see Goodman 1996 for further details).

The *European Court of Justice* (ECJ) consists of fifteen judges and nine advocates-general. Judgments of the ECJ on matters relating to the interpretation and application of European law have been of great importance for the operation of the EC. As the supreme court of the EU, the ECJ gives a coherent and uniform interpretation of Community law and ensures compliance by the member states. The *Council* consists of ministers of the member countries. Decision-making in the Council is on the basis of either unanimity or qualified majority, depending on the issue at hand. In case of a qualified majority, countries have a different number of votes. Germany, France, Italy, and the UK cast ten votes; Spain eight; Belgium, Greece, the Netherlands, and Portugal five; Austria and Sweden four; Denmark, Finland, and Ireland three, while Luxembourg has two votes. A qualified majority requires 62 out of 87 votes. When the Council meetings comprise ministers of economics or finance, it is known as *Ecofin*. Since its establishment in 1974 the *European Council* has become a very powerful body. Comprised of the French president, the government heads, the ministers of foreign affairs, and the President and one Vice-President of the European Commission, it has had a hand in all major decisions.

The mid-1970s can be characterized as a low point in European monetary integration. The Marjolin Committee, which was asked to review the prospects for achieving EMU in 1980, was very clear: 'Europe is no nearer to EMU than in 1969. In fact, if there has been any movement it has been backward' (cited in Gros and Thygesen 1998: 20).

The situation changed at the end of the 1970s when the French president Valéry Giscard d'Estaing and the German Chancellor Helmut Schmidt took the initiative for the European Monetary System (EMS). The aim of the EMS was to create a 'zone of monetary stability' in Europe (see section 1.2).

During the 1980s the discussion focused again on EMU. No doubt the signing of the Single European Act (SEA) in 1986 and the commitment to complete the internal market by 1992 were important in furthering EMU. Initially regarded as rather modest in nature, the SEA succeeded in developing renewed momentum for European integration, not least by establishing a clear deadline for completion of the internal market. It was argued that in order to reap the full gains from the internal market, exchange rate risks and transaction costs were to be banished. This view is apparent from the title of an important study by the European Commission: *One Market, One Money* (Emerson, *et al.* 1992). Although many economists do not subscribe to the view that fixed exchange rates are needed to capture the gains from the Single Market (see, for example, Kenen 1995), the argument gained popularity under policy-makers.

Another important consideration, in some European countries at least, was the dissatisfaction with the German dominance in the EMS (see section 1.2). A monetary union was considered the proper answer to this problem. At the Hannover summit in June 1988 the European Council decided to establish a committee that should propose concrete stages leading to EMU. The committee was chaired by Jacques Delors, the President of the European Commission at the time. By June 1989 the committee had already presented its report. Although it did not offer a specified timetable, the committee proposed a gradual process towards EMU, eventually leading to entirely fixed exchange rates. The first stage would involve a concerted effort to co-ordinate national monetary policies. In stage two, the exchange rates of currencies destined to enter the monetary union would not be realigned save 'in exceptional circumstances'. With stage three would come a single currency under a new central bank's authority. According to the Delors Report, under permanently fixed exchange rates 'there would be a need for a common monetary policy, which would be carried through new operating procedures . . . This shift from national monetary policies to a single monetary policy is an inescapable consequence of monetary union and constitutes one of the principal institutional changes' (paragraph 24). Although not strictly necessary for the creation of a monetary union, the Delors Committee argued in favour of a single currency as this 'would clearly demonstrate the irreversibility' of the monetary union (paragraph 23).

Subsequent negotiations eventually led to the Maastricht Treaty, establishing EMU (see Box 3 for a chronology). Many of the suggestions of the Delors Committee found their way into the Treaty. As suggested in the Delors Report, the first stage of EMU had already started at 1 July 1990 with the liberalization of capital controls (see section 6.1 for further details).

Ratification of the Treaty turned out to be difficult. Denmark rejected the Maastricht Treaty at a referendum in June 1992. The rejection, with a slight majority, came as a huge shock. For the time being, the other countries proceeded with their own ratification, shelving the Danish problem until later. In the end, the problem was solved at the European Council meeting in Edinburgh in December 1992. Denmark declared that it would not participate in the third stage of EMU and that it would not participate in the common defence policy. On this basis, a new referendum was called in May 1993, and the Danish voters now voted in favour with a modest majority (Szász 1999).

In France, where the Maastricht Treaty was put to a referendum after the Danes initially had said no, the majority in favour was a wafer-thin 51 per cent. Ratification was tortuous and contentious in other countries too. The growing anti-Maastricht sentiment in Germany was reflected in a number of appeals to the Federal Constitutional Court alleging that the Treaty violated the German constitution. It was only after the Court ruled that this was not the case that Germany could deposit the instruments of ratification, being the last member to do so, and thus enabling the Treaty to come into force on 1 November 1993 (ibid.).

Perspectives for EMU became dim with the currency crises in 1992/93 (section 1.2). Many sceptics asked what hope there could be for a monetary union among countries unable to keep national currencies aligned. For instance, the prime minister of the UK, John Major, wrote in *The Economist* that continuing 'to recite the mantra of full economic and monetary union . . . will have all the quaintness of a rain dance and about the same potency'. Although the currency crises for some time led to lingering doubts, with the start of the second stage of EMU on 1 January 1994 it became clear that EMU was becoming more and more likely.

From an economic perspective there are pros and cons for a monetary union. Before we turn to the costs and benefits of a monetary union, we will discuss the European Monetary System, as this is widely considered to be the predecessor of EMU.

1.2 The European Monetary System: Phases and Crises

1.2.1 Development of the EMS

After the other European countries had endorsed the initiative of the French President Giscard d'Estaing and the German Chancellor Schmidt, the European Monetary System started in March 1979. The cornerstone of the EMS was the Exchange Rate Mechanism (ERM). Although frequently used as synonyms, the EMS and the ERM have to be carefully distinguished. For one thing, all EU member countries were part of the EMS, but not all countries participated (all of the time) in the ERM. Furthermore, the EMS was more complex than the ERM. It also implied the birth of the *European Currency Unit* (ECU). The ECU was a basket of EMS currencies, with the weight of each currency depending on the relative economic importance of the countries concerned. Initially it was foreseen that the ECU should also play an important role in the ERM.

Box 3 Major Steps towards Economic and Monetary Union

October 1970	Report of the Werner Committee published
March 1971	Council of Ministers endorses EMU by 1980
March 1972	European 'snake in the tunnel'
July 1978	European Council endorses plan for EMS
March 1979	Start of EMS
February 1986	Signing of Single European Act
June 1988	Delors Committee established by European Council
April 1989	Report of the Delors Committee published
June 1989	European Council decides about start of stage I of EMU
July 1990	Stage I of EMU begins (lifting of capital controls)
October 1990	European Council decides on start of stage II of EMU
December 1990	Start of intergovernmental conferences on EMU and political union
December 1991	European Council adopts Treaty on European Union
June 1992	First referendum in Denmark rejects Maastricht Treaty
August 1992	Crisis in Exchange Rate Mechanism (ERM) begins
September 1992	Referendum in France approves Maastricht Treaty
May 1993	Second referendum in Denmark approves Maastricht Treaty
November 1993	Maastricht Treaty enters into force
January 1994	Start of stage II of EMU; European Monetary Institute established
December 1995	European Council decides that the name of new currency will be euro
June 1997	Adoption of Stability and Growth Pact
June 1997	Decision about ERM II
May 1998	European Council decides about membership of EMU
May 1998	Decision about bilateral central rates of the EMU currencies
May 1998	Executive Board of ECB appointed
June 1998	Establishment of ECB
January 1999	Start of stage III of EMU; decision on euro rates
January 2002	Distribution of euro coins and banknotes to start

However, the ECU played a larger role in international financial markets as various governments, institutions, and corporations issued loans denominated in ECU. It was also possible to have a bank deposit denominated in ECU. Another main role was the function of unit of account within the European Union (for example, the EU budget was expressed in ECU: see Chapter 5).

Within the ERM each currency was kept within a band defined by a grid of central rates for the various pairs of currencies. This band was defined as plus and minus 2.25 per cent of the central rate. These central rates could be changed by mutual consent.[2]

[2] Szász (1999: 60) argues that to enable French participation everything possible (for example, expressing the central rates in ECU) 'was done to make the European Monetary System, as finally agreed, look different from the snake. But in essence it was not. The exchange rate mechanism was exactly the same.'

Whenever an exchange rate reached the edge of the band, the central banks of both countries concerned were supposed to intervene on the foreign exchange market. To facilitate interventions, countries had access to short-term credit facilities, of which the most important was the Very Short Term Facility (VSTF). Initially eight countries joined the ERM, but Italy was allowed to adopt a wide band of plus or minus 6 per cent instead of the narrow band.

The ERM went through a number of phases that can be clearly distinguished:

- a turbulent start (1979–1983)
- a calmer intermediate phase (1983–1987)
- no realignments (1987–1992)
- crises (1992–1993)
- tranquillity restored (1993–1998).

Initially, there were frequent and substantial realignments (see Table 1.1). For instance, in September 1979 a number of currencies were already devalued vis-à-vis the German mark. This was a pattern to be repeated many times. Although it was originally foreseen as a symmetric system, the ERM developed in practice very much as a target zone in which the mark functioned as nominal anchor (see Box 4 for a discussion). The realignments in the initial phase intended to offset cost and price disparities. They were generally not accompanied by domestic stabilization measures (Ungerer, *et al.* 1990). However, Gros and Thygesen (1998) see some progress during this period, especially if compared to the experience of the 'snake'. Realignments became more visibly a joint responsibility and they were sufficient to prevent serious misalignments.

The second phase of the ERM started in March 1983 after the French government decided to change its policy. Instead of stimulating domestic demand by expansionary fiscal and monetary policies, which led to substantial capital outflows, the Mitterrand government now opted for a stable exchange rate vis-à-vis Germany. Although some realignments took place, both their frequency and magnitude were substantially lower than in the previous phase. The realignments were also smaller than the cumulated inflation differentials vis-à-vis Germany, thus leading to changes in real exchange rates. During this second phase a shift occurred in the operational setting from (obligatory) interventions at the fluctuation margins towards (voluntary and therefore more intentional) intra-marginal interventions in German marks and timely increases in interest rates, which was more or less sealed by the *Basle-Nyborg* agreement of September 1987.

This agreement marked the beginning of a 'new EMS' (Giavazzi and Spaventa 1990), where all member countries were encouraged to commit themselves more firmly to the 'hard-currency' option. To this end credit facilities were extended in time and could be used for intra-marginal interventions. It was also agreed that the countries would aim for a better balance between the instruments for operating the ERM. Especially interest-rate differentials should be used more actively. There was another important institutional change during this period: restrictions on capital flows were removed in most countries as an adjunct to the 1992 programme to complete the

Box 4 Was the ERM a German Mark Zone?

The ERM is often conceived as a German mark zone (that is, a system in which the Bundesbank determined monetary policy in the participating countries). In turn, these other countries would acquire (part of) the credibility of the Bundesbank.

If a country aims at a stable exchange rate vis-à-vis the German mark, it will generally have to follow German interest rate changes. This can easily be seen. Suppose capital is mobile (that is, there are no restrictions on international capital flows). If a country, say the Netherlands, would not follow an increase of German short-term interest rates, it would make the Dutch guilder a less attractive currency to invest in. The resulting decline in demand for guilders would affect the exchange rate.

The Bundesbank is widely perceived as a very credible central bank, which has, no doubt, its roots in the relatively good inflation performance of Germany after the Second World War. By pegging their currency to the German mark—that is, by tying their hands—the central banks of the other countries were believed to acquire at least part of the credibility of the Bundesbank (Giavazzi and Pagano 1988). The increased credibility was thought to lower disinflation costs. This can be explained as follows. If the monetary authorities of a country lack credibility, it is quite costly to reduce inflation. Although the central bank may announce its intentions to reduce inflation, trade unions and financial markets will not consider this announcement credible and, consequently, will not behave differently. Only by tough measures (high interest rates) will economic agents learn that the central bank is serious. During this process unemployment will be high. Suppose, a country would instead peg its currency to the German mark. Given the purchasing-power parity, this fixes the inflation rate at the German level. As the Bundesbank is perceived as credible, economic agents will revise their inflation expectations accordingly, thereby reducing actual inflation. Now unemployment does not increase.

There exists an extensive body of research on the character of the ERM. This research has not shown decisively that the Bundesbank indeed set monetary policy for the other countries, nor has it shown that these other countries acquired a great deal of credibility from the Bundesbank (Kenen 1995). Various studies find that the leader–follower model is not supported by the data. For instance, Fratianni and von Hagen (1992) find that policy reactions run in both directions (that is, from Germany to the other countries and vice versa). There is only mixed evidence that ERM membership has fostered price stability and reduced disinflation costs. For instance, Collins (1988) and Egebo and Englander (1992) do not find support for this view. However, other authors report more supportive results. For instance, Bini Smaghi (1994) concludes that ERM countries achieved a larger reduction of inflation than the other OECD countries, in particular the European ones.

internal market. It was widely believed that these controls provided at least temporary protection against speculative attacks.[3]

In the period 1987–92 the sequence of devaluations came to a halt. The central rates and the bands of the ERM were considered to be very credible. Apart from the rebasing of the Italian lira in January 1990, when it moved from the wide to the narrow fluctuation band, there were no realignments.[4] This third phase of the ERM was also marked by new entries: the Spanish peseta in June 1989, the British pound in October 1990, and the Portuguese escudo in April 1992. The new currencies all had fluctuation margins of 6 per cent. During this period it looked as if exchange rates were almost fixed. However, this turned out to be illusory. The fourth phase of the ERM was very turbulent. Anticipations of a smooth transition to monetary union, which had stabilized expectations and, hence, the operation of the ERM, were cast in doubt due to the outcome of the Danish referendum on the Maastricht Treaty. In August 1992 the British pound fell close to the ERM floor and the Italian lira even fell below it. Eventually, the two currencies left the system. Except for the Dutch guilder, all currencies came under attack between September 1992 and August 1993.

Only after the fluctuation margins were increased to 15 per cent (except for the German mark and the Dutch guilder which kept the 2.25 per cent margins) did the foreign exchange markets become more tranquil. During this fifth phase of the ERM membership broadened again. Austria joined the ERM in January 1995. In November 1996 the Italian lira re-entered the ERM, as participation in the exchange rate system was one of the convergence criteria for participation in EMU. In October 1996 the Finnish marka joined and in March 1998 the Greek drachma entered the ERM. There were some realignments in this period. In March 1995 the Spanish and Portuguese currencies were devalued by 7 and 3½ per cent, respectively. In 1997 the Irish punt rose in the slipstream of the British pound to its upper limits against all other currencies. On the eve of EMU this prompted a unique occurrence in the history of the ERM: the Irish currency was revalued by 3 per cent against the German mark in March 1998.

During this phase of the ERM most currencies moved over time very closely to their central rates. Given the 'no devaluation' criterion in the Maastricht Treaty, as well as the desire to sustain exchange rate stability and nominal convergence in the run-up to EMU, the central banks prevented large deviations from central rates (with the exception of the Irish punt). As a result, and contrary to most expectations, monetary and exchange rate policies were not loosened and exchange rates soon returned to within what would otherwise still have been the narrow band. In fact, the central rates became for many countries (Austria, Belgium, Denmark, France, Germany, Luxembourg, and the Netherlands) eventually the irrevocably fixed rates in EMU.

---

[3] However, this view has not gone unchallenged. See Gros and Thygesen 1998 for further details.

[4] The wide band was replaced with the narrow band, leaving the upper limit unchanged and raising the lower limit, thereby effectively raising the central rate against the German mark. The actual exchange rate did not change.

Table 1.1 Realignments in the ERM, 1979–1993 (Realignments vis-à-vis German Mark)

	France	Italy	Netherlands	Belgium	Denmark	Ireland	Spain	Portugal
24 September 1979	−2.0	−2.0	−2.0	−2.0	−5.0	−2.0		
30 November 1979	—	—	—	—	−5.0	—		
23 March 1981	—	−6.0	—	—	—	—		
5 October 1981	−8.5	−8.5	—	−5.5	−5.5	−5.5		
22 February 1982	—	—	—	−8.5	−3.0	—		
14 June 1982	−10.0	−7.0	—	−4.25	−4.25	−4.25		
21 March 1983	−8.0	−8.0	−2.0	−4.0	−3.0	−9.0		
22 July 1985	—	−8.0	—	—	—	—		
7 April 1986	−6.0	−3.0	—	−2.0	−2.0	−3.0		
4 August 1986	—	—	—	—	—	−8.0		
12 January 1987	−3.0	−3.0	—	−1.0	−3.0	−3.0		
8 January 1990	—	−3.7	—	—	—	—		
14 September 1992	—	−7.0	—	—	—	—	—	—
16 September 1992	—	—	—	—	—	—	−5.0	—
23 November 1992	—	—	—	—	—	—	−6.0	−6.0
1 February 1993	—	—	—	—	—	−10.0	—	—
14 May 1993	—	—	—	—	—	—	−8.0	−6.5
Cumulative	**−25.5**	**−44.1**	**−4.0**	**−24.4**	**−27.0**	**−37.1**	**−17.8**	**−12.1**

Source: De Nederlandsche Bank.

1.2.2 The ERM Crises

What caused the crises in the ERM in 1992/3? Following Eichengreen and Wyplosz (1993), we may discern four possible, but not mutually excluding, explanations.

First, persistent inflation differentials vis-à-vis Germany and rising labour costs in some countries (notably Italy) eroded their competitiveness. As explained in the previous section, after 1987 there were no realignments, apart from the 'technical' one for the Italian lira. If price increases in certain countries exceed those of Germany, the countries concerned will lose competitiveness. The prices of their products in German marks will increase more than those of local producers. So, exporting firms in these countries either lose market share, or their profits are cut: both outcomes will not be sustainable. The problem with this argument is, however, that it cannot explain the timing of the crisis in 1992. In other words, there has to be some kind of a trigger mechanism for a crisis to occur. For this purpose, one could point at the negative impact that the Danish referendum on the Maastricht Treaty had, seriously affecting prior beliefs in continued stability and a smooth transition towards EMU. As long as EMU was on track, officials and markets may have believed that misalignments might in time be corrected by adjustments in domestic wages rather than by a realignment. Valid as this first explanation may be for at least some countries (for example, Italy), it cannot explain the difficulties of currencies like the Belgian and French franc.

Second, the asymmetric shock of German unification required exchange rate changes. The demand pressure on home goods due to the enormous transfers to the former German Democratic Republic (GDR) required a real appreciation of the German mark. Such an appreciation would raise the relative price of domestic goods. (Alternatively, one could motivate the required appreciation by referring to its demand-reducing effect to offset the expansionary impact of the transfers to the former GDR). A proposal from the Bundesbank for a realignment in 1989 was turned down. According to this view, the collapse of the ERM came from the unification shock and the inability to allow a revaluation of the German mark. As with the previous explanation, proponents of this view point to the Danish referendum to explain the timing of the crisis.

Third, speculative attacks occur because of inevitable policy shifts. As inflationary pressures in Germany increased after unification, the Bundesbank raised interest rates. Consequently, the other ERM countries were forced to raise their rates as well. In this view, the austerity measures required to defend prevailing parities led to rising unemployment. If this was considered to be too costly from a political point of view, financial market participants may have expected a future policy shift. This can be explained by a simplified model based on Ozkan and Sutherland (1994).

(The log of) output (y) is assumed to depend on the interest rate (i) and the (log of the) exchange rate (s, foreign currency per unit of domestic currency). This gives:

$$y_t = -ai_t + \beta s_t \text{ with } \alpha, \beta > 0 \tag{1.1}$$

Assuming uncovered interest parity:

$$i_t = i_t^* + E(s_{t+k} - s_t) \qquad (1.2)$$

where the last term of equation (1.2) denotes the expected depreciation. Suppose that the foreign interest rate is a stochastic variable, i.e. $i_t^* = \eta_t$. In case of a credibly fixed exchange rate ($Es_{t+k} = s_t$), this implies that equation (1.1) becomes:

$$y_t = -a\eta_t + \beta s_t \qquad (1.1')$$

So every shock in the foreign interest rate (like the one after German unification) affects domestic output. A flexible exchange rate would make it possible to offset a shock. Suppose now that there is a certain critical level for the domestic interest rate (i_{max}) above which the output effects of a stable exchange rate are no longer thought to be acceptable. Once that level is reached, policy-makers will no longer stick to the fixed exchange rate. If financial markets expect such a regime shift to occur, this may make the moment at which this shift actually occurs endogenous. This is very easy to be seen. Once financial markets expect a depreciation (that is, if it is no longer believed that the exchange rate will remain fixed), this will raise domestic interest rates, which makes it more likely that i_{max} will be surpassed. So it is crucial in this reasoning that financial markets are not given any reason to believe that the critical level of the interest rate is close. Unfortunately, various French politicians at the time raised questions about the 'hard currency' approach, which may have fed expectations that a regime shift was likely, thereby making it in fact more likely. Although there is some evidence that financial markets indeed expected a policy shift, these expectations turned out to be wrong for the case of France. After the broadening of the band in August 1993, French policy-makers stuck to their franc fort policy.

Fourth, self-fulfilling speculative attacks occur, which are not related to economic fundamentals. In this explanation monetary policy will become less restrictive, causing the currency to depreciate, if an attack takes place. The attack may provoke policy changes that would not occur in its absence. There are, in other words, multiple equilibria. In this respect the explanation is fundamentally different from the third one, where there is a unique equilibrium (that is, the exchange rate is only attacked if existing policies are (thought to be) non-sustainable). Self-fulfilling attacks are different as the attack provokes the policy shift. Without the attack, policy would not change. This type of speculative-attack model therefore focuses on the reasons why a government faced with an attack might choose to switch to an expansionary policy even if it originally does not want to do so. According to Eichengreen and Wyplosz (1993) the intrinsic reason why monetary policy would shift after an attack is to be found in the Maastricht Treaty which makes exchange rate stability a precondition for EMU participation. Once this condition can no longer be fulfilled after an attack, a country no longer has the incentive to pursue the policies of austerity required for entry. This argument overlooks the simple fact that the exchange rate stability criterion applies to the last two years preceding EMU. A devaluation in 1992 or even 1993 would thus be irrelevant from this point of view, given that the earliest date for EMU was 1997 anyway (Gros and Thygesen 1998). Also, the prediction of less restrictive policies was not vindicated in most countries. Only the UK eased monetary policy after the British pound had left the ERM.

So explanations abound. What do financial market participants have to say about the cause(s) of the ERM crises? Eichengreen and Wyplosz (1993) report the results of a survey of foreign exchange traders who were asked to indicate how important various factors were in causing the crises, ranging from very important to not important. High German interest rates were considered to be very important by 68 per cent of the respondents. Asked for when they thought changes in ERM exchange rates were imminent almost 47 per cent of the respondents answered: just after the Danish referendum.

Before the crises of 1992/3 governments and others began to view the ERM as an (almost) fixed exchange rate regime. As was pointed out in section 1.1, a process started to go all the way towards monetary union. Before we turn to this transition towards EMU in more detail, we will first analyse whether a monetary union is beneficial from an economic point of view. This analysis is based on the 'theory of optimal currency areas (OCA)' as pioneered by Mundell (1961), McKinnon (1963), and Kenen (1969) and further elaborated upon by various authors (see De Grauwe 1997).

1.3 The Costs and Benefits of a Monetary Union

1.3.1 The Benefits of a Monetary Union

The benefits of monetary union include lower transaction costs, reduced exchange rate volatility and uncertainty, more price transparency, and a better functioning internal market. Transaction costs are lower since international transactions in the monetary union no longer require to exchange currencies. Furthermore, the administration and treasury management of firms operating in more than one country are simplified. According to estimates of Emerson, *et al.* (1992) these benefits of monetary union amount to 0.3 to 0.4 per cent of European GDP. However, other authors find somewhat different results. For instance, Prast and Stokman (1997) report lower estimates for the Netherlands (0.2 per cent of GDP). An additional reduction of transaction costs stems from the fact that it is no longer necessary to hedge exchange risks. Prast and Stokman estimate these costs in the case of the Netherlands around 0.1 per cent of GDP.

Obviously, these benefits imply less turnover for the financial sector. Estimates by Reuters (1997) show that before EMU trade between the German mark and other European currencies amounted to on average almost 9 per cent of the total currency trade in the industrial countries. Still, this redistribution should not be confused with a welfare loss. Furthermore, EMU offers new possibilities for the financial sector.

If exchange rate uncertainty has a negative impact on trade and international investment, monetary union will lead to a better international allocation of the means of production. However, most empirical studies find hardly any support for a negative relationship between exchange rate uncertainty on the one hand and trade and investment on the other. Various possible explanations for this rather counter-intuitive result come to mind. First, in most empirical studies exchange rate uncertainty is proxied by observed exchange rate variability, which is not necessarily a good yardstick. A prime example is provided by the history of the ERM. Between 1987 and 1992 observed exchange rate variability of the participating currencies was very low. Interest rates in various countries were, however, substantially above German levels. According to uncovered interest rate parity (see section 6.1) financial markets therefore expected a depreciation of high interest rate currencies, but there was, no doubt, uncertainty about the timing. So focusing on actual exchange rate changes would not take this uncertainty into account.

A second explanation for the lack of a negative impact of exchange rate uncertainty could be the level of aggregation of most studies. For instance, Stokman (1995) reports significant negative effects of exchange rate variability for five EU member countries. In contrast to most previous studies, the analysis of Stokman is based on disaggregated data.

A third explanation has been provided by Krugman (1989), arguing that observed exchange rate variability may not affect trade if setting up this trade would involve a high level of sunk costs, for instance, in the form of investment in marketing and distribution. Exchange rate fluctuations would in that case be reflected in variations in profit margins. A study by the European Commission (1995) on the impact of exchange rate movements on trade in the internal market in the period 1987–95 provides various examples of this.

A third alleged benefit of monetary union is that the internal market will function better owing to more price transparency. After all, prices are in a (full) monetary union expressed in the same unit of account. Transparent pricing will increase competition because it will be easier for companies to sell across the euro zone and for consumers to shop around. This advantage is estimated to be around 0.15 per cent for the Netherlands by Prast and Stokman (1997). In this view, a common currency will strengthen a process that is already visible. For instance, between 1985 and 1993 the variation coefficient of the prices of consumer products in the EU declined from 22.5 per cent to 19.6 per cent (European Commission 1996). Still, substantial differences in prices will remain in EMU due to lasting differences in national tax systems. We will return to this issue in section 4.3.

Finally, as pointed out before, it is often claimed that EU member states cannot obtain the full gains from the Single Market without a single currency. The most compelling argument is that currency fluctuations strongly affect competitive positions in the EU, possibly giving rise to political charges of competitive depreciation and exchange dumping. This could trigger protectionist responses, thereby endangering the Single Market (Buti and Sapir 1998).

1.3.2 The Costs of a Monetary Union

The costs of a monetary union mainly derive from the loss of an instrument of economic policy (that is, the exchange rate). In a monetary union the participating countries have either entirely fixed exchange rates or a common currency. So they can no longer change the price of their own currency vis-à-vis other currencies. The seriousness of this loss depends on three factors: the need for exchange rate adjustments, the effectiveness of exchange rate adjustments, and the availability of other instruments. We will discuss these issues in turn.

The need for exchange rate adjustments depends on the importance and character of economic shocks. A *shock* may be defined as an unanticipated disturbance of an equilibrium without having its cause in the system itself (Emerson, *et al.* 1992). Various types of shocks may be distinguished. A first distinction to be made is between demand and supply shocks, the difference being from where the shock originates. For instance, productivity shocks originate at the supply side, whereas an increase in government spending is an example of a demand shock. A second distinction is between country specific and general shocks. Country specific shocks only hit one country (for example, a decline in foreign demand), in contrast to general shocks, which hit all countries (for example, an increase in oil prices). Shocks that hit only one country are by definition asymmetric. However, general shocks may also have an asymmetric impact, depending on the structural characteristics of the economies being hit. For instance, an oil price hike affects oil importing countries differently from oil exporting countries.

The more important asymmetric shocks are, the higher are the costs of giving up the exchange rate instrument. We may illustrate this as follows. Assume that France and Germany are the two countries considering a monetary union. Suppose that for whatever reason consumers shift their preferences away from French-made to German-made products. In other words, there is an asymmetric demand shock. In France output will decline as a result of the shift in aggregate demand. The country faces a current account deficit and unemployment will rise. In Germany the situation will be the reverse: output increases, there is a current account surplus and shortage of labour. Both countries face an adjustment problem. By adjusting the exchange rate, these problems could be resolved. Suppose that the French franc is devalued vis-à-vis the German mark. French products will become cheaper and, consequently, demand for French products will increase. Output and employment in France grow, and the current account deficit is reduced. In Germany the opposite occurs (De Grauwe 1997).

So, provided that an exchange rate adjustment has the effects as assumed so far, a devaluation of the French franc will contribute to solving the adjustment problem.

But does it? Are exchange rate changes really effective in making up for differential developments in demand, or in costs and prices? The answer to this question crucially depends upon whether the steps outlined above are the end of the story or not. If the situation after the devaluation of the French franc is not an equilibrium, there is more to happen. Why would the post-devaluation situation not be an equilibrium? A devaluation of the franc implies higher domestic prices as import prices have gone up. So real wages are reduced. Suppose trade unions would not accept such a situation and demand higher wages. If they succeed, the initial advantage of the devaluation will evaporate. It is also possible that wage contracts are indexed (that is, employees are compensated for price increases). In both cases, the real wage will not decline and a devaluation of the nominal exchange rate will not be effective. If real wages are rigid (that is, nominal wages respond quickly to changes in the exchange rate), the case against giving up the exchange rate instrument is less compelling even if countries in a monetary union are being hit by asymmetric shocks. The effectiveness of an adjustment of the nominal exchange rate is determined by the openness of the country and the degree of (explicit or implicit) indexation of wages (see De Grauwe 1997).

How much stabilization capacity the euro zone countries have sacrificed due to monetary union remains uncertain (Eichengreen 1998). Anecdotal evidence from the 1990s, when Italy and the UK withdrew from the ERM, suggests that exchange rate changes retain their power. However, Bergin and Moersch (1997) report that although the countries that depreciated their currencies had booming exports, this was not translated into faster overall economic growth. This could be explained by the fact that countries that depreciated their currencies after 1992 (including Italy, Spain, Finland, and Sweden) took the opportunity to cut their government budget deficits.

There is quite some evidence that for most of the European countries the effects of a devaluation wither away (Emerson, *et al.* 1992). However, this does not imply that giving up the possibility of de/revaluations is cost-less, since there are benefits of exchange rate changes in the short run. When a country devalues, it makes the necessary adjustment of wages and prices somewhat less painful (De Grauwe 1997).

What about alternative adjustment mechanisms? Let us return to the example above. If wages in France and Germany are flexible the following will happen. French workers facing increasing unemployment will reduce their wage claims. So, French products will become cheaper. In Germany the excess demand for labour will push up wages, making German products more expensive. Both effects will restore equilibrium.

A second mechanism that could lead to a new equilibrium is labour mobility. If the French unemployed workers move to Germany, where there is an excess demand for labour, both the French and German labour markets would move towards equilibrium. There is no need for French wages to decline and for German wages to increase.

So, in principle the adjustment problem after the asymmetric demand shock will be solved if prices and wages are flexible and/or mobility of labour is sufficiently high. For instance, Americans readily move to where the jobs have shifted, even if this means crossing state lines. However, it is widely believed that Europeans are loath to migrate within their own country, let alone moving abroad. Furthermore, wages in the EU are often conceived as notoriously inflexible (see section 5.2 for a discussion). Under these conditions, changing the nominal exchange rate may alleviate the adjustment problem, even if only temporarily.

Box 5 The Costs of Introducing the Euro

Apart from the costs as outlined in the main text, the introduction of the euro is also costly in another sense: banks, firms, and consumers face (one-time) adjustment costs. Every coin-using machine has to be modified, and all sorts of computer programmes need to be adjusted, from simple lists of prices to stock exchange quotations. Estimates of these costs vary considerably across sectors. This is owing to the fact that some of these costs are related to the so-called millennium problem, while it is also not easy to distinguish between improvements that were already scheduled to take place anyway and specific adjustments due to the introduction of the euro.

In 1995, the European Banking Association estimated the total costs for the banking sector in Europe to be around 10 mrd euro. However, aggregating national cost estimates for the banking sector yielded higher estimates (Bundesverband Öffentlicher Banken Deutschlands 1997). A survey of the International Securities Market Association (ISMA) led to estimated adjustment costs ranging between 110,000 euro to 8 mrd euro for each of its members (Scobie 1997). A survey under Dutch firms yielded an estimate of almost 1 per cent of GDP for the total conversion costs. Firms also expected benefits from EMU. The period after which the conversion costs had been recouped ranged between 0.8 and 2.3 years (Prast and Stokman 1997).

Finally, there is a third adjustment mechanism: fiscal policy. If fiscal policy in France would stimulate demand, whereas German fiscal policy turned restrictive, the effects of the asymmetric demand shock would also be counteracted. How this synchronization of fiscal policies is arranged—be it at some federal level or through coordination—is of less concern here.[5] The point is that fiscal policy may also alleviate the adjustment problem in case of a demand shock.

1.3.3 Costs and Benefits Compared

The huge literature on the costs and benefits of a monetary union in Europe can be nicely summarized by Figure 1.1 (from De Grauwe 1997). On the vertical axis the degree of real divergence is shown (that is, the degree to which countries face asymmetric shocks). As pointed out above, more divergence makes the relinquishment of national monetary policy more costly. The horizontal axis measures how well the alternative adjustment mechanisms are working (that is, how flexible wages are and/ or how mobile labour is). More labour market flexibility makes the loss of national monetary policy less costly. Above the line asymmetric shocks are so frequent and large while the alternative adjustment mechanisms are so weak that the costs of monetary union exceed the benefits. In contrast, below the line monetary union would, on balance, be beneficial.

---

[5] In Chapter 5 we will discuss the need for some kind of European stabilization policy scheme, similar to that in federal states like Germany, the US, and Canada.

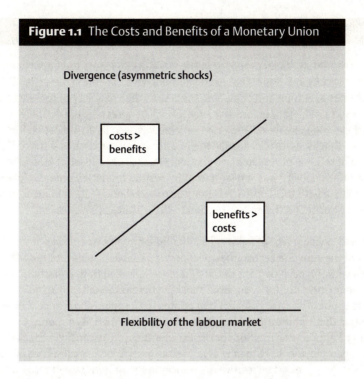

Figure 1.1 The Costs and Benefits of a Monetary Union

So the crucial question then becomes where we should locate the 11 EMU countries. Is an EMU with 11 member countries beneficial from a purely economic point of view? And can the position of the 'outs' be explained by this analysis? Until quite recently most authors concluded that the divergence among the EMU member countries was so high and the flexibility so low that EMU as it exists now was not considered an optimum currency area. Box 6 discusses the literature on asymmetric shocks in the European Union.

No matter how important asymmetric shocks have been in the past, in assessing the economic case for EMU the crucial question is how likely these shocks will be in the future. Two views have been put forward on this issue. According to a study by the European Commission (Emerson, *et al.* 1992) further economic and monetary integration will lead to less divergence (that is, income and employment will tend to diverge less between the countries involved). In contrast, Krugman (1991) argues that trade integration will lead to regional concentration of industrial activities. In Europe a similar concentration of industries will take place as in the US (like in Silicon Valley). This concentration process is caused by economies of scale. Trade in Europe will change from intra-industry trade to inter-industry trade. Due to this concentration process, sector-specific shocks may become region-specific shocks, thereby increasing the likelihood of asymmetric shocks. Figure 1.2 summarizes both views (De Grauwe 1997).

Which view is correct? Three comments are in order. First, if the concentration process as foreseen by Krugman develops along regional lines (for example, the European automobile industry concentrates in a region that is partly in France, in

Box 6 The Importance of Asymmetric Shocks in the European Union

Various methods have been proposed in the literature to assess the importance of asymmetric shocks in Europe. First, some authors have examined the variability of real exchange rates in Europe and compared them with the variability of real exchange rates in existing monetary unions (for example, Eichengreen 1991; De Grauwe and Vanhaverbeke 1993). Real exchange rate variability is seen as an indication for asymmetric shocks, as it reflects adjustment after the occurrence of a shock. The conclusion of this line of research was that only in a (small) subset of EU countries real exchange rate variability was similar to that in existing monetary unions. However, a serious problem with this approach is that the real exchange rate is influenced both by asymmetric shocks and the policy reaction to those shocks (Bayoumi and Eichengreen 1994).

Cohen and Wyplosz (1989) followed a different approach. The development in two countries of the sum of a certain macroeconomic variable (like output growth) is compared with the development of the difference between both countries. The sum is regarded as an indicator for symmetric shocks, whereas the difference indicates asymmetric shocks. In their research that relates to Germany and France, Cohen and Wyplosz find that symmetric shocks are more prevalent than asymmetric shocks. Weber (1991) applied this method for the EU countries at the time. He concludes that shocks in unemployment are mainly asymmetric, except for a small subset of countries. Demand shocks—proxied by relative differences in the growth rate of retail sales—are primarily symmetric. However, this approach suffers from the same problem as the first one: cause and effect are not distinguished.

A third approach employs so-called Vector Auto Regressions (VARs). A system of equations is estimated in which all variables are 'explained' by their own lagged values and those of the other variables. By imposing certain restrictions it is possible to differentiate between demand and supply shocks. Bayoumi and Eichengreen (1994) estimated VARs for EU member countries for the period 1963–90. They find that supply shocks generally have a higher correlation than demand shocks, which indicates that supply shocks are more symmetric than demand shocks. Table B6.1 is reproduced from this study. It shows that the correlation of demand and supply shocks is quite high in only a small group of countries. Especially in Ireland, the UK, Finland, and in the southern member countries there is much asymmetry. This suggests that a monetary union of all EU member states is not optimal. The position of the UK and Greece as being 'out' is in line with the results of this study. However, this approach can also be criticized. The restrictions imposed can be questioned. It is, for instance, assumed that demand shocks only have a temporary effect on output, whereas supply shocks have a permanent impact.

Helg, et al. (1995) estimate VARs at the industry level. They differentiate between country-specific, industry-specific, and local shocks. The first type of shocks influence all industries in a country, whereas the second affects an industry in Europe. The third type refers to shocks only hitting one industry in one country. Helg, et al. find that country-specific shocks are relatively important. However, in a small subset of countries the asymmetry is quite low. This result is broadly in line with the findings of Bayoumi and Eichengreen (1994).

A final strand of literature focuses on the synchronization of business cycles. For instance, Artis and Zhang (1997, 1999) studied the synchronization of the business cycles of a number of European countries vis-à-vis Germany. This analysis is based on the correlation of the cyclical components of GDP growth. Artis and Zhang conclude that after the establishment of the ERM, apart from the UK, there is more synchronization with the German business cycle.

The general conclusion that can be drawn from the research on asymmetric shocks is that only in a so-called 'core-group' of countries is divergence quite low, whereas in the Union as a whole it is rather high. The position of some 'outs' is in line with this general conclusion. This does not imply, however, that this is the actual reason for their non-participation in EMU.

Germany, and in Italy), a sector-specific shock cannot be countered by simple exchange rate adjustments. In other words, economic integration is likely to rob the exchange rates of their capacity to deal with these shocks. Only if a sector is for the most part concentrated in one country might an exchange rate adjustment be helpful in case of a sector-specific shock.

Second, Table 1.2 shows that, until now, the share of intra-industry trade in the euro area has increased. Third, recent research provides some support for the view as put forward by Emerson, *et al.* (1992). For instance, Frankel and Rose (1996) find that the more countries trade with each other the more business cycles in these countries are synchronized. Similar results are reported by Artis and Zhang (1997; 1999) and Fatás (1997) who analyse the influence of monetary integration. They find that over time countries participating in the ERM show a strong synchronization of business cycles, in contrast to countries which do not participate.[6] In other words, it follows from these studies that if EMU furthers integration the likelihood of asymmetric shocks will diminish. Table 1.3 is based on the work of Artis and Zhang, and Fatás. It clearly follows from the table that most correlation coefficients are higher after the introduction of the ERM, the exceptions being Denmark and Greece (employment growth) and the UK (GDP growth).

Although there is less asymmetry according to these figures, this does not imply that economic developments are fully synchronized. After 1979 employment growth of the EU countries shows considerable divergence. Figure 1.3 shows the mean and standard deviation of the annual growth rates of employment in the 15 EU member states. The asymmetric shocks of German reunification and the recession in Finland after the enormous decline in exports to the former Soviet Union are clearly visible.

Divergence in EMU may not only be diminished because of further trade and monetary integration. Also, asymmetric shocks originating in diverging national economic policies will be reduced. This applies of course for monetary and exchange rate policy, but also national fiscal policies will be restricted owing to the Stability and Growth Pact (see section 4.2 for further details).

---

[6] A problem of these studies is that correlation is considered as an indicator for synchronization. As in many other studies, shocks and reactions to those shocks are not distinguished properly.

Table B6.1 Correlation of Demand and Supply Shocks in the European Union

	Germany	France	Netherlands	Belgium	Denmark	Austria	Italy	UK	Spain	Portugal	Ireland	Sweden
Correlation of supply shocks												
France	0.52											
Netherlands	0.54	0.36										
Belgium	0.62	0.40	0.56									
Denmark	0.68	0.54	0.56	0.37								
Austria	0.41	0.28	0.38	0.47	0.49							
Italy	0.21	0.28	0.39	-0.00	0.15	0.06						
UK	0.12	0.12	0.13	0.12	-0.05	-0.25	0.28					
Spain	0.33	0.21	0.17	0.23	0.22	0.25	0.20	0.01				
Portugal	0.21	0.33	0.11	0.40	-0.04	-0.03	0.22	0.27	0.51			
Ireland	-0.00	-0.21	0.11	-0.02	-0.32	0.08	0.14	0.05	-0.15	0.01		
Sweden	0.31	0.30	0.43	0.06	0.35	0.01	0.46	0.41	0.20	0.39	0.10	
Finland	0.22	0.12	-0.25	0.06	0.30	0.11	-0.32	-0.04	0.07	-0.13	-0.23	-0.10
Correlation of demand shocks												
France	0.30											
Netherlands	0.21	0.34										
Belgium	0.36	0.53	0.52									
Denmark	0.34	0.32	0.20	0.30								
Austria	0.32	0.50	0.29	0.56	0.30							
Italy	0.22	0.62	0.24	0.49	0.06	0.44						
UK	0.09	0.20	-0.05	-0.03	-0.00	-0.15	0.05					
Spain	-0.10	0.53	0.11	0.26	0.25	0.30	0.43	0.23				
Portugal	0.24	0.47	0.05	0.45	0.30	0.60	0.63	0.24	0.32			
Ireland	0.06	0.09	0.39	0.00	0.34	-0.12	-0.08	0.25	0.02	-0.01		
Sweden	0.10	0.18	0.29	0.36	0.18	0.02	0.25	0.18	-0.01	0.08	0.30	
Finland	0.10	0.47	0.32	0.60	0.36	0.53	0.65	0.16	0.40	0.54	0.17	0.33

Figure 1.2 Two Views on the Relationship between Economic and Monetary Integration and Divergence

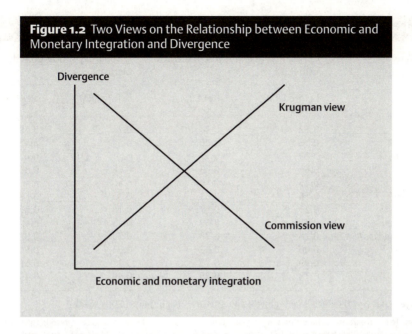

Table 1.2 Intra-industry Trade as Percentage of Manufactures Trade, 1970–1997

	1970	1980	1990	1997
Austria	53	65	79	78
Belgium	77	86	83	89
Finland	21	35	41	51
France	82	84	86	90
Germany	70	75	79	81
Ireland	27	61	54	42
Italy	70	61	67	70
Netherlands	68	69	77	77
Portugal	28	41	53	64
Spain	43	69	75	81

Source: OECD, *Economic Outlook* (Dec. 1998).

Note: 1996 for the Netherlands, Portugal, and Spain.

Table 1.3 Correlation of Employment and GDP Growth before and after ERM

	Correlation of employment growth with EU12		Correlation of GDP growth with Germany	
	before ERM	after ERM	before ERM	after ERM
Belgium	0.52	0.94	0.72	0.79
Denmark	0.56	0.00	n.a.	n.a.
Germany	0.73	0.77	n.r.	n.r.
France	0.61	0.75	0.68	0.85
Greece	0.45	−0.10	n.a.	n.a.
Ireland	0.56	0.61	0.33	0.58
Italy	0.21	0.57	0.18	0.67
Luxembourg	0.42	0.69	n.a.	n.a.
Netherlands	0.28	0.78	0.73	0.82
Portugal	0.06	0.32	0.33	0.55
Spain	0.09	0.79	0.37	0.58
UK	0.73	0.75	0.49	0.44

Source: Fatás (1997) (employment growth) and Artis and Zhang (1997) (GDP growth).

Notes: The correlation of the employment growth is vis-à-vis EU12 and relates to the periods 1966–1979 and 1979–1992. The correlation of GDP growth is vis-à-vis Germany and relates to 1961–1979 and 1979–1993; 'n.r.' means not applicable and 'n.a.' means not available.

Figure 1.3 Employment Growth in the European Union, 1980 –1996 (Mean and Standard Deviation)

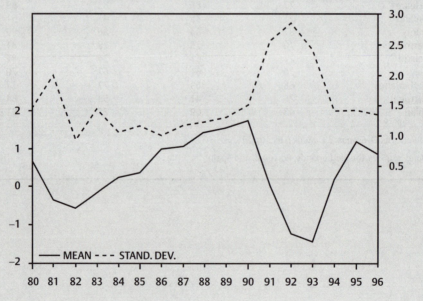

Source: OECD, *Economic Outlook* (various issues).

1.4 The Transition to Economic and Monetary Union

ALTHOUGH economic arguments like those presented in the previous section have played a role in the (academic) debate about monetary union, it is important to realize that political considerations were more important in shaping EMU. According to Szász (1999), the relations of Germany with Eastern Europe had long been a major reason for German integration in Western Europe and to meet French wishes for monetary integration. This had been the case for Willy Brandt's Ostpolitik as well as for German unification, which initially was received rather critically in at least some European countries. On both occasions German initiatives towards the East required support in the West, and co-operation with France was one of the keys to that support. Indeed, some observers have argued that the German concession that EMU would start automatically in 1999 was made in response to the support that the German Chancellor Kohl sought for German unification (Kenen 1995). According to Szász (1999), for France European integration is the way to safeguard its influence in both Europe and the world. Through EMU France—and, no doubt, other countries too—wanted to obtain influence on monetary decision-making in Europe. But—as will be explained below—Germany attached conditions to EMU which France had no choice but to accept. If genuinely respected, these will prevent the French government from exerting influence on monetary decision-making (see also Chapter 2).

The Maastricht Treaty defined a precise transition process towards EMU. The first stage towards EMU started on 1 July 1990, prior to the signing of the Treaty. During this phase member countries should abolish all remaining capital controls and monetary co-operation and convergence was to increase.

The second stage started on 1 January 1994 with the creation of the *European Monetary Institute* (EMI). The two main tasks of the EMI were (1) to strengthen monetary co-operation and (2) to make the preparations required for the establishment of the ESCB, for the conduct of a single monetary policy and for the creation of a single currency in the third stage of EMU. The creation of the EMI was clearly a compromise between countries favouring the establishment of the ECB in Stage Two of EMU and countries in favour of strict convergence before any move to EMU. The latter opposed any gradual transfer of monetary responsibilities during Stage Two, as this might interfere with the pursuit of price stability in individual countries.

At the beginning of the second stage several new rules took effect. Central banks were no longer allowed directly to provide credit to governments. Similarly, 'bail outs' of public entities and forced investments in public debt were prohibited. In this stage the member countries also must endeavour to avoid excessive deficits. Finally, governments had to grant independence to their own central banks.

If a majority of the member states would fulfil certain *convergence criteria* in 1996, EMU (that is, the third stage) could begin in 1997. As there were not enough qualifying countries, it became clear that EMU would start on 1 January 1999. The same convergence criteria were then to be used to identify the countries that were ready to participate. These convergence criteria relate to: price stability, sustainable fiscal policy, exchange rate stability, and long-term interest rates (see Box 7).

Economists are not used to analysing the process of European monetary integration in political terms. That is, perhaps, the reason that the convergence criteria—notably those referring to fiscal policy—met with so much criticism (see section 4.1). Still, the amendments to the EC Treaty agreed in Maastricht are the outcome of a political process in which economic arguments were not decisive. For instance, it is widely believed that from an economic point of view Germany had not much to gain by the move to the third stage of EMU. Indeed, according to De Grauwe (1997) the fundamental interest of Germany was to keep a monetary union small. In the past, Germany set monetary policies in the European Monetary System. This dominant position had its roots in the strong reputation of the Bundesbank and its pursuit of price stability as the major objective of monetary policy. In EMU the dominating role of Germany would evaporate. This was, of course, precisely an important reason for other countries to join the third stage of EMU. Their overriding political objective was not to be left out of the monetary union. According to De Grauwe (1997), the conditions for entry to the third stage of EMU had different meanings for the various participants. For Germany they were a way to exclude some countries, while for others they were a mechanism to show that they could join by their own efforts and that they were not second-class countries.

Box 7 Defining Convergence

The Maastricht Treaty contains four convergence criteria:

1. *price stability*: an average inflation rate (measured on the basis of the consumer price index) that does not exceed by more than 1.5 percentage points that of, at most, the three best performing member countries.
2. *sustainable fiscal position*, meaning that there is no excessive deficit. An excessive deficit exists if:

- the budget deficit is higher than 3 per cent of GDP, unless, either the ratio has declined substantially and continuously and has reached a level that comes close to 3 per cent, or the excess over the 3 per cent reference value is only exceptional and temporary and the deficit remains close to 3 per cent;
- the ratio of gross government debt to GDP exceeds 60 per cent, unless the ratio is sufficiently diminishing and approaching the reference value at a satisfactory pace.

3. *exchange rate stability*, meaning that the currency has respected the 'normal' fluctuation margins of the ERM, without severe tensions for at least two years (especially no devaluation on the initiative of the member country concerned).
4. *low interest rate*, meaning that the average long-term interest rate should not exceed by more than 2 percentage points the interest rates in, at most, the three best performing countries in terms of price stability.

The gradual process towards EMU has been criticized by some economists, who argued that there was no need for convergence. For instance, De Grauwe (1997) forcefully argues that the easiest way to force inflation convergence is starting a monetary union. After all, in a monetary union the inflation rate is more or less the same in the participating countries. Allowing a highly indebted country into the union would also facilitate the reduction of the government budget deficit because it is likely to lead to a lower interest burden. A long transition process could be hazardous as incidents might disrupt it.

Despite these criticisms, the European governments stuck to the gradual approach. In December 1995 the European Council decided that the third stage of EMU was to be divided in three sub-stages:

- From 1 January 1999 until the end of 2001 national currencies will continue to be in circulation (with irrevocably fixed exchange rates). Transactions between financial institutions will be in euros and individuals and firms have the choice of an account in their own currency or in euros. New issues of government debt will be made in euros.

- During 1 January 2002 and at the latest 1 July 2002 euro banknotes and coins will replace national currency.

- From 1 July 2002 onwards the euro will be the single currency. At that time, national currencies have lost their legal-tender status.

On the basis of a report by the EMI, the European Council took a decision in June 1997 about the principles of a new Exchange Rate Mechanism (ERM II), which will be discussed more extensively in section 3.4.

On 2 May 1998 the European Council decided unanimously that 11 countries (Austria, Belgium, Finland, France, Germany, Ireland, Italy, Luxembourg, the Netherlands, Portugal, and Spain) fulfilled the convergence criteria to join EMU. This decision was final. Although it was sometimes suggested otherwise, under the Maastricht Treaty a member country cannot decide for itself whether or not to participate in Stage Three. Only the UK and Denmark have a special position in this regard. The UK has maintained the right to opt out, and participation of Denmark in EMU is subject to a national referendum. This is arranged for in two protocols to the Treaty.[7]

At the same time, the ministers of Finance agreed with the national central banks, the European Commission and the EMI that the ERM bilateral central rates would be the irrevocably fixed rates in the third stage of EMU. The Maastricht Treaty determined that at the start of the third stage of EMU one ECU should equal one euro. As the ECU also comprised a number of currencies of countries that would not join the euro area, the euro conversion rates could only be established at the start of EMU (see Box 1).

The decision of the European Council on EMU membership was mainly based on an

---

[7] The UK protocol states that the country shall not be obliged to move to Stage Three without a separate decision to do so by its government and parliament. The Danish protocol notes that a referendum may be needed before Denmark can participate in Stage Three and grants Denmark an exemption if it cannot participate.

assessment of convergence. The most important obstacle for most member states were the public finance criteria. In 1996 many countries did not satisfy the debt and deficit criteria. Through additional policy measures (including accounting measures and privatization) most member states fulfilled the criteria, except Greece (most criteria) and Sweden (exchange rate criterion).

On 25 May 1998 the governments of the EMU countries appointed the members of the Executive Board of the ECB. The appointment took effect from 1 June 1998 and marked the establishment of the ECB and the ESCB. With the establishment of the ECB, the EMI had completed its task and went into liquidation. The third stage of EMU started on 1 January 1999.

1.5 Conclusion

DESPITE the scepticism of many economists EMU started in 1999. Various economists were critical about monetary union for basically two reasons. First, there were serious doubts whether the EU fulfilled the traditional optimal currency area criteria. However, more recently, various authors have argued that these criteria may be endogenous (that is, further trade and monetary integration may reduce divergence).

Second, some authors questioned the wisdom of the transition process towards EMU as foreseen in the Maastricht Treaty. The criticism referred to the necessity and the contents of the convergence criteria. With the benefit of hindsight it can be concluded that, apart from the serious crises in the ERM in 1992 and 1993, the transition process towards EMU has been remarkably smooth.

The ECB is now in charge of monetary policy in Europe. So the next chapters are about the E(S)CB. Chapter 2 will discuss the institutions as such, while Chapter 3 is about monetary policy of the ECB.

Chapter 2

EMU and the European (System of) Central Bank(s)

Introduction

THE Maastricht Treaty has made the ECB and national central banks very independent. Nowadays it is widely believed that a high level of central bank independence and an explicit mandate for the bank to restrain inflation are important institutional devices to assure price stability. It is thought that an independent central bank can give full priority to low levels of inflation. In countries with a more dependent central bank other considerations (notably, re-election perspectives of politicians and a low level of unemployment) may interfere with the objective of price stability. In that context the German central bank is often mentioned as an example. The Deutsche Bundesbank was relatively autonomous; at the same time, Germany had one of the best post-Second World War inflation records among the OECD countries. Indeed, the statutes of the ECB are largely modelled after the law governing the Bundesbank. After a short description of the ESCB (section 2.1), this chapter reviews the arguments for central bank independence (section 2.2), followed by an analysis of the independence of the ECB and the ESCB (section 2.3). We conclude that, on paper, the ECB is indeed a very independent institution. Some critics have complained, however, that the democratic accountability of the ECB is poorly arranged for in comparison with various national central banks. Indeed, the basic argument for the democratic accountability of central banks is that delegation of power to non-elected officials can only be acceptable in a democratic society if central banks are one way or another accountable to democratically elected institutions. So this chapter ends with a discussion of the accountability of the ECB (section 2.4).

2.1 The European (System of) Central Bank(s)

THE *European System of Central Banks* consists of the European Central Bank and the national central banks. The basic tasks to be carried out by the ESCB are to:

- define and implement monetary policy in EMU
- conduct foreign exchange operations
- hold and manage the official foreign reserves of the countries participating in the euro
- promote the smooth operation of payment systems.

The ECB and the national central banks of the countries that have adopted the euro are often referred to as the *Eurosystem*. If all member states participate in the euro, Eurosystem and ESCB will be synonymous. The *ESCB* is governed by the decision-making bodies of the ECB: the Governing Council, the Executive Board, and the General Council (see Figure 2.1). In contrast to the ECB and the national central banks, the ESCB (and hence the Eurosystem) has no legal personality and no decision-making bodies of its own.

The Statute of the ECB is set out in a separate protocol to the Maastricht Treaty, which implies a solid legislative base, since most of the provisions of the Protocol can only be changed through an amendment of the Treaty itself. Furthermore, the Treaty establishes that the ECB has its own budget, independent from that of the European Union. This makes it impossible for Community institutions to interfere with the

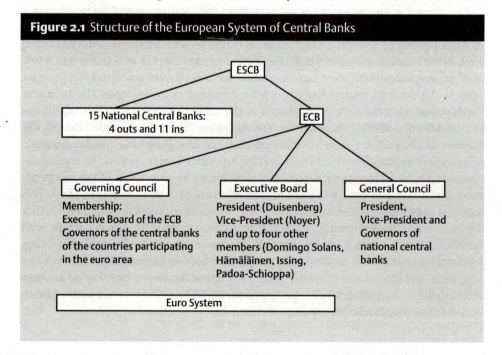

Figure 2.1 Structure of the European System of Central Banks

ESCB

15 National Central Banks:
4 outs and 11 ins

ECB

Governing Council

Membership:
Executive Board of the ECB
Governors of the central banks
of the countries participating
in the euro area

Executive Board

President (Duisenberg)
Vice-President (Noyer)
and up to four other
members (Domingo Solans,
Hämäläinen, Issing,
Padoa-Schioppa)

General Council

President,
Vice-President and
Governors of
national central
banks

Euro System

administration of the ECB and keeps the budget separate from the financial interests of the Community.

The *Governing Council* of the ECB is the most important decision-making body of the ECB. It consists of the Executive Board of the ECB and the governors of the national central banks of the countries in the euro area. The main responsibility of the Governing Council is to take decisions in relation to the tasks entrusted to the ESCB. The Governing Council is, for instance, responsible for monetary policy, including decisions about intermediate objectives and interest rates (see Chapter 3 for further discussion). The ECB adheres to the *principle of decentralization*. This principle stipulates that, to the extent deemed possible and appropriate, the ECB shall have recourse to the national central banks to carry out operations, which form part of the tasks of the Eurosystem. In order to ensure that the decentralized approach does not hamper the smooth functioning of the Eurosystem, the national central banks, as operational arms of the ECB, have to act in accordance with ECB guidelines and instructions (ECB, *Monthly Bulletin* (July 1999)).

When taking monetary policy decisions, the members of the Governing Council of the ECB do not act as national representatives, but in a fully independent personal capacity. This is reflected in the principle of 'one person, one vote'. According to the Statute, the Governing Council has to meet at least ten times a year. Current practice is for the Governing Council to meet every two weeks. Within the Governing Council eleven out of the seventeen members come from national central banks. This implies that national central banks have an important say in monetary policy decisions. In this respect the ECB is quite different from other central banks in federal countries (see Box 8 for further details).

The *Executive Board* of the ECB consists of the President, the Vice-President, and up to four other members. The Executive Board implements monetary policy decisions taken by the Governing Council. In doing so, it may give instructions to national central banks. The European Council appoints members of the Executive Board. Their term in office is eight years and is not renewable. A system of staggered appointments has been applied for the appointment of its first members.

Finally, the *General Council* of the ECB comprises the President, the Vice-President and the governors of all fifteen national central banks. During the negotiations about the Maastricht Treaty it became clear that not all EU member countries would join EMU at its start. A two-track path to EMU seemed inevitable. Governments who had reason to fear that they would be on the slow track, wanted all of the national central banks to participate in the ECB's Governing Council, even if some governors would not be able to vote. Other governments wanted to exclude non-participating countries from any formal role. A compromise was reached in the form of the General Council (Kenen 1995). The General Council has to contribute to the work of the ESCB in various areas (for example, collecting statistics and laying down employment conditions of the ECB's staff). One of its most important tasks is to prepare for the irrevocable fixing of the exchange rate of the slow track countries. The General Council has no role in making monetary policy. The President of the ECB informs the General Council about monetary policy decisions taken. Current practice is that the General Council meets every three months in Frankfurt.

Box 8 Decentralization of the ESCB Compared to Other Federal Central Banks

Critics of the ESCB sometimes argue that its decentralization is a design flaw. The structure of the ESCB is more decentralized than other federally organized central bank systems, such as the German Bundesbank and the Federal Reserve System in the US. Within the ESCB national central banks have more power than in the other federal systems. First of all, the ESCB has a decentralized *voting system*. Within the Governing Council 11 out of the 17 members come from national central banks. This is a relatively high number compared with the 9 votes from the Land central banks within the Bundesbank's Central Bank Council of 17 members. It is also high in comparison with the 5 members from the regional Federal Reserve Banks within the decision-making Federal Open Market Committee of 12 members. The Governing Council of the ESCB is supposed to set short-term interest rates according to conditions in the whole euro area, but there is a risk that national central bankers in the Council will be influenced by conditions in their home country weakening the credibility of the ESCB. Some critics (from large countries) believe that small countries are over-represented in the ESCB's Council.

Table B8.1 shows that at the moment of writing, central bankers coming from Austria, Belgium, Finland, Ireland, Luxembourg, the Netherlands, and Portugal have 9 of the 17 votes on the Governing Council in comparison with only 2 votes for central bankers from Germany, although Germany's GDP is twice the combined GDP of these small countries. However, the designers of the ESCB have deliberately (on the insistence of Germany) chosen the principle of *one (wo)man, one vote* to stress the collective responsibility of the Governing Council.

Table B8.1 Number of Votes and GDP per Vote in the ECB's Governing Council

Countries	Number of votes	GDP per vote (mrd euro)
Luxembourg	1	14
Finland	2	52
Ireland	1	64
Portugal	1	86
Netherlands	2	160
Austria	1	182
Belgium	1	214
Spain	2	235
Italy	2	505
France	2	614
Germany	2	933

Source: 'Euro Towers or Fawlty Towers?', *The Economist* (31 October 1998).

Note: GDP in mrd euro (ECU) in 1997. Data from OECD.

Apart from voting power, the ESCB is also quite decentralized in other respects (Angeloni, 1999). For one thing, it has a decentralized budget process. Furthermore, national central banks may have their own portfolios and non-ESCB related activities.

Finally, the size of the ECB's staff is small both compared with the staff at the participating national central banks and with other federally structured central banking systems (Table B8.2).

Table B8.2 Relative Size of Central Bank Staff of ECB and ESCB

Central bank systems	Total staff	Staff of Economic Department
Federal Reserve System	25,000	830
of which: board	1,700	374
ratio board/total	7%	45%
Bundesbank	15,881	223
of which: directorate	2,579	72
ratio directorate/total	16%	32%
ESCB	63,000	870
of which: ECB	576	99
ratio ECB/ESCB	0.9%	11%

Source: Angeloni 1999.

Note: Federal Reserve System staff based on 1996 data (partially estimated), Bundesbank staff based on 1998 data and ESCB staff based on 1997 data.

The ECB's capital is 5,000 mln euro. The Governing Council may increase this amount. The national central banks are the sole holders of this capital. The subscription of capital is based on the shares of the member countries in the GDP (50 per cent) and population of the EU (50 per cent). Table 2.1 shows the capital subscription shares of the various countries. Central banks of countries in the euro zone had to pay 100 per cent of the subscribed capital. The General Council has decided that the central banks of Denmark, Greece, Sweden, and the UK should pay 5 per cent of their subscriptions to the capital of the ECB. This represents their contribution to operational costs of those activities of the ECB in which they participate.

Net profits of the ECB shall be allocated as follows. An amount not exceeding 20 per cent of the net profit shall be transferred to the general reserve fund of the ECB. The remaining profit will be distributed to the shareholders (that is, the national central banks) in proportion to their paid up shares.

Where does central bank profit come from? While central bank money is an asset for the private sector because it serves as a medium of exchange, as the unit of account and as a store of value it is not a true liability for the central bank. Except for the negligible cost of printing the money, the central bank incurs no other cost in producing it. The monetary base therefore measures the central bank's wealth from money creation. With the introduction of the euro, each member country will have to exchange its monetary base for euros. Countries whose share in the monetary base exceeds their share in equity capital will lose seigniorage wealth, and countries with the opposite relationship between these values will gain. Sinn and Feist (1997) have calculated the distribution of gains and losses under the assumption of an

Table 2.1 Seigniorage Gains and Losses in an All-inclusive Monetary Union

Country	(1) Share in ECB equity capital (%)	(2) Share in seigniorage wealth	(3) Difference (1) – (2)
Austria	2.37	3.5	−1.13
Belgium	2.89	2.7	0.19
Denmark	1.66	1.2	0.46
Finland	1.40	0.9	0.50
France	16.87	10.9	5.97
Germany	24.41	35.8	−11.39
Greece	2.06	1.9	0.16
Ireland	0.84	0.7	0.14
Italy	14.96	12.6	2.36
Luxembourg	0.15	0.0	0.15
Netherlands	4.28	4.4	−0.12
Portugal	1.93	1.4	0.53
Spain	8.83	12.7	−3.87
Sweden	2.66	2.1	0.56
UK	14.71	9.3	5.41
Total	100%	100%	

Source: ECB (http://www.ecb.int) and Sinn and Feist 1997.

all-inclusive monetary union (Table 2.1). It follows that France and the UK are the two big winners of EMU. Italy would be another big winner. The biggest loser would be Germany, followed by Spain.

The primary *objective* of the ECB is to maintain price stability. The Maastricht Treaty is silent about the exact definition of price stability. As a subordinated—secondary— objective, the ECB is supposed to support the general economic policies in the European Union. The ESCB is obliged to act in accordance with the principle of an open market economy with free competition.

An important factor influencing the scope for the ECB to pursue monetary policy is the exchange rate regime, and here a division of responsibilities is arranged for between the Council of Ministers and the ECB. The Council is responsible for decisions about formal *agreements on an exchange rate system* for the euro vis-à-vis non-Community currencies. It has to decide unanimously about participation in an exchange rate system, either on the basis of a recommendation of the ECB or on the basis of a recommendation of the European Commission, or after consultations with the ECB in an endeavour to reach a consensus consistent with price stability. In either case the European Parliament must be consulted. The Council also has to decide by qualified majority, on a recommendation from the ECB or the Commission, and after consulting the ECB, about the adoption, adjustment, and abandonment of euro central rates within such an exchange rate system. Even though the Maastricht Treaty indicates that the chosen rates should be consistent with the objective of price stability, the final decision is very clearly one for the Council. In principle this could mean an interference with the objective of price stability. A binding exchange rate agreement might force the ECB to intervene on the foreign exchange market in such a way that the money supply increases, thus fuelling inflation (see section 3.3 for further details). Pegging of the euro and the US dollar would be an example of an exchange rate agreement. Although there is some support for such a scheme, a formal agreement to stabilize exchange rates at the global level does not seem likely (see Box 9).

If there is no formal exchange rate system, the ECB has control over exchange rate policy. However, the Council may formulate general orientations for exchange rate policy in relation to these currencies, but these orientations must not interfere with the objective of the ESCB to maintain price stability.

One important function of the ESCB is to promote the smooth operation of payment systems. For that purpose TARGET has been established (see section 3.3 for further details). Finally, the Council may confer on the ECB specific tasks concerning policies relating to the prudential supervision of credit institutions and other financial institutions (with the exception of insurance undertakings). This issue will be discussed in section 3.5.

Box 9 Duisenberg Hints at Euro Conflict

The following is an excerpt from an article in the *Financial Times*:

Wim Duisenberg, president of the European Central Bank foreshadowed a looming conflict with European governments when he warned politicians adopting an explicit exchange rate policy for the euro. Duisenberg said exchange rate target zones were unworkable and potentially inconsistent with the ECB's primary objective of stable prices. Many European governments support explicit target zones for the US dollar, the euro, and the yen, fearing that excessive appreciation of the euro against the dollar could stifle economic growth and increase unemployment. Mr Duisenberg said: 'We do not have an explicit exchange rate policy. We have a policy to ensure price stability. We have no exchange rate targets vis-à-vis another currency.' Yet Oskar Lafontaine and Dominique Strauss-Kahn, the German and French finance ministers, have both expressed support for target zones. Lionel Jospin, French prime minister said the euro should be strong, but not too strong 'because then we would lose what we won on the monetary front on the commercial front'. Read for this that an overvalued euro could damage exports and so cause job losses, something the governments in neither Paris nor Bonn can afford.

Source: Financial Times (8 Jan. 1999), 1–2.

2.2 Central Bank Independence: The Rationale

2.2.1 Defining Central Bank Independence

Before we discuss the arguments put forward in favour of an independent central bank, we first have to be clear what central bank independence really means. Central bank independence refers to three areas in which the influence of government must be excluded or drastically curtailed:

- independence in personnel matters
- financial autonomy
- policy independence.

These aspects will be discussed by turn, first in general terms, and in section 2.3 in greater detail with respect to the ECB.

In practice, it is not feasible to exclude government influence completely when appointments are made to such an important public institution as a central bank. So *personnel independence* refers to the influence that government has in appointment procedures. Various criteria are relevant here, like governmental representation in the governing body of the central bank, appointment procedures, terms of office, and procedures governing dismissal of the board of the bank.

It is clear that politicians can influence central bank policy if the government is able to finance its expenditure either directly or indirectly via central bank credits. In that case there is no *financial independence*. Direct access to central bank credits implies that monetary policy is subordinated to fiscal policy. Indirect access may result if the central bank is cashier of the government or if it handles the management of government debt. In these cases restrictions may be necessary to prevent government interference with monetary policy.

Policy independence is related to the room of manoeuvre given to the central bank in the formulation and execution of monetary policy. As has been pointed out by Debelle and Fischer (1995), it may be useful to distinguish between goal independence and instrument independence. A central bank has goal independence if it can decide on the formulation of its ultimate objective(s). In practice, most central bank laws formulate one or more objectives. However, if the central bank has been trusted with various (possibly conflicting) goals—such as achieving low inflation and low unemployment—it has quite some scope in setting its priorities. In that case the central bank has considerable *goal independence* since it is relatively free to choose the final goals of monetary policy. It could, for instance, decide that price stability is less important than output stability, and act accordingly.

Finally, a central bank must wield effective instruments in order to defend its objective(s). A bank that has *instrument independence* is free to choose the means by which it seeks to achieve its goals. Clearly, if government approval is required of the central bank's use of policy instruments, no instrument independence exists.[1] Although the instruments of the ECB have to be market-oriented, the ECB has almost complete instrument independence. The Maastricht Treaty states that neither the ECB, nor a national central bank, nor any member of their decision-making bodies shall seek or take instructions from Community institutions or bodies, from any government of a member state, or from any other body.

2.2.2 Central Bank Independence and Inflation Performance

Why would central bank independence, *ceteris paribus*, yield lower rates of inflation? The theoretical reasoning in this field stresses the *time inconsistency problem* (Kydland and Prescott 1977; Barro and Gordon 1983). The basic idea behind the time-inconsistency problem can be explained as follows. Suppose, the policy-maker announces a certain inflation rate that (s)he considers optimal. If private-sector agents take this announced inflation rate into account in their behaviour, it becomes at that time optimal for the government to renege and to create a higher than announced inflation rate. The reason for this is that a burst of unexpected inflation yields certain benefits. For instance, unexpected inflation reduces real wages, thereby increasing employment. Of course, this is only part of the story. The next step is to add rational expectations. Under rational expectations economic agents know government's incentive to create unexpected inflation and they take this into account in forming their expectations. Government has no other choice than to vindicate these. It is clear that the inflation rate will be higher than in the situation where government would stick to its promise. No matter which factors exactly cause the dynamic inconsistency problem,[2] in all cases the resulting rate of inflation is sub-optimal. So in the literature devices have been suggested to reduce this so-called *inflationary bias*.

Rogoff (1985) has proposed to delegate monetary policy to an independent and 'conservative' central banker. *Conservative* means that the central banker is more averse to inflation than the government, in the sense that (s)he places a greater weight on price stability than does the government. Why would a central banker be more inflation-averse than the government? Two main differences have been pointed

---

[1] It will be clear that if the central bank is obliged to finance budget deficits, there is also no instrument independence. In that sense financial independence and instrument independence are related; instrument independence is, however, much broader.

[2] Apart from the lower unemployment rate resulting from surprise inflation, there are other sources of the time inconsistency problem that originate with the public finances. For example, the incentives for the government to inflate change after the public has settled for a nominal interest rate, taking into account its expected rate of inflation. Initially, there is an incentive to abstain from fuelling inflation as this yields a low nominal interest rate. However, after positions in government bonds have been taken, policy-makers have an incentive to create inflation thereby reducing the real value of outstanding government debt.

out in the literature between preferences of the government and those of the central bank (Cukierman 1992). One relates to possible differences in the time preference of political authorities and that of central banks. For various reasons, central banks tend to take a longer view of the policy process than do politicians. For instance, central bankers do not have to worry about re-election prospects. The other difference concerns the subjective weights in the objective function of the central bank and that of government officials. It is often assumed that central bankers are relatively more concerned about inflation than about other policy goals such as achieving high employment levels and adequate government revenues.

If monetary policy is set at the discretion of a 'conservative' and independent central banker, a lower average time-consistent inflation rate will result. The central insights of this literature can be explained as follows. It is assumed that policy-makers seek to minimize the following loss function (L), which represents the preferences of the society:

$$L^G = \frac{1}{2}\pi_t^2 + \frac{\chi}{2}(y_t - y_t^*)^2 \tag{2.1}$$

where y_t is output, y^* denotes desired output and χ is government's weight on output stabilization ($\chi > 0$). Output is driven by a simplified Lucas supply function:[3]

$$y_t = (\pi_t - \pi_t^e) + u_t \tag{2.2}$$

where π is actual inflation, π^e is expected inflation, and u_t is a random shock. Policy-makers minimize (2.1) on a period-by-period basis, taking the inflation expectations as given. With rational expectations, inflation turns out to be:

$$\pi_t = \chi y_t^* - \frac{\chi}{\chi + 1}u_t \tag{2.3}$$

The first term at the right-hand side of equation (2.3) is the inflationary bias. A country with a high inflationary bias has a credibility problem, as economic subjects realize government's incentives for surprise inflation. The second term in equation (2.3) reflects the degree to which stabilization of output shocks influences inflation. Suppose that a 'conservative' central banker is put in charge of monetary policy. Conservative means that the central banker is more inflation-averse than government. The loss function of the central banker can therefore be written as:

$$L^{cb} = \frac{1 + \varepsilon}{2}\pi_t^2 + \frac{\chi}{2}(y_t - y_t^*)^2 \tag{2.4}$$

where ε denotes the additional inflation aversion of the central banker. The preferences of the central banker do not matter, unless (s)he is able to determine monetary policy. In other words, the central bank should be able to pursue monetary policy without (much) government interference. This can simply be modelled as follows (Eijffinger and Hoeberichts 1998):

$$M_t = \gamma L^{cb} + (1 - \gamma)L^G \tag{2.5}$$

---

[3] The natural rate of output is normalized and the slope is set at one.

where γ denotes the degree of *central bank independence* (that is, to which extent the central banker's loss function affects monetary policy-making). If $\gamma = 1$, the central bank fully determines monetary policy M. With rational expectations and minimizing government's loss function, inflation will be:

$$\pi_t = \frac{\chi}{1 + \gamma\varepsilon} y_t^* - \frac{\chi}{1 + \gamma\varepsilon + \chi} u_t \qquad (2.6)$$

Comparing equations (2.3) and (2.6), it is immediately clear that the inflationary bias (the first term at the right hand of the equations) is lower for positive values of γ and ε. In other words, delegating monetary policy to an independent and 'conservative' central bank will yield a lower level of inflation.[4] There is an optimal level of independence cum conservativeness ($\gamma\varepsilon^*$). Under certain assumptions, this is shown graphically in Figure 2.2.[5] Optimal means that the loss function of the society (eq. 2.1) is minimized. This optimum is not necessarily one with zero inflation, as it also depends on output stabilization.

It also follows from equation (2.6) that both independence and the inflation aversion of the central bank are relevant here. If the central banker would have the same

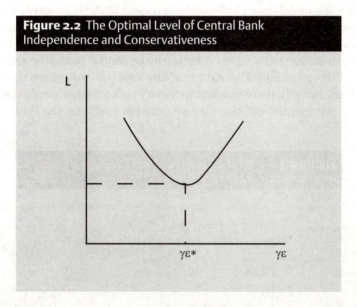

Figure 2.2 The Optimal Level of Central Bank Independence and Conservativeness

[4] The solution to reduce the inflationary bias by delegating monetary policy to a conservative and independent central banker has been criticized by McCallum (1995). His argument is that if the time inconsistency problem is present when the government performs monetary policy, it remains when policy is delegated as government can still create surprise inflation by changing the terms of delegation. In other words, delegation does not resolve the time inconsistency problem, it merely relocates it. Implicitly it has been assumed in the analysis as presented above, that the costs of changing the 'rules of the game' are prohibitive. Jensen (1997) addressed this issue in a model where the choice of delegation is part of the strategic interaction and where a formal commitment technology is considered explicitly. When it is costly to change delegation, Jensen shows that delegation to some extent reduces the time inconsistency problem. However, only in the special case where costs are all that matter for the government is the inconsistency problem resolved completely by delegating monetary policy to a conservative and independent central banker.

[5] In writing this part we benefited from discussions with Helge Berger.

inflation aversion as government (i.e. $\varepsilon = 0$), independence does not matter. And similarly, if the central bank is fully under the spell of government (i.e. $\gamma = 0$), the conservativeness of the central bank does not matter. There are various combinations of γ and ε that may yield the same outcome, including the optimal one. We can illustrate this in Figure 2.3. The lines drawn represent different levels of the loss of society. There is an optimal level of $\gamma\varepsilon$, that is, the product of independence and conservativeness of the central bank. Hence, a lack of independence may be compensated by appointing more conservative central bankers.

From a practical point the concept of a 'conservative' central banker seems, however, void, if only because the preferences of possible candidates for positions in the governing board of a central bank are generally not very easy to identify and may change after they have been appointed. So, it is hard to find some real-world example of a 'conservative' central banker. Still, one could argue that the statute of the central bank could be relevant here. Whether or not the statute of a central bank defines price stability as the primary policy goal, can be considered as a proxy for the 'conservative bias' of the central bank as embodied in the law (Cukierman 1992).

Apart from a *legislative approach* to create by law an independent central bank and to mandate it to direct its policies towards achieving price stability—which is the approach that has mainly been followed with respect to the ECB—other mechanisms have been suggested to overcome the incentive problems of monetary policy. The so-called *contracting approach* regards the design of monetary institutions as one that involves the structuring of a contract between the central bank (the agent) and the government (the principal). The nature of the contract will affect the incentives facing the bank and will, thereby, affect monetary policy (Persson and Tabellini 1993). Walsh (1995) has pointed out that the government could set the central banker's

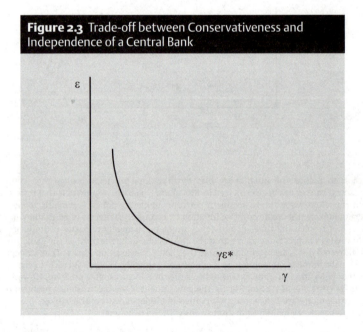

Figure 2.3 Trade-off between Conservativeness and Independence of a Central Bank

rewards contingent upon realized inflation. The Walsh solution takes the form of a contract between the government and the central bank. The contract is structured such that a linear tax is imposed upon the central bank for any inflation in excess of the inflation target. In all other respects, the central bank is given complete discretion when setting policy. It turns out that an inflation contract can be designed so as to eliminate the inflation bias, whilst ensuring that the central banker's stabilization of the real economy is at the optimal level.

So from a theoretical point of view it can be argued that an independent central bank may reduce the inflationary bias of monetary policy-making. What about the empirical evidence? A substantial amount of empirical research supports the inverse relationship between central bank independence and the level of inflation (see Eijffinger and De Haan 1996 and Berger, de Haan, and Eijffinger 2000). This evidence generally consists of cross-section regressions in which average inflation over a certain period is 'explained' inter alia by some measure of central bank independence.[6] Some of these measures are explained in more detail in Box 10.

The negative relationship between indicators of central bank independence and inflation in OECD countries is quite robust, particularly if various control variables are included in the regression. However, it should be noted that a negative correlation does not necessarily imply causation. The correlation between both variables could be explained by a third factor (for example, the culture and tradition of monetary stability in a country).

2.3 Independence of the E(S)CB

IN the previous sections it has been argued that an independent (and conservative) central bank may improve the inflation performance. How independent is the ECB in comparison with national central banks? We will answer this question in two steps. First, based on the general definition of central bank independence as provided in the previous section, the legislation for the ECB is described. Second, we will present various indicators of central bank independence for the ECB and compare them with those for the G7 countries as far as they do not participate in the euro area.

2.3.1 Independence of the ECB

As pointed out in section 2.1, the Governing Council of the ECB will formulate monetary policy in the EMU. The Executive Board must implement monetary policy in

---

[6] The use of legal indicators for central bank independence has been criticized by Forder (1996), who argues that there is no theory that says it matters what the rules say. There is only a theory that says it matters what the behaviour is. Of course, one could conjecture that regulations concerning the position of the central bank may (at least partially) shape the options for the central bank to pursue the kind of policies that it deems necessary.

Box 10 How to Measure Central Bank Independence?

In the literature various indicators for central bank independence have been constructed which differ in the weights given to the different aspects of central bank independence. They have in common that they are all based on the law(s) governing the central bank. This implies that these indicators may differ due to diverging interpretations of the law. Section 2.3 presents the scores of the ECB for the various indicators.

The pioneering attempt to measure legal central bank independence of Bade and Parkin (1988) was extended by Alesina (1989). His index focuses on questions like: Does the central bank have final authority over monetary policy? Are there government officials on the governing board of the bank? Are more than half of the board members appointed by the federal government?

Grilli, Masciandaro, and Tabellini (1991) present indices of political and economic independence. The first focuses on appointment procedures for board officials, the length of their term in office, and the existence of statutory requirements to pursue monetary stability. The economic independence indicator focuses on the extent to which the central bank is free from government influence in implementing monetary policy. Generally the total score on the political and economic independence is employed as an indicator for legal central bank independence.

Eijffinger and Schaling (1993) have constructed an index which centres on three items: the location of the final responsibility for monetary policy, the absence or presence of a government official on the board of the central bank, and the fraction of board appointees made by government. Central bank laws under which the central bank is the final authority get a double score. The number of positive answers plus one gives the total score on this index.

Cukierman (1992) provides an index which is the aggregate from sixteen basic legal characteristics of central bank charters, which in turn are grouped into four clusters: 1. the appointment, dismissal, and legal term of office of the governor of the central bank; 2. the institutional location of the final authority for monetary policy and procedures to resolve conflicts between the government and the bank; 3. the importance of price stability in comparison to other objectives; 4. the stringency and universality of limitations on the ability of government to borrow from the central bank.

accordance with the guidelines and decisions of the Governing Council. The members of the Executive Board are appointed by the governments of the member countries, on a recommendation from the European Council after it has consulted the European Parliament and the Governing Council of the ECB. The term of office of Board Members is eight years and the mandate is not renewable. This ensures the *personnel independence* of the members of the Executive Board.

From the start of the second stage of EMU in 1994 it was no longer allowed for central banks to provide credit to their respective governments, though they were allowed to act as 'fiscal agent'. So, the *financial independence* of the ECB also seems to be warranted. However, there is nothing that the ECB precludes to engage in operations at the secondary market for government bonds, which may have exactly the same outcome as direct provision of credit. The Stability and Growth Pact (see section 4.2) may be regarded as an additional safeguard to ensure that national governments remain sufficiently solvent so that the ECB does not have to bail them out.

From section 2.1 it will be clear that the ECB has little *goal independence*, since its primary objective is price stability. Still, the Maastricht Treaty does not define price stability. Although many central bankers and economists would consider an inflation rate between zero and 2 per cent consistent with price stability, one may wonder whether a somewhat higher inflation rate is still in accordance with the mandate of the ECB. So, there is some room for manoeuvre for the ECB with respect to the goals of monetary policy (see section 3.2 for further details). As pointed out before, one possible threat to the primary objective for the ECB may come from formal exchange rate arrangements.

The Maastricht Treaty includes various provisions to ensure that the ESCB will be independent. Neither the ECB nor a national central bank, nor any member of their decision-making bodies shall seek or take instructions from Community institutions or bodies, from any government of a member state or from any other body. Every member state (also those with a derogation, that is the EU countries outside the eurozone) must ensure that its national legislation, including the statutes of its national central bank, is compatible with the Treaty and the Statute of the ESCB. So, the *instrument independence* of the ECB seems guaranteed too.

2.3.2 Independence of the ECB: A Comparison

In order to compare the independence of the ECB with those of national central banks, we have calculated the scores for the ECB for various indicators of legal central bank independence. Table 2.2 summarizes the indices as discussed in Box 10 and compares the scores for the ECB with those of the other G7 countries, as far as they are not part of the euro area. As the Statute of the ECB is largely modelled after the law governing the Bundesbank, we start by providing the scores for the Bundesbank (before the start of EMU).

The ECB score for the Alesina index is 4, since the ECB has final authority over monetary policy, there are no government officials on the Governing Council, and more than half of the members of the Governing Council are not appointed by the European Council. For the same reasons the score on the Eijffinger-Schaling index is 5. As only two questions used to construct the index of Grilli, *et al.* are not answered in the affirmative (namely, 'is the governor not appointed by the government?' and 'are all policy board members not appointed by the government?'), the total score of the ECB for this measure is fourteen. The score for the Cukierman index is based on our interpretation of the various issues taken into account in constructing this indicator.

It follows from Table 2.2 that the ECB is indeed very independent, and may be regarded as even more independent than the Bundesbank. This is certainly true if one takes into account that in Germany the law which describes the functions of the

Table 2.2 Central Bank Independence: A Comparison

Measure	Alesina	Grilli, Masciandaro, Tabellini	Eijffinger-Schaling	Cukierman
Maximum total score	4	16	5	1.00
personnel independence	2	6	2	0.20
financial independence	1	5	—	0.50
policy independence	1	5	2	0.30
of which				
instrument independence		3		0.15
goal independence		2		0.15
Germany	4	13	5	0.66
Canada	2	11	1	0.46
Japan	3	6	3	0.16
UK	2	6	2	0.31
US	3	12	3	0.51
ECB	4	14	5	0.94

Source: Eijffinger and De Haan 1996.

Bundesbank could be changed by simple parliamentary majority, whereas in the case of the ECB a unanimous decision of all member states is required. Even though the ECB's independence is properly arranged for, this does not imply that there will be no conflicts between the ECB and national governments (see Box 11 for an example).

2.4 Accountability of the E(S)CB

IN contrast to the concept of central bank independence, there is no consensus in the literature about the concept of central bank accountability. Various authors hold different views on the definition and crucial elements of democratic accountability. In a general sense, we define *accountability* as meaning that policy-makers can be and will be held to account for the economic performance of the targets in their care. In other words, policy-makers will be held responsible for how close indicators for the economic performance come to the target values set. In a democratic society parliament represents the view of the electorate. Therefore, it is crucial that either the central bank is directly accountable to parliament, or that the central bank is accountable to government who in turn is, of course, accountable vis-à-vis parliament. In the latter case, government should have instruments to influence the central bank (for example, the possibility to override policy decisions of the central bank).

In our view the concept of central bank accountability has three main features: 1. decisions about the *ultimate objectives* of monetary policy; 2. *transparency of actual*

Box 11 The Struggle for the ECB Presidency: Central Bank Independence in Practice

With the historic launch of the euro, the President of the ECB, Wim Duisenberg, has arguably become one of the world's most powerful central bankers. Although he has only one of seventeen votes on the bank's Governing Council, the President of the ECB is the 'face' of the ECB. Duisenberg was born in the Netherlands in 1935. He studied economics at the University of Groningen, where he received his Ph.D. in 1965. He worked for the IMF and was minister of Finance and head of the Dutch central bank before he joined the EMI. After serving as EMI's President, Duisenberg was widely expected to become the ECB's first President. Still, his appointment was a prime example of political tinkering. Although there was broad support for Duisenberg's candidacy, the French government proposed a rival candidate Jean-Claude Trichet, France's central bank president and former director of the Treasury. A political deadlock was the result.

   A proposal simply to split the term was considered to be incompatible with the Statute of the ECB. After intense negotiations and fierce political fights (the German central bank president is reported to have clashed with the German prime minister about the latter's willingness to compromise with the French), the problem was eventually solved. Duisenberg was elected for a full eight-year term. However, it was announced that Duisenberg would not stay on for this entire term, given his age. Ever since, there has been a quarrel about the details of this agreement. The French government takes the view that it was agreed that Duisenberg would step down after four years, to be replaced by a Frenchman. However, Duisenberg has always denied that such an agreement exists and that only he himself can decide when he will leave.

monetary policy; 3. final responsibility with respect to monetary policy (see also Amtenbrink 1999). In the next section we will discuss this concept in more detail. We continue by analysing how the democratic accountability of the ECB is arranged for in the Maastricht Treaty. We also discuss how the ECB deals with accountability in practice.

2.4.1 Democratic Accountability of Central Banks

Decisions about the *ultimate objective(s)* of monetary policy should be taken by parliament and not be left to the central bank. So, the central bank law—as enacted by parliament—should provide the ultimate objective(s) of monetary policy. The less a central bank is bound to specific objectives, the more difficult it becomes to evaluate the bank's performance, since a suitable yardstick is missing. As the evaluation of the performance of the central bank is the crucial element of accountability, a clearly stated objective is essential.

   It is also important that the objective(s) are clearly defined. The quantification of policy objectives (for example, a maximum inflation rate) may enhance accountability. A good example is the Reserve Bank of New Zealand, which has price stability as its primary objective. The governor of the Reserve Bank of New Zealand has to agree with the government a tight range for inflation. In this so-called Policy Target Agreement (PTA) a target for the inflation rate is provided.

Finally, in case of various objectives a clear prioritization should be provided, since otherwise it is left to the central bank to decide which of the statutory objectives is given priority at any given time.

In the past, the statutes of most European central banks were rather vague in terms of final objectives, or contained various (possibly conflicting) objectives without giving indications as to their prioritization. For instance, the primary objective of the German Bundesbank was the defence of the value of the currency. Even more vague was the objective of the Dutch central bank, which was to regulate the value of the guilder in a welfare enhancing way.

Transparency forms one of the central elements of democratic accountability. Information concerning the behaviour of the central bank is crucial for the evaluation of its performance. Without this information a well-founded judgement on whether the bank has fulfilled its tasks will be impossible.

It is fairly straightforward to analyse transparency in terms of the model of section 2.2. Suppose that there is uncertainty about the preferences of the central banker (that is, how inflation averse is the central banker?). An easy way to model this is to assume that there are preference shocks, leading to a higher or lower level of conservativeness. The central banker has private information about the realization of the uniformly distributed preference shock on the interval [–h, h]. The loss function of the central bank now becomes:

$$L^{cb} = \frac{1 + \varepsilon - x}{2} \pi_t^2 + \frac{x}{2}(y_t - y_t^*)^2 \text{ with } x \sim U[-h, h] \text{ and } h < \varepsilon \tag{2.7}$$

Inflation will be higher in comparison to the situation framed by equation (2.6) if it is not clear how conservative the central bank is. A positive preference shock makes the central bank less conservative leading to higher (expected) inflation and a stronger reaction to supply shocks. A negative preference shock (–h) has an opposite effect. However, the effect on inflation of a positive preference shock is larger than the effect of a negative one. Because of this asymmetry, a lower variance of preference shocks (more transparency) decreases (expected) inflation and reduces the credibility problem.

Transparency can be accomplished in various ways. A central bank could, for instance, be required regularly to publish monetary policy reports in addition to the annual central bank report. These reports should include details on its past performance and future plans for monetary policy in accordance with the primary objective. This is even more important where a clear objective is missing because in this case the central bank can only be judged on the basis of its own statements. On the basis of these reports (or other information), the central bank should be required to explain publicly to what extent it has been able to reach its objectives. According to some observers, transparency is enhanced by a requirement to publish the minutes of meetings and/or the (reasoned) decisions of the governing board of the bank. The new

Bank of England Act 1998, for instance, prescribes publication of the minutes of the Monetary Policy Committee.

Proponents of an accountable central bank argue that ultimately democratically elected politicians should bear the *final responsibility* for monetary policy. Two issues may be considered crucial here: the relationship with parliament and the existence of some kind of override mechanism.

The relationship between the central bank and parliament has to play a major role in any evaluation of the democratic accountability of the central bank itself. Indeed, while the transparent conduct of monetary policy supports parliament in its decision-making process about the performance of the bank, institutionalized contacts support the overall transparency of monetary policy. Parliament has the opportunity to review the performance of the central bank with regard to monetary policy on a regular basis, while the central bank at the same time can explain and justify its conduct. These contacts should be provided for in the legal basis of the central bank because informal and, thus, non-binding arrangements in this respect put the central banker in a much stronger position vis-à-vis parliament. It may be argued that parliament always holds the ultimate responsibility for monetary policy since it can change the legal basis of the bank. Parliament's legislative power can function as a mechanism of *ex ante* control whereby parliament sets the rules with which the central bank must comply. Moreover, it can function as a mechanism of *ex post* accountability because parliament may decide to change the legal basis of the bank in reaction to actual policy. This mechanism of democratic accountability in the hand of the national parliaments has practically vanished in EMU. The Maastricht Treaty insulates national central banks from any amendments to their legal bases which could infringe the independence of the ESCB and the ECB, or national central banks in performing ESCB-related tasks. This surely excludes any amendments of a national central bank statute redefining the relationship between the bank and government, as this would by definition concern the independence of the bank.

Proponents of a monetary policy that is performed independently from government generally reject override mechanisms. Nevertheless, such a mechanism may be one way to enhance accountability, especially if the central bank is not directly accountable to parliament. Coming back to our model of section 2.2, an override mechanism could be modelled as follows (Lohmann 1992):

$$L^G = \frac{1}{2}\pi_t^2 + \frac{\chi}{2}(y_t - y_t^*)^2 + \delta c \qquad (2.8)$$

where c ($c > 0$) denotes the cost of overriding decisions of the central bank and $\delta = 0$ (no overriding) or $\delta = 1$ (overriding). It is intuitively clear that owing to the possibility of overriding the central bank the inflationary bias will increase ($\pi^G > \pi^{cb}$).[7] In other words, the credibility problem of government will increase if it has the possibility to put aside decisions by the central bank.

---

[7] When there is no overriding, inflation will be: $\pi^{cb} = \dfrac{y_t^* + \pi_t^e + u_t}{2 + \varepsilon}$; with overriding inflation will be: $\pi^G = \dfrac{y_t^* + \pi_t^e + u_t}{2}$.

Government should explain to parliament why it has (not) used the override, and parliament in turn can decide whether it agrees with government. So, eventually parliament decides about monetary policy. The question that arises in this context is whether an override mechanism is per se an infringement of the independent position of the central bank. The key to the answer is that in examining override mechanisms attention has to be paid to the type of override mechanism and the procedure for its application. Generally, three types of override mechanisms can be distinguished, including (in descending order): the right to issue instructions, the right to approve, suspend, annul, or defer decisions, and the right to censor decisions on legal grounds. The first one, in particular, may enhance accountability. For instance, until recently, under the Dutch Bank Act 1948, the minister of Finance had the right to give the Dutch central bank certain instructions concerning the conduct of monetary policy. Whether he really used this right (which indeed he never did) is of limited importance. By abstaining from giving instructions, the minister and thus the government implicitly approved of actual policy which made government accountable vis-à-vis parliament. Similarly, the Reserve Bank Act 1989 gives the New Zealand minister of Finance the right to override the objective of price stability. The central bank remains in charge of monetary policy but should aim for the objective as specified by the government. This type of override mechanism is of a very different nature than, for example, the right that the German government had to suspend a decision of the governing council of the Bundesbank, since only the first gives the government the power really to change monetary policy. It is important to realize that the simple fact that government can override the central bank does not necessarily add to the democratic accountability of monetary policy. Indeed, it may, as opponents of such mechanisms emphasize, only open a floodgate for political influence on monetary policy. Therefore, the conditions under which an override mechanism could be applied have to be laid down in detail *ex ante*. The procedure for the application for the override mechanism also needs to be transparent. The decision to apply the override mechanism should be made public. Furthermore, the procedure to apply an override should provide for some kind of review, such as a possibility for the central bank to appeal, in order to ensure that the override is being used carefully.

2.4.2 The Democratic Accountability of the European Central Bank

In this subsection we will first compare the accountability of the ECB with that of the central banks of the G7 countries as far as they do not participate in the euro area. We focus on accountability as prescribed in the law governing the central banks. The next step is to show that the ECB goes further than its legal basis, especially in terms of transparency.

Table 2.3 compares the accountability of various central banks, quantifying the three crucial aspects of central bank accountability we have distinguished in section 2.4.1.

Table 2.3 Comparing (Legal) Accountability of Various Central Banks

Various aspects of accountability	Bank of Canada	Bank of Japan	Bank of England	Federal Reserve System	ECB
1. Does the central bank law stipulate the objectives of monetary policy?	*	*	*	*	*
2. Is there a clear prioritization of objectives?	—	—	*	—	*
3. Are the objectives clearly defined?	—	—	*	—	*
4. Are the objectives quantified (in the law or based on document based on the law)?	—	—	*	—	—
Subtotal on *ultimate objectives of monetary policy*	1	1	4	1	3
5. Must the central bank publish an inflation or monetary policy report of some kind, in addition to standard central bank bulletins/report?	*	—	*	*	—
6. Are minutes of meetings of the governing board of the central bank made public within a reasonable time?	—	—	*	*	—
7. Must the central bank explain publicly to which extent it has been able to reach its objectives?	*	*	*	*	*
Subtotal on *transparency*	2	1	3	3	1
8. Is the central bank subject to monitoring by parliament (is there a requirement—apart from an annual report—to report to parliament and/or explain policy actions in parliament)?	*	*	*	*	*
9. Has the government the right to give instructions?	*	*	*	—	—
10. Is there some kind of review in the procedure to apply the override mechanism?	*	*	*	*	—
11. Has the central bank possibility for an appeal in case of an instruction?	—	—	—	—	—
12. Can the central bank law be changed by a simple majority in parliament?	*	*	*	*	—
13. Is past performance a ground for dismissal of a central bank governor?	—	—	—	—	—
Subtotal on *final responsibility*	4	4	4	2	1
Total on accountability	**7**	**6**	**11**	**6**	**5**

Source: De Haan, Amtenbrink, and Eijffinger 1999.

Although the legal basis of the ECB defines an explicit *primary objective*, it is up to the Governing Council of the ECB to quantify price stability. In October 1998 the Governing Council defined price stability as an annual increase in the Harmonised Index of Consumer Prices (HICP) for the euro area below 2 per cent. The Governing Council explicitly announced that price stability is to be maintained over the medium term (see section 3.2 for further details).

As far as *transparency* is concerned, the legal basis of the ECB foresees the publication of reports on the activities of the ESCB on at least a quarterly basis. In addition, the ECB has decided to publish a Monthly Bulletin. Furthermore, the Governing Council of the ECB has decided that it will regularly inform the public about its monetary policy decisions. The Council will meet every fortnight. The first meeting in every month will be followed by a press conference. When policy decisions are made, the reasoning behind specific decisions will be communicated to the public immediately after the meeting at which they have been taken. Minutes of the meetings will not be published. However, the idea behind presenting the reasoning of the Governing Council serves, of course, exactly the same goal as publishing minutes (that is, the explanation of the decisions taken). The only difference is that minutes could also reveal voting patterns in the Governing Council. As the Council has a clear collective responsibility the usefulness of making voting behaviour public seems limited.

With respect to the *final responsibility for monetary policy*, it should be noted that the relationship between the ECB and the European Parliament (EP) cannot be easily compared with that between a national parliament and a national central bank. First of all, the EP is not a true legislative. Although in various cases it decides together with the Council, in a number of important areas the EP only plays a consultative role. The EP clearly has not the power to change the legal basis of the ECB. Apart from some minor amendments, a change of the institutional structure of the ECB would require an amendment of the Maastricht Treaty.

A somewhat more meaningful role is given to the EP with regard to appearances of members of the ECB before the EP. Apart from the yearly presentation of an annual report of the activities of the ESCB by the President of the ECB, the EP can ask the members of the Executive Board to appear before the Committee for Monetary and Economic Affairs. The ECB has gone some way here as Duisenberg has already expressed his willingness to appear before the EP at least four times a year, apart from the presentation of the Annual Report.

Neither the Maastricht Treaty nor the ESCB Statute contains any provisions that would enable the Council or any other Community institution to override the ECB with regard to monetary policy. The reason for this is apparent as every effort was put into insulating the ECB from any political influence from either Community institutions or member states. The legal bases of the national central banks participating in the ESCB are also not allowed to include override mechanisms.

2.5 Conclusion

FROM 1999 onwards the Eurosystem, with the ECB at its centre, is responsible for monetary policy-making in the euro area. The ECB will have a hard job matching the reputation of its neighbour in Frankfurt, the Bundesbank. Still, the Maastricht Treaty has given the ECB a very independent position and a relatively clear mandate to strive for price stability. In both respects the ECB is in a better position than the Bundesbank to live up to expectations. It is widely believed that an independent central bank with a clear mandate for price stability may be helpful in containing inflation. However, the drafters of the Maastricht Treaty seem to have forgotten that the democratic accountability of a central bank is also important. This could be owing to the idea among policy-makers that there is a trade-off between independence and accountability. Although this might be true regarding the final responsibility for monetary policy, transparency of monetary policy will certainly be beneficial to the position of the central bank. The ECB seems to be aware of this and has made it clear that it strives for a transparent conduct of monetary policy. After having described the institutional set-up of the E(S)CB, the following chapter will discuss its monetary policy.

Chapter 3
European Monetary Policy

Introduction

A **COMMON** monetary policy in the euro zone countries is a novelty. In the past, the German Bundesbank determined monetary developments in most of Europe. Policy decisions were mainly based on the economic situation in Germany. In contrast, in striving for its objective of price stability the ECB has to take the economic situation in the entire 'euroland' into account. How this should be done—(that is, which strategy the ECB should follow) was discussed extensively before the monetary union started. However, no consensus was reached. The European Monetary Institute summarized the options (mainly inflation targeting and monetary targeting) and it was left to the ECB to decide upon its strategy.[1] Section 3.1 first discusses the main differences between both options, before the actual monetary strategy of the ECB is outlined in section 3.2. Next, the monetary instruments of the ECB are explained. Moreover, we will give an analysis of the transmission mechanism of European monetary policy and the balance sheet of the ECB (section 3.3). As has been described in the previous chapter, not all EU member states participate (yet) in EMU. Section 3.4 therefore provides an analysis of the relationship between the 'ins' and the 'outs' and the 'new' Exchange Rate Mechanism (ERM II). Finally, section 3.5 deals with the ECB and banking supervision.

---

[1] EMI (1997). An update of this report with a detailed description of the monetary policy instruments and procedures of the ESCB was published by the ECB (ECB 1998).

3.1 The Monetary Policy Strategy: Options

DURING the discussion about the monetary strategy of the ECB, it became clear that the ECB would have to choose between two options: monetary targeting and inflation targeting. The differences between the approaches are illustrated in Table 3.1. A main difference between both strategies is the choice of the intermediate target.

In both strategies the ultimative objective is price stability. Why worry about inflation? Central bankers and most economists view price stability as a worthy objective since they believe inflation to be costly. Some of these costs involve the average rate of inflation, while others relate to the variability and uncertainty of inflation. Generally a difference is made here between expected and unexpected inflation (Buti and Sapir 1998).

Expected inflation can affect the allocation of the economy's resources in three ways. First, inflation places a tax on money balances when those balances pay less than the market rate of interest. Consumers and businesses will make more trips to the bank to avoid holding significant amounts of currency. These costs are generally referred to as *shoe leather costs*. A second cost arises because many tax systems are defined in nominal terms. As a result higher nominal incomes which are only due to inflation can lead to a higher tax burden relative to income (bracket creep). Some studies report that inflation exacerbates the distortions inherent in tax and benefit systems considerably (Feldstein 1999). A third cost of expected inflation are so-called *menu costs*, or costs to firms of changing prices (reprinting price lists, informing customers, and so on).

The most important consequence of unexpected inflation is redistribution of wealth. Its implications are harder to gauge since losses to some parties are matched by gains to others. Still, the point is that this redistribution may be significant and is always arbitrary. Many economists believe that higher inflation also leads to more inflation uncertainty. Uncertainty about the rate of inflation can introduce serious costs. It may lead to a risk premium in interest rates, possibly lowering investment. Furthermore, it may undermine the functioning of markets. In a market economy, households and businesses base their decisions on prices of goods and assets. In other words, prices are signals upon which the resource allocation is based. Relative prices, not individual prices, provide these signals. Under fluctuating inflation it is very often not clear whether relative prices have changed or the general price level. In other

Table 3.1 Monetary Policy Strategies

Strategy	Operational target	Intermediate target	Ultimate objective
Monetary targeting	Short-term interest rate	Money supply (growth)	(Trend) inflation
Inflation targeting	Short-term interest rate	(Expected) inflation	Inflation target

words, valuable signals provided by markets are distorted, thereby hindering the efficient allocation of resources both across uses and across time. This is especially true in case of hyperinflation.

Empirical evidence suggests that the benefits of price stability for economic growth are significant. Several studies conclude that countries with lower inflation appear, on average, to grow more rapidly (see, for example, Barro 1997).

The general conclusion from the preceding analysis is that businesses and households perform poorly when inflation is high and unpredictable. The question then becomes how to reach price stability.

In the *monetary targeting* approach some target (zone) for the growth rate of one (or sometimes more) monetary aggregate(s) is announced and aimed at in order to reach price stability. The policy of the Bundesbank is probably the most famous example of the monetary targeting strategy. It involved three steps: (i) the selection of the inflation objective; (ii) the derivation of the intermediate monetary target and announcement of the target as well as the range for permissible deviations; and (iii) the steering of the growth of the money stock within the target range in response to excess inflation and changes in the external value of the German mark.

There are three prerequisites for a successful monetary targeting policy:

- The demand for money function should be stable.
- The targeted monetary aggregrate should be under the control of the central bank.
- The intermediate target should be a leading indicator for inflation.

A *stable money demand* function means that the relationship between money demand and its determinants is predictable. For instance, if policy-makers raise interest rates, they can predict within reasonable bounds what the effects of their policy on money demand will be. Absence of such a stable relationship would make focusing on money growth as intermediate target senseless. A stable money demand function also implies a predictable relationship between the money stock and the ultimate objective of monetary policy. Most studies on the stability of the European money demand function (that is, aggregated money demand functions) conclude that it is more stable than money demand in individual member countries (see Box 12 for a further analysis). However, one may wonder whether stability of aggregated money demand functions has anything to say about the stability of the demand for money function in the EMU, since the latter constitutes definitely a new regime.

With respect to controllability it is clear that the broader is the monetary aggregate chosen, the more difficult it may be to control its rate of growth by manipulating the short-term interest rate. A broader aggregate includes many instruments that bear interest (see Box 14 for details about monetary aggregates). Raising short-term interest rates will lead to substitution by economic subjects from non-interest-bearing to interest-bearing assets. This substitution leaves the broad monetary aggregate unaffected.

Whether a monetary aggregate is a leading indicator for future inflation is, of course, of prime importance in a monetary targeting strategy. Still, it is also relevant in an inflation targeting approach. For some countries there are indications that some broad monetary aggregates like M3 contain relevant information to predict inflation.

Box 12 The Stability of European Money Demand Function in Stage Three

Browne, Fagan, and Henry (1997) have surveyed around sixty papers on the theoretical and empirical aspects of money demand functions in EU countries. Money demand functions have been estimated for nearly all EU countries, in particular for Germany. Early studies of money demand have focused on a narrow money aggregate (M1), while more recent ones have examined the broad money aggregate (M3). Money demand is expressed as a function of prices, real income, one or more market interest rates (or a weighted average of interest rates), and sometimes currency substitution proxies (such as the exchange rate of the US dollar vis-à-vis the ECU or German mark). Most studies have been carried out using quarterly data with samples usually beginning at, or soon after, the late 1970s. There seems to be a consensus that the EU-wide money demand function is stable in the long run, especially in comparison with national money demand functions. Income elasticities for narrow money are found to be close to unity and for broad money generally exceeding unity, while interest elasticities have the expected sign and are normally significant. Although currency substitution effects are usually significant as well, they are quite small.

What explains the relative stability of EU-wide money demand compared with the national money demand? The first explanation is that changes in national money stocks due to trade, tourism, or capital flows can contribute to instability in national money demands, but mostly cancel out at an EU-wide level. Second, if currency substitution is confined to currencies of other EU countries, it will be neutralized within Europe leaving EU-wide money aggregates insulated. Third, since the ERM apparently operated as an asymmetric system with Germany as the anchor country, the money stock in individual non-anchor countries was largely demand-determined and, as they account for the bulk of the non-anchor European countries, EU-wide money stock is more closely related to the demand variables. Fourth, the dominant central bank in the ERM—the Bundesbank—was deliberately not targeting any EU-wide (or sub-EU-wide) money stock which would have jeopardized the stable relationship between money and prices (*Lucas critique*). Fifth, the relatively limited extent of major financial innovations in some EU countries and the different timing of these innovations across EU countries could also have contributed to a more stable European money demand function.

Arnold (1994) emphasizes that the sources of EU-wide money demand stability before and in Stage Two are crucial for its stability in Stage Three of EMU. If stability is caused by the averaging-out of shocks within the EU (first explanation), then it will only persist to the extent that these shocks will not be more synchronized in the third stage. If it is caused by the neutralization of currency substitution (second explanation), we may expect the stability of European money demand to continue into Stage Three. However, if stability is due to the asymmetry of the ERM, the lack of EU-wide monetary targeting or the limited and varying financial innovation (third, fourth, and fifth explanation), then there is a 'major risk' that the stability of European money demand may not continue in Stage Three. Nevertheless, the third stage of EMU implies a regime shift causing new sources of instability, in particular with respect to large and unpredictable disturbances in the velocity of money. Monetary targeting may, therefore, result in too much volatility of the European (short-term) interest rate with detrimental effects on output and unemployment.

Various European countries have at times followed a monetary targeting strategy. As Table 3.2 shows, money targeting can hardly be considered as a success: targets were very often missed, also in Germany.

It is sometimes argued that an inflation targeting strategy eschews an intermediate target. In a way this is correct: an intermediate target for money growth is quite different from expected inflation. The money target is aimed for, while the expected inflation rate—without policy changes taken into account—may not be the preferred policy outcome that should be aimed at. However, both money growth targets and inflation forecasts have one important thing in common: policy decisions are primarily based on these variables. If money growth is above the intermediate target, policy will turn more restrictive. The same happens if expected inflation is above the level considered being consistent with price stability.

An *inflation targeting* approach was first introduced in New Zealand in 1989. The Governor of the Reserve Bank of New Zealand can, under certain circumstances, be dismissed if the inflation rate exceeds a certain target, (set in the so-called 'Policy Target Agreement'). Thus, the government imposes an explicit inflation target on the central bank and makes the Governor explicitly accountable for meeting this target. Such a system of inflation targeting is in the literature referred to as the contracting approach (see section 2.2).

Inflation targeting is pursued in a more moderate way in Canada, Sweden, and the United Kingdom. For instance, in Canada inflation targeting has been implemented with formal target bands for reducing the inflation rate (CPI). These inflation-reduction targets were announced in early 1991 both by the Bank of Canada and the government to prevent a further wage–price spiral and to reduce the prevailing inflationary expectations, but also to realize price stability and to gain credibility (Freedman 1994). The loosest way of inflation targeting can be found in the United Kingdom. At the end of 1992 the British government set a target range of 1 to 4 per cent for the inflation rate (RPIX). Since 1993 the Bank of England has published a quarterly Inflation Report providing the expected time path of inflation. However, the inflation targets, set by the government, are a reference value for UK monetary policy, but involve no costs if not realized (see Bernanke, *et al.* 1998 for further discussion).

A concern often raised with respect to inflation targeting is that its effectiveness is relatively hard to assess. Since interest rate changes affect inflation through many different channels with 'long and variable' lags, monetary policy has to rely on a number of indicators to choose a time path for the instrument that is consistent with the inflation target. Furthermore, inflation is not entirely (others would perhaps say, entirely not) under the control of the monetary authorities, since it is affected also by a myriad of other factors, which implies that the central bank should not be held entirely responsible for inflation (Issing 1994). However, this argument also holds to a certain degree for the monetary targeting approach because money growth is not directly controlled by the central bank.

Although there are definitely some differences between the two strategies, these differences should not be exaggerated. Indeed, inflation targets are an essential ingredient of German monetary policy serving as the basis in the strategy of the

Table 3.2 Money Targeting Marksmanship in Europe, 1975–1998

Country	Period[a]	Average deviation[b]	Average absolute deviation[c]	Average width of target range[d]	Target achieved[e]
Germany[f]	1975–1998	0.98	1.70	2.53	42%
Central Bank Money	1975–1987	0.92	1.72	2.67	38%
M3	1988–1998	1.05	1.69	2.40	45%
France	1977–1998	−1.00	2.53	1.88	22%
M2	1977–1985, 1987–1990	−0.11	1.60	1.71	23%
M3	1986–1987, 1991–1998	−2.16	3.74	2.10	20%
UK	1976/77–1991/92	2.93	3.34	4.00	42%
£M3	1976/77–1986/87	4.24	4.74	4.00	25%
M1	1982/83–1983/84	3.70	3.70	4.00	0%
PSL2	1982/83–1983/84	2.60	2.60	4.00	50%
M0	1984/85–1991/92	0.86	1.34	4.00	75%
Netherlands[g] Liquidity ratio	1977–1980	0.45	0.45	—	0%
Italy (M2)	1984–1998	0.81	1.87	2.78	33%
Spain	1978–1994	2.00	2.80	3.59	47%
M3	1978–1983	0.57	1.40	4.17	83%
ALP	1984–1994	2.78	3.56	3.27	27%
Greece	1975–1997	1.33	5.02	2.50	11%
M1	1975–1987	0.22	6.02	—	15%
M3	1983–1997	2.29	4.16	2.50	7%
Portugal (L−)	1987–1989	0.98	1.58	3.63	67%
EU average[h]	1975–1998	1.14	2.91	3.00	31%

Source: Houben 1999.

Notes:

[a] Relates to the period during which money targeting was implemented, respectively the sub-period during which a specific money aggregate was targeted.

[b] Indicates the average deviation (in per cent of the initial money stock) between the money growth outcome and the point target or the mid-point of the target range.

[c] Indicates the average absolute deviation (in per cent of the initial money stock) between the money growth outcome and the point target or the mid-point of the target range.

[d] Indicates average width of target range in years that target ranges (rather than point targets or ceilings) were announced.

[e] Percentage number of targets achieved. Point targets are assumed to have been met when the outcome was within ±0.5% points of the target.

[f] On the basis of rounded figures, the Bundesbank considers the money targets in 1980 (5–8%), 1981 (4–7%) and 1991 (3–5%) to have been met (outcomes 4.9%, 3.5%, respectively 5.2%). This would improve the overall target achievement ratio from 42% to 54%.

[g] Target related to the *minimum* decline in the Liquidity ratio (that is, M2 as a percentage of GDP); deviations are expressed in per cent of GDP.

[h] Excluding the Netherlands, which expressed money targets in per cent of GDP rather than in percentage growth rates.

Bundesbank, which is typically characterized as monetary targeting (Eijffinger 1996). We can illustrate this argument with the quantity theory equation of Fisher (see Box 13).

Cukierman (1995) argues that the choice of the intermediate target involves a trade-off between controllability and visibility. While the central bank may presumably exert a reasonable control over the money stock, announcements about its growth rate may not have an immediate and substantial impact on inflationary expectations, given the 'long and variable' lag between money growth and inflation. In contrast, announcements about inflation targets are more likely to influence inflationary expectations, but, as already pointed out above, the controllability of the rate of inflation is less. An interesting conclusion that follows from Cukierman's model is that when reputation is very high, inflation targets are more efficient than money growth targets. This suggests that when the ECB could inherit the credibility of the Bundesbank, inflation targeting should be used. On the other hand, one could

---

Box 13 The Quantity Theory Equation of Fisher

The *quantity theory equation* of Fisher can be written as follows:

$$\dot{m} + \dot{v} = \dot{p} + \dot{y} \tag{3.1}$$

where $\dot{m}$ is the growth rate of the money stock (supply), $\dot{v}$ is the (relative) change of the velocity of money, $\dot{p}$ is the inflation rate (relative change of the price level) and $\dot{y}$ is the growth rate of real output. Rearranging equation (3.1) with respect to money growth gives the following equation:

$$\dot{m} = \dot{p} + \dot{y} - \dot{v} \tag{3.2}$$

This equation being an identity suggests that there is a stable relationship between money growth and inflation depending on real output growth and the change of money velocity. Monetary targeting means that the central bank sets a target (zone) for money growth in order to aim for a certain inflation rate (target) conditional on the expected real output growth and the predicted velocity of money.

The calculation of a target zone for M3 by the Bundesbank was not only based on the expected economic growth in real terms and the predicted velocity of money, but also on normative inflation (lying within a range of 0 to 2 per cent inflation). Thus the Bundesbank implicitly assumed an inflation target too in calculating its monetary target for M3 (von Hagen 1995). The reasoning also may be reversed in the sense that every inflation target implicitly assumes a monetary target, although the weight on the monetary aggregate in predicting expected inflation might be relatively less. Therefore, the debate during Stage Two between representatives of the Bundesbank insisting on monetary targeting and those of the Bank of England promoting inflation targeting was, in our opinion, somewhat artificial because it is basically a matter of *relative weights* given to the various information variables. It is exactly the uncertainty about these relative weights which has been the main argument for the Governing Council of the ECB to combine elements of monetary and inflation targeting at the start of Stage Three. We will discuss this in section 3.2.

argue that perhaps the best way for the ECB to inherit the credibility of the Bundesbank is to follow the same strategy.

3.2 The Monetary Policy Strategy of the ECB

As explained in the previous chapter, the primary objective of the ESCB is price stability. However, the Maastricht Treaty does not provide for a specific definition of this objective. In October 1998 the Governing Council of the ECB agreed that price stability is defined as a year-on-year increase in the *Harmonised Index of Consumer Prices* (HICP) for the euro area of below 2 per cent. The HICP is a comprehensive measure for inflation, reflecting the focus of the general public on consumer goods. It is the only harmonized price index currently available in the euro area. By choosing this definition, the ECB does not take asset inflation into account.

The aim of an inflation rate 'below 2 per cent' clearly delineates the maximum rate of inflation deemed to be consistent with price stability. The wording 'year-on-year increases' implies that persistent price decreases—that is to say deflation —would not be considered to be consistent with price stability either. The Governing Council explicitly announced that price stability is to be maintained over the medium term, thereby acknowledging that price levels may be temporarily distorted by short-term factors. The wording 'for the euro area' highlights that area-wide developments, instead of specific national or regional factors, will be the only determinants of decisions regarding the single monetary policy.

The monetary policy strategy of the ECB rests on two 'pillars' (ECB, *Monthly Bulletin* (Jan. 1999)). The first pillar is a prominent role for money. As inflation in the long run is considered to be a monetary phenomenon, the ECB Governing Council has announced a quantitative reference value for money growth. The second pillar is a broadly based assessment both of the outlook regarding price developments and of the risks to price stability in the euro area as a whole. According to the ECB, the chosen strategy ensures as much continuity as possible with the existing strategies of national central banks, notably the Bundesbank. At the same time, it gives due consideration to the unique situation created by the transition to Monetary Union.

The Governing Council will regularly analyse the relationship between actual monetary growth and the pre-announced reference value. If the deviation of monetary growth from the reference value indicates a threat to price stability, monetary policy will react accordingly. However, the ECB will not change interest rates in a mechanistic fashion. That is why the ECB does not speak of a target for monetary growth, but rather of a reference value. The reference value refers to the growth rate of M3, which is a broad monetary aggregate.

As explained in the previous section, central banks that follow an inflation targeting approach—like the Bank of England—often publish inflation forecasts. In an inflation targeting approach, the intermediate target for monetary policy does not

consist of a growth rate for money, but expected inflation. Whenever expected inflation threatens to become too high, monetary policy will become more restrictive. In
determining expected inflation, the monetary authorities may use all kinds of information, including money growth rates. The second pillar of the ECB monetary policy
strategy bears some resemblance to this approach. It allows the ECB to change policy
also if money growth is close to the reference value, but where there are other indications that inflation may become too high. The President of the ECB has announced
that from 2000 onwards the ECB inflation forecasts will be published.

Money fulfils three functions in the economy. It serves as a medium of exchange, as
the unit of account, and as a store of value. The better a certain asset fulfils the
functions typically performed by cash, the higher its 'degree of moneyness'. This is
generally measured by the degree of liquidity of the asset. The lower the transaction
costs incurred when making a payment using the purchasing power embedded in the
asset, and the less volatile the nominal value of the asset is over time, the higher its
liquidity will normally be. Given that many different assets are substitutable, and that
the nature and features of financial assets, transactions, and means of payment are
changing over time, it is not always clear how money should be defined and which
financial assets are included in a certain definition of money. For these reasons,
central banks usually define and monitor several monetary aggregates. These range
from very narrow aggregates such as base money to broader aggregates, which
include currency, bank deposits, and certain types of securities. The Eurosystem has
defined a narrow (M1), an 'intermediate' (M2), and a broad aggregate (M3). These
aggregates differ with respect to the degree of moneyness of the assets included (see
Table 3.3).

Why focus on M3?[2] As pointed out before, in selecting a monetary aggregate to
serve as intermediate target, three criteria are relevant:

- Stability of money demand.
- Leading indicator properties of money.
- Controllability of a monetary aggregate.

Table 3.3 Definitions of Euro Area Monetary Aggregates			
Liabilities	M1	M2	M3
Currency in circulation	X	X	X
Overnight deposits	X	X	X
Deposits with agreed maturity up to 2 years		X	X
Deposits redeemable at notice up to 3 months		X	X
Repurchase agreements			X
Money market fund (MMF) shares/units and money market paper			X
Debt securities up to 2 years			X
Source: ECB, *Monthly Bulletin* (Feb. 1999).			

[2] The following parts are based on ECB, *Monthly Bulletin* (Feb. 1999).

Broad aggregates normally show higher stability and better leading indicator properties than narrow aggregates. In contrast, in the short term narrow aggregates are easier to control via official interest rates than are broad aggregates. On balance, the ECB considered the properties of M3 best.

Broad money growth in the euro area has slowed down since 1990. Since the mid-1990s M3 and M2 growth rates have been fairly similar. Furthermore, Figure 3.1 demonstrates that movements in M1 are generally more volatile than those in M3. Since end-1996, M3 growth has stabilized at rates of between $3\frac{1}{2}$ and 5 per cent. At the same time, lower interest rates in the euro area and the improved outlook for price stability have made the most liquid assets more attractive, causing M1 growth to increase.

In setting the *reference value* for monetary growth, the Governing Council of the ECB has taken account of price stability (that is, inflation below 2 per cent) and of a growth rate of 2 to 2½ per cent per annum for trend real GDP. Furthermore, the medium-term trend decline in velocity of money is considered to lie in the approximate range of ½ to 1 per cent each year (see below). Based on these considerations, the Governing Council decided to set the first reference value for monetary growth at 4½ per cent. In December 1999 the Coucil decided not to change the reference value. This growth rate is determined on the basis of the latest three-month moving averages of the monthly year-on-year growth rates for M3. The derivation of the reference value on the basis of trend output and trend velocity indicates that monetary policy is expected to be implemented in a counter-cyclical fashion, since above-trend production growth is generally associated with above-trend money growth—and vice versa.

It is worth while reviewing the ECB's analysis on the velocity of money as this is a crucial factor in determining the reference value for the growth rate of M3. The income velocity of M3 is defined as the ratio between the nominal GDP and (nominal) M3. Velocity has shown a relatively smooth downward trend over the last two decades (see Figure 3.2). Between mid-1992 and mid-1995 this downward trend was

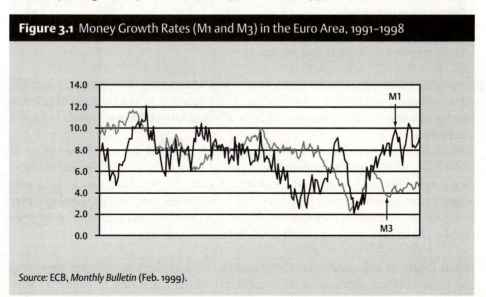

Figure 3.1 Money Growth Rates (M1 and M3) in the Euro Area, 1991–1998

Source: ECB, *Monthly Bulletin* (Feb. 1999).

Box 14 European Monetary Aggregates

The ECB takes the consolidated balance sheet of the Monetary Financial Institutions (MFI) sector as the basis for deriving monetary aggregates in the euro area. The MFI sector comprises those institutions, whose liabilities may be of a monetary nature, including central banks, credit institutions, and other financial institutions, mainly money market funds. For the purpose of defining monetary aggregates, the 'money holding' sector comprises non-MFI euro area residents. Currency in circulation and overnight deposits form the narrow definition of money, referred to as M1. Adding deposits with a maturity of up to two years and deposits redeemable at notice of up to three months gives M2. Finally, M3 is obtained by summing M2 with specific marketable liabilities of the MFI sector (repurchase agreements, money market fund (MMF) shares/units and money market paper, together with debt securities issued with an original maturity of less than two years). Central government deposit liabilities with a monetary character (like post office accounts, national savings accounts and treasury accounts) are included in the definition of monetary aggregates of the Eurosystem.

Table B14.1 Monetary Aggregates in the Euro Area, 1997–1999 (Mrd Euro, End of Period)

	1997	1998	1999 (Nov.)
Currency in circulation	318	324	330
Overnight deposits	1,297	1,458	1,578
M1	1,615	1,777	1,907
Deposits with maturity <2 years	890	886	859
Deposits redeemable at notice up to 3 months	1,162	1,232	1,261
M2	3,667	3,894	4,028
Repurchase agreements	205	177	158
MMF shares/units and money market paper	272	303	423
Debt securities up to 2 years	73	68	81
M3	4,218	4,442	4,689

Source: ECB, Monthly Bulletin (Jan. 1999; Jan. 2000).

temporarily distorted. The exchange rate crises, substantial movements in interest rates, and also incidental factors—such as major changes in the taxation of interest income in some countries—appear to have affected monetary developments during this period.

What is the trend for M3 velocity? As can be seen from Figure 3.2, the estimate of the velocity trend depends on the sample period. For example, over the period 1983–98 the trend decline was around 1 per cent per annum, whereas over more recent periods, starting around the early 1990s, the trend decline was smaller, coming closer to ½ per cent. The Governing Council of the ECB therefore chose a range of ½–1 per cent for the trend decline in velocity, rather than a single figure.

Will inflation be the same in all EMU countries? It is difficult to envisage persistent and large inflation differentials in a monetary union consisting of countries with

Figure 3.2 M3 Velocity Trends for the Euro Area, 1993–1998

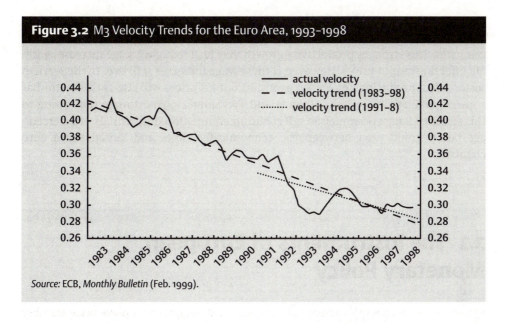

Source: ECB, *Monthly Bulletin* (Feb. 1999).

comparable economic characteristics. However, short-term differentials can be significant owing to differences in relative positions of the business cycle or tax changes. Evidence for Spanish regions suggests that the average differential between the lowest and highest inflation rate in these regions is well below 1 percentage point, although inflation differentials may exceed 3 percentage points. The standard deviation of regional bilateral inflation differentials is often above 2 (see Table 3.4).

If goods can be freely moved across national borders, price arbitrage makes it unlikely that inflation differentials in economically homogenous areas will accumulate to large price differentials. However, inflation differentials may show persistence

Table 3.4 Inflation Differentials across Spanish Regions: Standard Deviation and Maximum Differential (1978–1998)

	Andalucia	Canarias	Cataluña	Galicia	León	Madrid	Valencia
Andalucia	—	2.2	0.7	0.7	0.8	1.3	1.0
Canarias	3.1	—	2.2	2.4	2.1	2.2	2.6
Cataluña	1.2	3.4	—	0.7	0.7	1.2	1.0
Galicia	1.2	3.7	1.1	—	0.8	1.3	0.8
León	1.2	3.2	1.2	1.2	—	1.0	0.7
Madrid	1.3	3.1	1.7	2.0	1.1	—	1.0
Valencia	0.9	3.3	1.1	1.3	1.2	1.2	—

Source: OECD 1999.

Note: The numbers above the diagonal are the standard deviations of annual inflation rate differentials between two regions over the whole period. The numbers below the diagonal are the largest absolute inflation differentials observed during the sample period.

between more- and less-advanced euro zone countries. In so-called catching-up countries, productivity in manufacturing is likely to grow faster than in the other EMU countries. This stronger productivity growth may lead to higher wage increases without affecting output prices. However, if these wage increases spill over to the services sector, often producing non-traded goods, its output prices will rise as this sector has a lower productivity growth. Alberola and Tyrväinen (1998) estimate that owing to this so-called Balassa–Samuelson effect sustained inflation differentials of 2 percentage points could exist between the economically more- and less-advanced euro countries.

3.3 The Instruments of European Monetary Policy

THIS section reviews the arsenal of monetary instruments to achieve price stability in euroland. In drafting the Maastricht Treaty and the Statute of the ECB policymakers have deliberately chosen for indirect, market-oriented instruments. This means that direct instruments, like restrictions on (the growth of) bank credit, are excluded because of their distortionary effects on banking competition. The ECB has the following monetary instruments at its disposal:[3]

1. A *deposit facility* for mopping up liquidity from the banks at rates below market rates. The rate of this facility acts as a floor (lower limit) for short-term money market rates.
2. A *marginal lending or Lombard facility* providing liquidity to the banks at rates usually above market rates. The rate on this facility thus acts as a ceiling (upper limit) for short-term money market rates.
3. *Open market operations* with a fixed frequency and at a fixed term for steering and fine-tuning money market rates in the (very) short run.
4. *Minimum reserve requirements* whose average level is set on a monthly basis with an averaging facility.[4]

The first two instruments, deposit and marginal lending facility, are also called the standing facilities because of the availability of these instruments on the initiative of the banks within the euro zone. The standing facilities constitute a corridor for the (interbank) money market rate and signal the view of the ECB on the desired interest rate development in the medium run. Within that corridor the money market rate is

---

[3] This is based on ECB 1998.

[4] An *averaging facility* implies that the level of bank reserves may drop below the required level as long as this is compensated during the remaining time of the maintenance period. The required reserves are determined on the basis of the balance sheets of the banks at the end of a given calendar month. The maintenance period starts during the following calendar month starting on the 24th day of each month and ending on the 23rd day of the following month.

steered and fine-tuned by means of open market operations. This flexible and market oriented money market management was also applied by the Bundesbank and other national central banks.

The main refinancing operations are regular liquidity providing reserve trans-actions or repurchase agreements (repos) which have a weekly frequency and a maturity of two weeks. These operations are initiated by the ECB and executed by the national central banks on the basis of standard tenders. The rate of these weekly repos is the best indication of the stance of monetary policy in the (very) short run as this instrument provides the bulk of refinancing to the banks. Although they are not standardized, the ECB does not exclude the use of outright transactions, foreign exchange repurchase agreements, and swaps to provide liquidity to the banks and the issuance of central bank paper to absorb liquidity.

Minimum reserve requirements imply that banks are obliged to hold deposits at the central bank as a percentage (ratio) of their eligible monetary liabilities. The ECB applies a minimum reserve ratio of 2 per cent against the following liabilities: over-night deposits, deposits and debt securities with a maturity up to 2 years, and money market paper. The reserves are fully remunerated using the average of the repo rate over the maintenance period. The ECB is able to broaden the range of financial institutions that hold reserves at the central bank in order to avoid possible disinter-mediation and its detrimental effects on bank activity in euroland.

Until the establishment of the ECB, there was a lively debate between European central bankers about the need for minimum reserve requirements (ratios) as a monetary instrument. On the one side, the Bank of England saw cash reserve requirements just as a 'tax on the banking system' (by which it actually means the City of London). The United Kingdom is one of the few industrial countries without reserve requirements.[5] According to the British view, reserve requirements would jeopardize the competitive strength of the European banks against their American and Japanese counterparts (Eijffinger 1996). On the other side, many national central banks, like the Bundesbank, considered the minimum reserve requirements a neces-sary instrument. They would have to be maintained as an average of a specified period in order to smooth short-term interest rate fluctuations in the money market and to stabilize the demand for central bank money (see Deutsche Bundesbank 1996).

On 7 July 1998 the Governing Council of the ECB decided to introduce a minimum reserve system because of its contribution to stabilizing money market interest rates and to enlarging the demand for central bank money and thus creating or increasing a structural liquidity shortage in the European money market. Without such a mini-mum reserve system, the ECB feared a high volatility of money market rates requir-ing the frequent use of open market operations for fine-tuning and, thereby, blurring central bank signals. Next to the aforementioned functions of money market man-agement, the minimum reserve system may also contribute to controlling money growth by increasing the interest elasticity of money demand, if the bank reserves are not (fully) renumerated (ECB 1998).

---

[5] Until 1999 Belgium was the only other EU country with no reserve requirements. Italy, the Netherlands, and Portugal applied paid reserve requirements, while Austria, Finland, France, Germany, Greece, Ireland, and Spain maintained a regime of unpaid reserve requirements.

Box 15 The How and Why of TARGET

TARGET, standing for the Trans-European Automated Real-time Gross Settlement Express Transfer System, is the real-time gross settlement system for the euro. It consists of the ECB payment mechanism (EPM) and all (15) EU national real-time gross settlement (RTGS) systems, which are interlinked in order to provide a uniform infrastructure for the processing of cross-border payments. TARGET is a real-time system (these payments reach their destination within a few minutes or even seconds). It is also a gross settlement system, in which each payment is handled individually with intra-day finality (settlements are final if the funds have been credited).

The three main objectives of TARGET are: (1) to provide a safe and reliable mechanism for the settlement of cross-border payments on an RTGS basis; (2) to increase the efficiency of intra-EU cross-border payments; and, most importantly, (3) to serve the needs of the Eurosystem's monetary policy. By connecting EU-wide national (inter-bank) money markets, TARGET implements a uniform European (inter-bank) money market interest rate, so that banks and other financial institutions in euroland can manage their liquidity positions efficiently and their arbitrage operations easily and swiftly.[6]

The ECB uses the monetary instruments to realize its intermediate targets (that is, money growth (M3) and (expected) inflation and other information variables) indirectly through the *short-term (inter-bank) money market rate*. The successful implementation of European monetary policy will be reflected in a uniform money market interest rate in the euro area. The linking of national money markets into an EMU-wide (inter-bank) money market is done by TARGET (Trans-European Automated Real-time Gross Settlement Express Transfer System). How TARGET works and why it has been developed is briefly described in Box 15. So, the European (inter-bank) money market rate acts as an operational variable, although it is not quantified to control credit expansion in euroland and, thereby, money growth, (expected) inflation, and other information variables. To this end, the ECB applies a system of indirect credit control that is also used in other major industrial countries, such as the United States and Japan. The transmission mechanism of European monetary policy is summarized in Table 3.5.

Decisions about interest rate changes are motivated by the ECB in terms of the two pillars underlying its monetary policy. For example, the interest rate increase of 3 February 2000 was motivated by Duisenberg both in terms of the first pillar ('monetary and credit growth') and the second pillar ('price and costs increases, including oil and non-energy commodity prices as well as producer prices'). Of course, the depreciation of the euro had also contributed to increases in import prices.

Another way of illustrating the monetary instruments of the ECB is by looking at its simplified balance sheet in Table 3.6 which reflects (the sources of) *base money*.[7] The

---

[6] ECB, http://www.ecb.int/.

[7] *Base money* (B) is the total liquid debt of the central bank against the banking sector (cash reserves of the banks) and the private sector (currency, that is, coins and banknotes in circulation).

Table 3.5 The Transmission Mechanism of European Monetary Policy

Monetary instruments	Operational variables	Intermediate variables	Ultimate obectives
Standing facilities (deposit and marginal lending facility) Open market operations (fixed term and frequency) Minimum reserve requirements (with averaging facility)	Short-term (inter-bank) money market rates (not quantified)	Money growth (M3), (expected) inflation, and other information variables	Primary objective: price stability (increase of HICP below 2%)

Table 3.6 The Balance Sheet of the European Central Bank

Net foreign assets	(NFA)	Bank reserves	(R)
Net domestic assets	(NDA)	Currency	(C)
Sources of base money		Base money	(B)

sources of base money are the net foreign and domestic assets of the central bank. The *net foreign assets* (NFA) are the international or official reserves of the ECB, such as gold and claims denominated in foreign currency, in net terms. Changes of net foreign assets are caused by foreign exchange interventions which are, generally, sterilized by central banks to exclude their effect on the monetary base and, thus, on the money supply. Changes in *net domestic assets* (NDA) reflect open market policy of the central bank in net terms. They include the marginal lending facility, the main refinancing operations (longer-term and fine-tuning) and other lending to the financial sector to provide liquidity in the euro area. The cash reserves of the banks, of course, are absorbed with the deposit facility and are locked in by means of the minimum reserve system restricting credit expansion to the private sector. Depending on the stability of the money multiplier (the ratio between M3 and B), base money growth will influence broad money growth in euroland.

Box 16 presents the consolidated opening financial statement of the ESCB. This consolidated financial statement is a detailed version of the balance sheet of the ECB in Table 3.6. According to Article 15.2 of its Statute, the ESCB is obliged to publish such a consolidated financial statement each week. The Governing Council of the ECB has decided that the reporting day for this weekly financial statement shall be Friday and that publication will take place on the following Tuesday.[8]

---

[8] ECB, Consolidated Opening Financial Statement of the European System of Central Banks (Eurosystem) as at 1 January 1999, Press release, 5 Jan. 1999 (http://www.ecb.int).

Box 16 Consolidated Opening Financial Statement of the Eurosystem at 1 January 1999 (mln euro)

Assets		Liabilities	
Gold and gold receivables, and claims on non-euro area residents denominated in foreign currency	329,940	Banknotes in circulation	341,708
		Liabilities to euro area financial sector counterparties denominated in euro	
Lending to financial sector counterparties of euro area		Current accounts (covering the minimum reserve system)	84,437
Main refinancing operations	144,924		
		Deposit facility	973
Marginal lending facility	6,372	*Liabilities to other euro residents denominated in euro*	
		General government	58,612
Other assets	215,924	Other liabilities	211,430
Total assets	697,160	Total liabilities	697,160

This simplified consolidated opening financial statement contains the assets and liabilities held by the ESCB vis-à-vis third parties as they arise in the accounts of the ECB and the eleven national central banks participating in Stage Three of EMU. It should be noted that claims and liabilities between the ECB and national central banks are cancelling out and are, thus, not shown in this consolidated financial statement. The purpose of the weekly financial statement of the ESCB is to provide a source of information, in particular on monetary policy operations and on foreign exchange interventions with counterparties. The data contained in this weekly financial statement refer to fixed reporting days (Fridays) and the weekly changes are, typically, the result of recurrent yearly and especially monthly fluctuations, such as governments' borrowing and redemption activities and the flows of tax payments.

The ESCB has *no* direct influence on the magnitude of the items 'banknotes in circulation' and liabilities to 'general government' which depend, respectively, on the preferences of the public for currency and on behaviour of national governments. In a few euro area countries the amount of Treasury deposits with the central bank is large and these deposits are the most volatile of the autonomous factors (that is, those changes in the balance sheet of central banks not resulting from monetary policy decisions). Treasury accounts are affected by any operation conducted by the Treasury, such as debt issuance, redemption and coupon payment activity, the collection of tax and social security contributions, the acquisition of goods and services, and the payment of wages, pensions, and other social security benefits. The euro area countries can be divided into three groups according to the volatility and size of the liquidity effects triggered by Treasury activity. The first group, where the volatility of the Treasury accounts is negligible, comprises Belgium, Germany, Luxembourg, the Netherlands, Austria, and Finland. In these countries the overnight balances on the Treasury's account with the central bank are low or even close to zero, therefore not affecting liquidity. In the second group (Ireland and Portugal) some volatility occurs on the Treasury's account with the central bank but this is limited in scale. Finally, in the case of the third group of countries, namely Spain, Italy, and, to a lesser extent, France, the liquidity effects of Treasury activities are considerable (ECB, *Monthly Bulletin* (July 1999)).

The ESCB may *directly* influence assets like 'gold and gold receivables' and 'claims on non-euro area residents denominated in foreign currency' if it intervenes in the foreign exchange market. Furthermore, it can determine the 'main refinancing operations' (repo's) being credit facilities to the euro area banks with a fixed frequency (2 weeks) and a fixed maturity (3 months). Next, banks have unlimited access to the 'marginal lending facility' (Lombard facility) against collateral for which they pay a higher rate than the repo rate. Finally, banks may stall end-of-day excess liquidity at the 'deposit facility' for which they receive a lower rate than the repo rate. Banks are also obliged to keep 'current accounts' at the ESCB to cover the minimum reserve requirements on an average basis during a certain period.

3.4 The Relation between the 'Ins' and the 'Outs'

THE relation between the 'ins' and the 'outs'—or, as some prefer to call them, the 'pre-ins'—has been formally arranged by the establishment of an *Exchange Rate Mechanism Mark II* (ERM II). According to the Maastricht Treaty, each member state that is not yet allowed to participate in the euro area shall treat its exchange rate policy as 'a matter of common interest' from the beginning of the third stage of EMU. In principle, this should also apply to the countries with an opting-out clause (Denmark and the UK). None the less, membership of ERM II is voluntary for all 'outs'. A member state not participating in the new exchange rate mechanism from the outset may join at a later date. Although the UK has recently expressed interest in joining EMU in due course—actually meaning after the next election of parliament—it will not participate in any exchange rate arrangement.

The basic aims of ERM II are the following. First, to safeguard the functioning of the Single Market and the stability of the euro for the 'ins' by excluding competitive devaluations by the 'outs'. Second, to achieve more convergence—especially in terms of (long-term) interest rates and budget deficits—between the 'ins' and 'outs'. Third, to ensure free entry to EMU for the 'outs' once they comply with the convergence criteria. At its meeting in Amsterdam in June 1997, the European Council decided to replace the 'old' Exchange Rate Mechanism of the EMS (ERM I) by the 'new' ERM II linking the currencies of the non-euro area to the euro. The operating procedures for ERM II have been laid down in an agreement between the ECB and the national central banks in the non-euro area.[9] Unlike ERM I, ERM II is designed as an *asymmetrical*, euro-centred exchange rate system. The main feature of ERM II is the wide fluctuation of ± 15 per cent between the euro and the currency of the country participating in the mechanism. The bilateral central rate and the upper and lower intervention rates (expressed as a percentage of the central rate) vis-à-vis the euro are quoted using the euro as the base currency. On 31 December 1998 the ECB, Danmarks Nationalbank, and the Bank of Greece have established by common accord the compulsory intervention rates for the Danish krone and the Greek drachma within the framework of ERM II. On 15 January 2000 the Greek drachma was revaluated. The euro central rates and compulsory intervention rates, in force as of 17 January 2000, are given in Table 3.7.[10] For Denmark the fluctuation margin around the central rate is only ± 2.25 per cent.

The only two member states not participating in ERM II are Sweden and the UK. Although Sweden has no opting-out clause, it can avoid being forced to enter the third stage of EMU by staying outside ERM II (even if it satisfies the other convergence criteria of the Maastricht Treaty). Both Sweden and the UK are, nevertheless, still constrained by the Maastricht Treaty in that they should consider their exchange rate policies as 'a matter of common interest' to avoid any distortion in the Single Market.

Analogous to the 'old' mechanism, another important feature of the ERM II is the automatic and unlimited intervention at the margins by both the ECB and the participating national central bank with the Very Short-Term Facility available. So, the 'new' mechanism involves a reciprocal commitment by credit lines between the ECB and respective central banks. It must be emphasized that these credit lines are of a very temporary nature because the debt should be repaid within 75 days after the end of the month in which the intervention took place. However, the ECB and the central banks concerned could suspend automatic intervention if this would conflict with

Table 3.7 Euro Central and Intervention Rates in ERM II

Currency	Fluctuation band	Euro
Danish krone	upper rate	7.62824 (+2.25%)
	central rate	7.46038
	lower rate	7.29252 (−2.25%)
Greek drachma	upper rate	391.863 (+15%)
	central rate	340.750
	lower rate	289.688 (−15%)

[9] ECB, Conventions and Procedures for the New Exchange Rate Mechanism (ERM II), Press release 12 Sept. 1998 (http://www.ecb.int).

[10] ECB, Euro Central Rates and Intervention Rates in ERM II, Press release, 17 Jan. 2000 (http://www.ecb.int).

the primary objective of maintaining price stability. There is even the possibility of allowing, for example, closer exchange rate links between the euro and other currencies in the exchange rate mechanism 'where, and to the extent that, these are appropriate in the light of progress towards convergence'.

The consequence of the asymmetrical design of ERM II will be, of course, that the 'outs' have to adjust their domestic fiscal and monetary policies. The stability of euroland may have a positive 'demonstration effect' to the 'outs', similar to the German mark-zone since the second half of the eighties (Eijffinger 1996).

If present non-EU countries (for example, the Czech Republic, Hungary, and Poland) joined the European Union in the near or distant future (see section 5.3), the character and importance of ERM II could change drastically. This would also imply that possible realignments (adjustments of the parities of the future 'outs') should not be excluded. The 1992 and 1993 currency crises within ERM I have shown that realignments may be necessary when the fundamentals between countries are diverging.

What is the EU policy on exchange rate agreements with non-EU countries? Exchange rate agreements with non-EU currencies can be separated into unilateral (U), bilateral (B), and multilateral (M) links. An overview of these links outside the European Union is in Table 3.8.

This table illustrates that the currencies of many European mini states (except the British Isles) have unilateral or bilateral links to EMU currencies and, thus, the euro. They may switch as of 1 January 2002 to use euro coins and banknotes. More interestingly, the euro has also a stable exchange rate in the West and Central African

Table 3.8 Unilateral, Bilateral, and Multilateral Links of Non-EU Currencies

Country	Currency	Formal link	Type
Andorra	French franc, Sp. peseta	French franc, Sp. peseta	B (euro)
Bosnia-Herzegovina	Bosnian kuna	German mark	U (euro)
Bulgaria	Bulgarian lev	German mark	U (euro)
Comoros	Comoros franc	Euro	U
Cyprus	Cypriot pound	Euro	U
Estonia	Estonian kroon	German mark	U (euro)
Gibraltar	Gibraltar pound	British pound	U
Guernsey	Guernsey pound	British pound	U
Isle of Man	Manx pound	British pound	U
Jersey	Jersey pound	British pound	U
Cape Verde	Cape Verde escudo	Euro	U
Monaco	French franc	French franc	B (euro)
San Marino	Italian lira	Italian lira	B (euro)
Vatican City	Vatican lira	Italian lira	B (euro)
West African MU	CFA franc	French franc	M (euro)
Central African MU	CFA franc	French franc	M (euro)

Source: Rabobank 1998; ECB, *Monthly Bulletin* (Aug. 1998).

Notes: Overseas regions of Denmark and France are excluded. *MU* refers to Monetary Union.

Box 17 The Question of the CFA Franc

The CFA (Communauté Financière Africaine) franc was established in 1948 as a currency for mostly former French colonies. The CFA franc is the currency of two monetary unions in Africa: the West African Monetary Union (Benin, Burkina Faso, Ivory Coast, Guinea-Bissau, Mali, Niger, Senegal, and Togo) and the Central African Monetary Union (Cameroon, the Central African Republic, Chad, Congo (Brazzaville), Equatorial Guinea, and Gabon). It has a fixed parity vis-à-vis the French franc (1 French franc = 100 CFA francs) with, in principle, full convertibility to the French franc and, thus, to the euro. The CFA countries hold 65 per cent of their international reserves at the Banque de France. Germany and other EMU countries stated that the CFA agreement falls, according to the Maastricht Treaty, under the competence of the EU. However, France denied this competence of the European Council because the CFA link is the responsibility of the French ministry of Finance (Treasury) and, consequently, a budgetary and not a monetary agreement. The European Commission and Ecofin have recognized the French competence in this case, although the European Council has to approve changes of the CFA agreement. Therefore, from 1 January 1999 onwards the CFA franc is linked to the euro with full convertibility guaranteed by the French Ministry of Finance.

Monetary Union owing to the fixed parity of the CFA franc vis-à-vis the French franc (see Box 17).

3.5 Banking Supervision

STABILITY of the financial sector is important for monetary authorities, as monetary and financial sector stability are closely connected (Arnold 1999). History provides many examples where problems in the financial sector led to monetary instability. The Great Depression in the US is probably the best known example where bank failures combined with an inadequate response by the monetary authorities resulted in a prolonged economic crisis.

What causes instability of the financial sector? The balance sheet of banks makes them vulnerable. Banks provide long-term loans, which are at least partly funded through deposits, which are generally withdrawable on demand. Lack of trust may cause depositors to withdraw their money. Apart from this traditional run on a bank, a liquidity crisis can also occur owing to illiquidity in money or capital markets. Doubt about the solvency of a bank may lead to a shift in portfolios away from bank liabilities in favour of government securities or corporate assets. A massive withdrawal of deposits or a shift in portfolios could force a bank to liquidate its loan portfolio on unfavourable terms. So, a process that starts as a liquidity crisis could lead to a solvency crisis. Furthermore, problems at one bank could easily spread towards the rest of the financial system. If various banks went bankrupt, the resulting decline in the money supply could lead to a serious recession. Deposit insurance and liquidity support by the central bank may prevent such a scenario.

However, the lender of last resort function of the central bank comes at the price of increased *moral hazard*. A bank may provide more risky loans in the knowledge that deposit holders are insured and the central bank may come to the rescue. A further problem of deposit insurance arises owing to *adverse selection*. The people who are most likely to produce the adverse outcome insured against (bank failure) are those who most want to take advantage of the insurance. Therefore, regulation and supervision are needed. Banking regulation generally consists of restrictions on bank assets holdings and capital requirements (see Box 18).

In some countries banking supervision is carried out by the central bank, whereas in others this task is performed by another institution, sometimes in close co-operation with the central bank (Table 3.9). Following the recent adoption by the UK[11] and Luxembourg of the separation approach, only six EU member countries have the central bank as the only authority responsible for banking supervision. According to Lannoo (1999) the development that central banks retreat from supervisory functions can be explained as follows. First, banking is becoming an increasingly complex business and less clearly defined. Leading banks are active in several jurisdictions as providers of a whole series of financial services. Linked to this are new developments in financial supervision, which increasingly emphasize the role of self-regulation and internal risk management in financial institutions. Finally, there is increasing acceptance that the government, not the central bank, should take responsibility for ultimate financial support. This was demonstrated earlier this decade in Norway and Sweden, but also more recently in France. In those cases there was no alternative but to rely on taxpayer funding, leading to more demand for political control of supervisory functions.

There are other arguments both for and against a separation of the responsibilities for monetary policy and supervision. The first argument in favour is the possibility of a conflict of interests between both activities. A central bank, responsible for supervision of the financial system and, thus, also for failures of financial institutions, could be tempted to admit lower (money market) interest rates or higher money growth than would be desirable from the perspective of price stability, in order to avoid such failures.

A second argument to separate the authority on financial stability from that on monetary stability is the bad publicity usually associated with failures or rescue operations. This bad publicity could harm the reputation of the central bank in its

---

[11] In the UK all financial supervisory tasks are now concentrated in the Financial Services Authority, including banking supervision (formerly belonging to the Bank of England). The FSA has rule-making powers and co-operates with exchanges and clearing houses. It is accountable to the government and parliament. The Bank of England remains responsible for ensuring the overall stability of the financial system, which involves monitoring and, when necessary, intervening in the market. A mega-supervisor has certain advantages. There are economies of scale in supervision, as well as some practical advantages. There is a one-stop shopping for conglomerate financial groups. Expertise is pooled and co-operation between the different functional supervisors is guaranteed. Still, the differences in risk profiles and in the nature of the businesses remain important arguments against a mega-supervisor, most importantly for banking as compared to the insurance business (Lannoo 1999).

Table 3.9 The Role of Central Banks in the European Union in Promoting Financial Stability

Country	Central bank responsible for financial stability?	Supervisor
Austria	Yes	Ministry of Finance
Belgium	Yes	Banking and Finance Commission
Denmark	Yes	Financial Inspectorate
Finland	Yes	Bank Inspectorate/Bank of Finland
France	Yes	Banque de France/Commission Banqaire
Germany	Yes	Federal Banking Supervisory Office and Deutsche Bundesbank
Greece	Yes	Bank of Greece
Ireland	Yes	Central Bank of Ireland
Italy	Yes	Banca d'Italia
Luxembourg	Yes	Commission de Surveillance du Secteur Finance (CSSF)
Netherlands	Yes	De Nederlandsche Bank
Portugal	Yes	Banco de Portugal
Spain	Yes	Banco de España
Sweden	Yes	Swedish Financial Supervisory Authority
UK	Yes	Financial Services Authority
EMU	No	National supervisors

Source: Update of Goodhart and Schoenmaker 1995.

function as a supervisory agency. A loss of reputation may also affect the credibility of monetary policy. However, formally separated responsibilities implies the risks of inter-agency conflict, long deliberations, and insufficient information exchange. This will become problematic when rapid decision-making about, for example, liquidity support is needed (Arnold 1999).

There are further arguments against a separation of financial supervision and the conduct of monetary policy. First, the central bank plays a crucial role in the smooth operation of the payments system and the associated financial risks. To limit these risks, the central bank wishes to supervise and regulate the participants of the payments system. Furthermore, the central bank has a function as 'lender of last resort' for the financial system and in that capacity has the task of supplying instantly enough liquidity in the case of liquidity problems or rescue operations.

The ECB is not entrusted with any direct responsibility related to prudential supervision of credit institutions and the stability of the financial system.[12] These functions are in the realm of the competent national authorities. In most EU countries the central bank plays a role here, albeit that the supervision is often entrusted to another agency (see Table 3.9). Limiting the ECB functions to monetary policy is part

---

[12] The Maastricht Treaty establishes, however, a simplified procedure that makes it possible without amending the Treaty, to entrust specific supervisory tasks to the ECB.

of a general trend of withdrawal from supervisory functions in central banking and fits with the home country control principles of the single market. Specific expertise in and knowledge of prudential control is situated at the local level, where the bulk of the operations of financial institutions are still located (Lannoo 1999).

Various critics have argued that the situation where the ECB puts its resources at stake while national supervisors remain responsible for supervision, creates a huge potential for inter-agency conflicts (Folkerts-Landau and Garber 1992). National supervisors may have interests of their own, like keeping national banks in business. Lacking expertise and the time to acquire any, the ECB is likely to follow the advice of the national supervisor if a crisis occurs. Led astray by possibly biased advice and information, the ECB may then create excess liquidity, thereby perhaps even compromising on its primary objective of price stability (Arnold 1999). Such operations will, of course, be sterilized should there be any impact of the operations on the money market.

This reasoning assumes that the ECB will act as lender of last resort. Surprisingly enough, no explicit reference is made in the Maastricht Treaty to the role of the ECB as a lender of last resort. This is not surprising as there is hardly any national central bank law that refers to this function. However, the ECB has a responsibility for promoting the smooth operation of payment systems, including the provision of financing facilities to credit institutions. In this respect there is a potential for the ECB to act in the capacity of a lender of last resort as far as the provision of short-term liquidity is concerned (OECD 1998a). Furthermore, the trend towards greater financial integration (see Chapter 6) will make it increasingly difficult to establish national dividing lines. Even when a bank problem can be identified as a national one, it may quickly become European in scope, warranting action by the central bank. Indeed, Goodhart and Schoenmaker (1995) find that in most banking problems in the history of industrial countries central banks have been involved. However, in crisis management the creation of central bank money is just one category of emergency action (Padoa-Schioppa 1999). The central bank may not be the provider of liquidity assistance. Funds may also come from the private sector (other financial institutions) or from the government (the taxpayers). In the latter case the European Commission will be involved in scrutinizing and authorizing such actions, since state aid must be compatible with the EU's competition legislation.

According to Padoa-Schioppa (1999) the textbook case for emergency liquidity assistance to individual institutions has been a rare event over the past decades. Furthermore, the emergence of the single euro money market lowers bank(s') liquidity risk, because the number of possible sources of funds is now considerably larger than in the past. If a liquidity crisis occurred, the Eurosystem has—at least according to Padoa-Schioppa—the necessary capacity to act.

Box 18 European Union Regulation on Credit Risk

The fact that the ECB only plays a limited role in supervising financial institutions does not imply that there is no European involvement. The increased integration of financial markets (see Chapter 6) and the need for a level playing field for banks from different countries has led to harmonization of banking regulation. Through the so-called Basle accord of June 1988, the supervision authorities in the most important industrial countries standardized bank capital requirements. The Basle capital requirements work as follows. Assets and off-balance sheet activities are allocated in four different categories, each with different weight to reflect the degree of credit risk. The lowest risk category carries a zero weight and includes items without default risk. Loans to OECD countries carry a 0 per cent weighting, claims on banks from OECD countries 20 per cent, residential (and commercial) mortgages 50 per cent, all other credits 100 per cent, including claims on non-OECD countries and commercial loans. Once all the bank's assets and off-balance sheet items have been assigned to a risk category, they are weighted by the corresponding risk factor and are added up. The bank must then meet two capital requirements. First, stockholders' equity capital and published reserves should at least be 4 per cent of total risk-adjusted assets. Second, total capital must come to 8 per cent of total risk-adjusted assets. The Basle accord formed the basis for the EU Solvency Ratio Directive (1989). A directive is a special type of EU legislation, which requires member states to change their national law in accordance with the contents of the directive. A further directive of 1992 limits the maximum exposure to one single counterpart. The value of an exposure to one client or a group of connected clients may not exceed 25 per cent of the bank's own funds. Furthermore, a credit institution may not incur large exposures above 800 per cent of its own funds.

It is important to realize that only part of the supervision regulation is harmonized. The non-harmonized part includes the different organizational arrangements for the conduct of supervision, the tools used by banking supervisors (for example reporting requirements, on-site inspections), provisions for the liquidation and restructuring of banks, and liquidity requirements. In 1999 the Basle Committee on Banking Supervision proposed a new capital adequacy framework to replace the 1988 accord. With regard to risk weights, the Committee proposes replacing the existing approach by a system that would use credit ratings for determining risk weights. More definite proposals will be set forth in the year 2000.

3.6 Conclusion

WHAT may we conclude about the design of European monetary policy? The ultimate objective of the ECB is to establish monetary stability in euroland by keeping the year-on-year increase in the Harmonised Index of Consumer Prices below 2 per cent. The Governing Council of the ECB has chosen an eclectic approach of targeting both broad money (M3) growth and (expected) inflation because of uncertainty regarding the stability of money demand, especially at the beginning of Stage Three. As the operational variable the ECB will use the (interbank) money market interest rate which will be uniform in the euro area. The ECB can control the money market interest rate by its monetary instruments, which are indirect and market-oriented. These instruments are: (1) a deposit facility; (2) a marginal lending or Lombard facility, together acting as a corridor for money market rates; (3) open market operations for steering and fine-tuning money market rates in the (very) short run within that corridor; and (4) minimum reserve requirements whose average level is set on a monthly basis with an averaging facility.

Furthermore, the relation between the 'ins' and 'outs' has been formally arranged by the 'new' Exchange Rate Mechanism (ERM II) linking the currencies of the non-euro area to the euro on a voluntary basis. At present, only the Danish krone and the Greek drachma have entered ERM II. Two EU member states, Sweden and the UK, have decided not to participate in the 'new' exchange rate mechanism. However, the character and importance of ERM II could change drastically, if present non-EU countries such as the Czech Republic, Hungary, and Poland joined the European Union in the near or distant future.

So far, the ECB is not entrusted with any general responsibility related to prudential supervision of credit institutions and the stability of the financial system.

Chapter 4
National Fiscal Policy in EMU

Introduction

IN June 1997 the European Council reached a final agreement on the Stability and Growth Pact. The Pact both extends and clarifies the so-called excessive deficit procedure as foreseen in the Maastricht Treaty. After an initial German proposal for a Stability Pact, the discussion in the EU has led to a *twin-track strategy*. The first track consists of a preventive, early-warning system for identifying and correcting budgetary slippage to ensure that government budget deficits will not exceed the ceiling of 3 per cent of GDP. The second track consists of measures (including sanctions) to correct excessive deficits quickly if they occur. Countries should in the medium term strive for a balanced budget. The Stability and Growth Pact has met considerable scepticism. Many economists have questioned the rationale for restrictions on national fiscal policy in a monetary union.[1] Therefore, we first analyse in section 4.1 the need for budgetary rules in a monetary union from a political economy perspective. It is argued that there are reasons that may justify certain fiscal policy rules. However, just as we cannot be sure that recommending a low-calorie diet for a person suffering from obesity will persuade that person to eat less, there is no guarantee that governments will be able to control their deficits by simply being told to have balanced budgets. After a review of the details of the Stability and Growth Pact, section 4.2 therefore compares the European rules with effective so-called Balanced Budget Rules of US states.

It is often argued that EMU will not only affect government borrowing, but also

---

[1] There are various arguments for lower deficits which have nothing to do with EMU and which will therefore not be discussed in this chapter. One particular argument that we will take up later is the rise in dependency ratios because of the ageing of the population. This will inevitably put a heavy burden on social spending in the years to come (see Chapter 6). By reducing their debt, governments can use the money otherwise spent on interest payments for higher social spending caused by the greying of the population.

governments' tax policies, be it through tax harmonization or tax competition. The final sections of this chapter discuss these issues.

4.1 The Need for Fiscal Rules in EMU

As explained in Chapter 2, the fiscal policy convergence criteria of the Maastricht Treaty also apply in EMU. Doubts about the effectiveness of the excessive deficit procedure as foreseen in the Treaty led to a proposal by the then German Minister of Finance (Waigel) for a stricter application of the rules on budgetary discipline. Germany proposed that under normal cyclical circumstances the budget deficit should not be higher than 1 per cent of GDP in order to create a safety margin below 3 per cent. It was also suggested that sanctions were to be imposed automatically, when the budget deficit exceeded the 3 per cent reference value. The German proposals for a Stability Pact were critically received. Especially the automatic imposition of sanctions was considered to be at odds with the Maastricht Treaty, which foresees discretionary decision-making during each stage of the excessive deficit procedure.

After intense discussions, the European Council eventually adopted the *Stability and Growth Pact*.[2] This consists of two Council regulations and a European Council resolution. The regulations relate to the excessive deficit procedure and to surveillance. The resolution, which expresses political commitment but has not the force of law, provides guidance to the Council and member states on the application of the pact. In contrast, the two Council regulations have the force of law. The details of the decisions by the Council will be discussed in the next section, but first we will deal with the question of whether it is necessary to restrict national fiscal policy in the EMU.

According to the founders of the Maastricht Treaty there is a definite need for certain mechanisms to ensure fiscal discipline of member states.[3] The most compelling argument for the Stability and Growth Pact is that if public debt is perceived as being on an unsustainable course, it may threaten price stability. As pointed out in Chapter 2, a high level of government debt may increase the inflationary bias. Following De Grauwe (1996) we may exemplify this as follows. We start with the government budget constraint:

$$\dot{b}_t = g_t - t_t + (r_t + \pi^e_t - \pi_t)b_{t-1}. \tag{4.1}$$

where b is the debt to GDP ratio (a dot represents a rate of change); g is the primary

---

[2] The Stability and Growth Pact was, as betrayed by its very name, a hard-fought compromise between German and French priorities. On a proposal of the French government, it was agreed by the European Council meeting in Amsterdam in June 1997 to include a Council Resolution on the co-ordination of employment policies in the EU.

[3] However, many economists do not share this view. See, for example, Buiter, Corsetti, and Roubini 1993 and Eichengreen and Wyplosz (1998). Eichengreen and von Hagen (1995) point out that fiscal restrictions in mature federations have been put in place for reasons unrelated to the existence of monetary unions.

government spending as a per cent of GDP; t is total tax revenues as a per cent of GDP; r is the real interest rate, π is the inflation rate, and π^e is the expected inflation rate. Note that we have written the nominal interest rate as the sum of the real interest rate and expected inflation. It follows from (4.1) that only the unanticipated component of inflation $(\pi^e - \pi)$ affects the budget constraint. Setting $\dot{b} = 0$ obtains the condition necessary to stabilize the debt-to-GDP ratio. A stable debt ratio may be considered as a condition for sustainability of fiscal policy. This gives:

$$t_t = g_t + r_t b_{t-1} + (\pi_t^e - \pi_t) b_{t-1}. \tag{4.2}$$

Assuming rational expectations, we can write the sustainability condition as follows:

$$t_n = g + rb \tag{4.3}$$

where t_n is the 'natural' rate of taxation given the level of spending, the accumulated debt, and the real interest rate. This is independent of inflation.

It will be clear that we have formulated the problem in a similar framework as in the models of Chapter 2. Unanticipated increases in inflation reduce the burden of the debt, very much like unanticipated inflation increases output in the short run. The long-run solvency constraint is similar to the natural rate of output growth. Assume now that the authorities aim at minimizing a loss function of the type:

$$L = t_t^2 + a\pi_t^2 \tag{4.4}$$

The equilibrium inflation rate is:

$$\pi^* = \frac{b}{a}(g + rb). \tag{4.5}$$

It follows that the level of the debt to GDP ratio, b, affects the equilibrium inflation rate. So, achieving convergence to a low debt to GDP ratio reduces the risk that the monetary union will have an inflationary bias.

Of course, one can argue that there are other options to reduce the inflationary bias (De Grauwe 1996). For instance, by reducing the term to maturity of government debt or by issuing indexed debt, the benefits of unanticipated inflation are reduced, and thereby the inflationary bias.

Furthermore, one can argue that governments have only limited influence on monetary policy, given the high degree of independence of the ECB (see section 2.3). Still, the ECB may be forced to an inflationary bail out, despite its independence. A worst case scenario might run as follows (Eichengreen and Wyplosz 1998). Suppose that the government of a country in the euro area gets into fiscal trouble, from which it cannot extricate itself. Investors fear suspension or (more likely) modification of payment on its public debt, and therefore sell their bonds. Consequently, bond prices start to plummet. Banks holding those bonds find their capital impaired, inciting depositor runs. Bond markets (and indirectly banks) in other EMU countries suffer adverse repercussions, as investors in public debt of other European states become demoralized. All this will increase the likelihood of a bail-out and, eventually, perhaps make it very difficult for the ECB to avoid getting involved.

Is such a scenario likely? Table 4.1 suggests that countries witnessing a rise in their government debt ratio also experience an expansion of government claims in bank portfolios. Still, the fifth column of Table 4.1 shows that in most countries the relative importance of banks' lending to government is not excessive. Nevertheless, the extra protection that the Stability and Growth Pact offers may be needed on two grounds.[4] First, EMU may lead to more government borrowing and second, financial markets may not be able to discipline governments (enough).

The creation of a monetary union may stimulate national governments to pursue less prudent fiscal policies. The argument goes as follows. In EMU governments may find it easier to borrow more. Before the monetary union, a would-be heavy borrower was limited by the size of its domestic capital market. If some government wanted to borrow more than the domestic market was able to supply, it must borrow in a foreign currency. This exposed the government to exchange rate risk. But with the euro in place, the 'domestic' capital market becomes much bigger which enables government to borrow more without taking on any exchange rate risk. Of course, the creditworthiness of this would-be heavy borrower will determine the interest rate that it has to pay on its debt. Countries that may get into financial troubles will have

Table 4.1 Government Debt and Bank Claims on Government

	Cumulative change of debt ratio, 1974–1996 (%)	Cumulative increase bank claims on government,[a] 1974–1996 (%)	Correlation between debt growth and bank claims	Banks' domestic claims on government (% of total domestic assets), 1996
Austria	54.1	11.1	0.84	n.a.
Belgium	74.2	15.8	0.93	24.5
Denmark	64.1	9.5	0.76	8.6
Finland	53.0	9.6	0.86	n.a.
France	35.9	5.3	0.20	6.8
Germany	41.4	9.2	0.58	13.9
Greece	89.5	21.0	0.90	22.1
Ireland	22.2	−20.2	−0.40	6.4
Italy	71.9	20.9	0.74	17.4
Netherlands	31.7	−7.9	0.31	10.2
Portugal	56.0	19.1	0.82	12.7
Spain	55.2	18.0	0.91	18.3
Sweden	48.1	2.0	0.30	6.6
UK	−10.3	−32.4	0.76	1.8

Source: Arnold 1999; ECB 1999.

Note: [a] As a percentage of capital accounts.

[4] An alternative solution, and indeed one supported by many academic economists (see, for example, Eichengreen and Wyplosz 1998) would be to rely on prudential supervision, and, perhaps, to reconsider the zero-weighting of government debt when assessing the capital adequacy of financial institutions. See section 4.2 for a further discussion.

to pay higher interest rates, which will restrain their borrowing (default risk premium). However, financial markets may believe that EMU provides an implicit guarantee of its members' debts, so that any default risk premium on the debt of the would-be heavy borrower will disappear, again encouraging the government to borrow more. Although the Maastricht Treaty provides for a no-bail-out clause, one may wonder whether this provision is really credible. If an EMU country experienced serious difficulties it is likely that the European Union would be politically harmed if other EU members did not assist this country. Reference to the experience of the US— where, for example, New York almost went bankrupt—may not be relevant here, since both the historical situation and the scale involved are quite different. In fact, not only the Union as such, but also other member states could be hurt as well owing to the financial problems of another EU country. A debt crisis in Italy, say, may spill over to the rest of the system. For example, financial institutions in other countries may hold Italian government bonds. Default by Italy may lead to defaults of these financial institutions, and may create a general crisis. To avoid this, the governments of other countries may decide to step in, despite the no-bail-out clause of the Maastricht Treaty.

In conclusion, the widening of the capital market and the possibility of a bail-out may lead to more government borrowing in the monetary union. There is, however, also a factor at work that may lead to less borrowing. In EMU national governments can no longer finance deficits by central bank credit. So the possibilities for government to finance budget deficits by money creation have been restricted, which may restrain governments. In principle, one cannot say which effect of EMU would be greater: the effect of less exchange rate risk and possible bail-out (tending to raise borrowing), or the effect of the loss of printing national money as a way to service their debts (tending to reduce it). Proponents of fiscal rules like the Stability and Growth Pact generally argue that a monetary union will reduce the fiscal discipline of national governments. Adversaries of rules hold the opposite view.

The second argument questions the view put forward by many economists that financial markets will be able to discipline governments' financial policies. This view goes as follows. Suppose that monetary union indeed stimulates more borrowing by some member countries. There is little danger that its EMU partners would suffer as a result, provided they had made it clear to the markets that there would be no bail-out. If capital markets were efficient, the default risk premium would be loaded exclusively on to the debt of the over-borrower; there would be no free riding. In other words, the would-be heavy borrowers face higher interest payments, which will provide them with an incentive to restrain fiscal policy.

This reasoning can, however, be criticized on various grounds. First, the no-bail-out promise is essential and, as already pointed out, one may question its credibility. Second, experience in less-developed countries, for instance, the Mexico crisis in 1995, and the New York financial crisis in the mid-1970s, show that markets react slowly to a threatening unsustainable fiscal position. In this regard it is also not encouraging that rating agencies have rather different views on the creditworthiness of EMU countries. Whereas Moody's assigned all EMU countries an AAA rating, Standard's and Poor's downgraded Belgium and Ireland from AAA to AA+, Italy, Spain, and

Finland to AA, and Portugal to AA– after the start of EMU (Arnold 1999). Third, the historical experience of many countries does not provide very convincing evidence that a higher interest burden stimulates governments to borrow less. Indeed, if anything, the record shows that the higher interest burden often only worsens government financial positions.[5] One could, of course, argue that in the case of very bad financial policies financial markets would eventually simply refuse to provide credit to a heavily indebted country. However, as the experience of the debt crises of some developing countries has shown, such a development is rather bumpy and may lead to contagion effects.

Suppose that financial markets do not have (enough) disciplining impact and a heavily indebted EMU member country experiences financing problems. Such a situation may lead to various undesirable outcomes. First, as pointed out above, the ECB will experience pressure to ease monetary policy to alleviate these problems. Although the ECB is *de jure* independent, it may de facto change its policies if confronted with a situation as sketched above. Second, it is very likely that not only does the long-term interest rate of the heavy borrower increase, but that the capital market rates in the entire euro area may go up. Whether this occurs depends critically on the degree of financial market integration in euroland (see Chapter 6) and at the world level. If financial markets are integrated worldwide, the additional borrowing may not affect interest rates, given the scale of such a world capital market. However, if such a world capital market does not exist, while financial markets in Europe are integrated, things may be different. If demand for loanable funds at this European capital market increases, the interest rate will rise. Although this attracts some capital from outside Europe, this capital inflow may not nullify the interest raising effects of government borrowing. This implies that excessive borrowing by a member country will harm other Union members.[6] If the governments of these countries were trying to reduce their debt-to-GDP ratios, they will be forced to follow more restrictive policies. Because of these externalities, it will be in the interest of the other countries that a control mechanism exists restricting the size of budget deficits in member countries. There may also be some effect of unsustainable national fiscal policies on the exchange rate of the euro, depending on the size of the country concerned.

Some critics argue that the Stability and Growth Pact deprives governments of the one power that they need most in a monetary union: the ability to use national fiscal policy to counteract recessions, which affect one member country more than the others.[7] They have not lost this ability altogether, but, so the critics argue, it will be

[5] However, De Haan and Sturm (1999) find evidence that countries facing a high interest burden reduce their primary deficit (that is, the budget deficit excluding interest payments) more than other countries.

[6] Buiter, Corsetti, and Roubini (1993) argue that this is in line with the working of the price mechanism. If the demand for bananas (or, for that matter, credit) goes up, the price of bananas will rise. This is exactly what ought to happen if the market system is to do its job of allocating resources efficiently. Implicit in this line of reasoning is that differences in deficit spending by countries reflect optimal policy decision-making. This may be criticized as there is ample evidence for non-optimal fiscal policy outcomes (see, for example, Alesina and Perotti 1995a).

[7] Defining a severe recession as a period in which GDP declines by 0.75 per cent or more, Buti and Sapir (1998) report that over the period 1961–96 there was no systematic tendency on average to loosen budgetary policy in the EU member states during severe recessions. Member states with high deficits and debt ratios even tightened their fiscal stance during severe recession episodes. This suggests that fiscal policy can only be used for stabilization purposes if the public finances are structurally healthy.

severely constrained. The consequences may go further than just economics. The danger is that in the event of a sharp recession in one or more countries there may be a political reaction against EMU. The Union may be blamed for the inability to moderate national recessions. Is such a scenario likely? In other words, how much room does the Stability and Growth Pact offer for stabilization purposes, and will this be enough?

Suppose that the EMU countries have a balanced budget in the medium term. Then they can let their budget deficit increase up to 3 per cent of GDP. This does not require discretionary policy measures: the working of *automatic stabilizers* will drive up deficits. In a recession government's revenues will go down, whereas outlays will go up. How large is the cyclical sensitivity of national budgets? One way to answer this question is to analyse the maximum difference between the actual deficit and the so-called 'cyclically adjusted deficit'. Table 4.2 provides estimates from the European Commission (Buti and Sapir 1998) on the cyclical component of budget balances. It follows that in most EU member states the cyclical component rarely surpassed the 3 per cent of GDP level. So, if countries stick to the medium-term objective of keeping their budget in balance, the Stability and Growth pact offers substantial room for automatic stabilizers to function.[8] However, the dampening effect of automatic stabilizers on output fluctuations differs significantly across countries. According to estimates of Buti and Sapir (1998), the average stabilizing impact after a shock is 28 per cent, the highest impact is 41 per cent (Finland), the lowest is 15 per cent (Greece). It is also quite low (18 per cent) in Portugal and Spain.

The fiscal rules of the Maastricht Treaty have also been criticized for their arbitrariness. Why would a deficit of 3 per cent be no problem, whereas a deficit of 4 per cent, say, would be excessive? At a more fundamental level, it has been argued that the sustainability of fiscal policy may differ across countries. So why should the same reference values then be used for all countries? For instance, countries with a higher real growth rate, other things being equal, can safely afford a higher deficit–GDP ratio (Buiter, Corsetti, and Roubini 1993).

It is undeniable that figures like 3 per cent and 60 per cent are arbitrary to a large extent.[9] However, this does not make them useless. Furthermore, the effectiveness of fiscal rules is enhanced if they are simple. From a political-economy point of view it is understandable that the same rules apply to all countries, despite their economic differences. Would it be acceptable for Italy, say, that Germany would be allowed a deficit ratio of 4 per cent, while for Italy the limit would be 3 per cent?

A final argument that has been put forward in support of rules like the Stability and Growth Pact, is that they offer protection against a 'deficit bias' that may exist in at least some European countries due to inefficient political decision-making. For instance, countries with frequent government changes, may find it difficult without

[8] According to the estimates of Buti and Sapir (1998), especially budgetary receipts are sensitive to economic fluctuations. The decrease in government revenue during a recession accounts on average for 80 per cent of the detorioration of the government deficit.

[9] The 3 per cent limit for the deficit and the 60 per cent reference value for the debt ratio are not inconsistent. If a country's nominal GDP would increase by 5 per cent (consisting of, say, 2 per cent inflation and 3 per cent real growth), and the country each year runs a deficit of 3 per cent, its debt ratio will eventually converge to 60 per cent of GDP. However, this process may take quite some time (Kenen 1995).

Table 4.2 Size of the Cyclical Component of Budget Balance for European Union Member States, 1961–1996

Member states	Lowest negative component (%)	Year	Highest positive component	Year
Belgium	−1.7	1986	2.0	1974
Denmark	−2.4	1981	2.6	1986
Germany	−1.8	1967	2.4	1991
Greece	−1.0	1987	1.6	1973
Spain	−2.1	1984, 1985	2.7	1990
France	−1.1	1985	1.6	1990
Ireland	−2.6	1993	2.0	1978
Italy	−1.2	1975	1.1	1980
Luxembourg	−3.3	1983	4.2	1974
Netherlands	−2.9	1983	1.8	1974
Austria	−1.2	1987	1.4	1991
Portugal	−2.4	1984, 1985	2.4	1973
Finland	−5.6	1993	5.3	1989
Sweden	−4.1	1993	3.2	1990
UK	−2.7	1982	3.1	1989
EU	−1.3	1983	1.6	1990

Source: Buti and Sapir 1998.

such rules to get their public finances in order. As with the (almost) fixing of exchange rates in the ERM (see section 1.2), the European fiscal rules 'tie government's hands'.

4.2 The Stability and Growth Pact

4.2.1 A Detailed Description

The most important elements of the Stability and Growth Pact are laid down in two Council regulations. They clarify the Maastricht Treaty's provisions regarding excessive deficits, in particular concerning the circumstances under which the 3 per cent reference value for the budget deficit may be exceeded. The regulations also clarify the timing and magnitude of the sanctions imposed if a member country has an excessive deficit. In addition, under the pact's provisions, participants in the monetary union commit themselves to a medium-term budgetary stance 'close to balance or surplus'. This objective is supposed to allow member states to deal with normal cyclical fluctuations, while keeping the budget deficit at or below the reference value.

Each year member states in the euro zone have to submit a so-called *stability programme*, which has to be updated annually. This programme must include the medium-term objective for the budgetary position of close to balance or in surplus and the adjustment path towards this objective. Acting by a qualified majority the Council decides whether to endorse the stability programme or whether to invite the member country concerned to adjust its stability programme. The Council will also monitor the implementation of the programme and may issue recommendations to implement adjustment measures.

Under the pact a *deficit in excess of 3 per cent is exceptional* if a country's GDP declines by at least 2 per cent in the year in question. Over the period 1961–96 such a situation occurred in 7 cases out of 475 (Buti and Sapir 1998). In addition, a recession in which real GDP declines by less than 2 per cent but more than 0.75 per cent may qualify with the concurrence of the Council. This occurred in 30 cases in the period 1961–96. The country concerned will have to show that its recession was exceptional in terms of its abruptness or in relation to past output trends. Countries in which output declines less than 0.75 per cent of GDP will not be able to claim exceptional circumstances. A government deficit over the reference value of 3 per cent is also considered exceptional and temporary when resulting from an annual event outside the control of the member state concerned and with a major impact on the government's financial position.

Figure 4.1 shows the *procedural steps* as foreseen in the *Stability and Growth Pact*. The Stability and Growth Pact introduces a strict time frame of ten months from the member country's submission of data to the European Commission to the actual application of sanctions by the Council. Twice a year member states have to provide budgetary data to the Commission. From the time of the reporting by the member country, the Council has a period of three months in which it has to decide whether the country concerned has an excessive deficit. If the Council decides by a qualified majority that an excessive deficit exists, it has to issue recommendations to bring the excessive deficit to an end. There is a maximum deadline of four months in which the member country concerned must take effective action. Within seven months from the submission of the report by a member country, the Council decides whether its recommendations have been implemented. Where it is found that the member state concerned acts in compliance with the recommendations made by the Council the excessive deficit procedure falls into abeyance. Otherwise, within eight months from the submission of the report the Council has to decide whether to notify the country concerned to take concrete measures for the deficit reduction. After the Council has requested for concrete measures, the member country has a maximum period of two months in which it can still avoid the application of sanctions by taking the necessary measures. If the member state fails to implement concrete measures or, if the Council finds that the measures are inadequate, it takes a decision to apply sanctions immediately.

Sanctions will take the form of a non-interest-bearing deposit. The *initial* deposit consists of a fixed component equal to 0.2 per cent of GDP and a variable component equal to 0.1 per cent of GDP for each percentage point that the government deficit is beyond the reference value of 3 per cent in the year that the deficit occurs (see Box 19

Figure 4.1 Time-scale for the Application of the Excessive Deficit Procedure

Time (ultimate dates)	Action
1 March (year *t*) or 1 September (year *t*)	Member states submit data on their public finances to the Commission
1 June (year *t*) or 1 December (year *t*)	The Council decides on the existence of an excessive deficit on the basis of a report by the Commission and issues recommendations to the member states concerned
1 October (year *t*) or 1 April (year *t* + 1)	The Council considers whether effective action has been taken and whether recommendations should be made public
1 November (year *t*) or 1 May (year *t* + 1)	The Council decides on measures to be taken by the member states concerned to correct the excessive deficit
1 January (year *t* + 1) or 1 July (year *t* + 1)	The Council imposes sanctions on the member states concerned
1 May (year *t* + 1) or 1 November (year *t* + 1)	The Council decides on an intensification of the sanctions or abrogation of the excessive deficit

for an example). An upper limit of 0.5 per cent of GDP is set for the annual amount of deposits. Additional deposits will be required each year until the deficit is corrected. This *additional* deposit equals 0.1 per cent of GDP for each percentage point that the government deficit is above 3 per cent. The deposit is, 'as a rule', converted into a fine if the member state has not corrected its excessive deficit within two years. The proceeds from the non-interest-bearing deposits and fines will be distributed among euro zone countries without an excessive deficit in proportion to their share in the total GNP of the euro zone.

4.2.2 Effectiveness of Stability and Growth Pact

If national fiscal policy is restricted, it is important that the restrictions are credible. The outcome of a cost-benefit analysis of breaking the rules must be such that it will stimulate governments not to break the rules. If absence of an excessive deficit is an entry condition for EMU, the presence of an excessive deficit should perhaps be a reason to dispel membership. This option is—perhaps understandably—however, not foreseen in the Maastricht Treaty. In other words, the excessive deficit procedure has to rely on other sanctions. An important issue that is stressed in the political-economy literature is that procedures should work fast so that the present government will not be able to shift responsibilities on to the next government. The

Box 19 Sanctions in the Excessive Deficit Procedure: An Example

Table B19.1 Sanctions if the Budget Deficit Exceeds 2 per cent of GDP

Year	Deficit	Deposits			Fines
		Fixed	Variable	Total	
2000	4.6	0.20	0.16	0.36	
2001	4.5		0.15	0.51	
2002	3.6		0.06	0.21	0.36
2003	2.5				

We assume that in the initial situation the country concerned had no excessive deficit. In the beginning of 2000 the Council decides that the country has an excessive deficit. As explained in the main text, within 10 months the country has to deposit an amount equal to 0.36 per cent of GDP, consisting of a fixed part of 0.20 per cent and a variable part of 0.16 per cent, being 10 per cent of the difference between the actual deficit (4.6 per cent) and the reference value (3 per cent). It is assumed that this sanction does not affect the behaviour of the country concerned. Consequently, the deposits grow to 0.51 per cent of GDP, consisting of 0.36 per cent of the year 2000 and 0.15 per cent of 2001, being 10 per cent of the difference between the actual deficit and the reference value. As the country still has an excessive deficit in 2002, the deposit of the year 2000 is transformed into a fine. Again the country has to deposit money. This time the amount is 0.06 per cent of GDP, being 10 per cent of 0.6 per cent. In 2003 the deposit is returned to the country, as the excessive deficit has disappeared. The fine is not returned.

credibility of the rules will be enhanced if there is no room for political tinkering since the rules apply to all countries in the same, automatic way which is determined *ex ante*.

Various authors (for example, De Grauwe 1997) argue that the enforcement of fiscal policy rules like the Stability and Growth Pact may be problematic. The experience with fiscal policy rules in the United States may be instructive here. With the exception of Vermont, US states have some legislation restricting government borrowing, but there is considerable variation in these rules across states. Therefore, the fiscal behaviour of US state governments provides a promising database for drawing inferences as to the effects of budget rules on policy outcomes.

Research on such fiscal policy rules in the US initially led to the conclusion that they were not effective. For instance, von Hagen (1991) found that constitutional limits on budget deficits had very little impact on the states' fiscal policy outcomes. However, recent and more extensive studies report that fiscal rules may be effective. For instance, Bohn and Inman (1996) have analysed the effectivity of fiscal rules in US states over quite a long period (1971–90) and conclude that various restrictions, including limits on debt issuance, are effective.

Inman (1996) argues that the evidence from the United States suggests four conditions for an effective *balanced budget rule* (BBR), which are summarized in Figure 4.2.

Figure 4.2 Aspects of Effective Fiscal Policy Rules

Specification of Balance Budget Rules (BBR)

Specification	Weak balance budget rules	Strong balance budget rules
Rule		
timing for review	*ex ante*	*ex post*
Override		
majority rule	allowed	not allowed
Enforcement		
access	closed	open
enforcer	partisan	independent
penalties	small	large
Amendment		
process	easy	difficult

Source: Inman 1996.

These conditions are first explained in some detail and, subsequently, applied to the Stability and Growth Pact.

The potentially most important distinguishing attribute of any BBR specification is whether the rule involves *ex ante* or *ex post* accounting. *Ex ante rules* apply only at the beginning of the fiscal year (that is, fiscal policy intentions), whereas *ex post rules* concern fiscal policy outcomes. The US experience suggests that weak BBR's use *ex ante* balance rules; strong BBR's use *ex post* accounting rules. A second attribute is whether politicians can put a certain rule aside if they think this to be appropriate. The US experience suggests that weak rules allow such a BBR override; strong rules do not. The third attribute of enforcement can be described along three dimensions: access to complain about adherence to the rules is closed or open, the enforcer is partisan or independent, and the penalties are economically insignificant or signifi-cant. The US experience suggests that strong enforcement of the BBR requires open access to a review panel or court to allow all potentially affected parties to claim a violation; closed access weakens the BBR. Further, for a strong BBR the enforcing review panel must be independent of (that is, not connected by partisan obligations to) the political bodies setting deficit policies. Also, if a violation is found, penalties must be enforceable and large enough to induce the political bodies setting deficit policies to prefer the balanced budget outcome over a deficit and the associated penalty. Finally, allowing the BBR to be amended by current political interests—the same interests preferring larger deficits—may weaken the BBR.

So what about the Stability and Growth Pact? Has it similar features as effective fiscal rules in the United States? First, the specification of the rule. As far as the *ex post* character is concerned, the European fiscal policy rules appear to score relatively well. The member states are judged on the basis of realized fiscal performance. Under the Stability and Growth Pact the time schedule is precise and relatively short. So in this respect the Stability and Growth Pact is a considerable improvement in comparison to the procedure as envisaged in the Maastricht Treaty.

Second, can the rules be set aside easily? One weakness in the Stability and Growth pact is that the same ministers who are responsible for drafting national budgets also have to decide whether they breach the 3 per cent criterion. This has led some observers to question the Stability and Growth Pact. Especially, if many countries at the same time have an excessive deficit, it remains to be seen whether the Council in that case would decide to apply the rules of the Stability and Growth Pact. Access is clearly limited, since the Council will only take decisions after the European Commission has written a report.

Third, the same argument that has been made with respect to the possibility for an override by the Council, can be made with respect to imposing sanctions. In comparison to the BBR's of US States, the sanctions due to breaching the deficit criterion are quite tough and could be expected to have a deterrent effect. However, as the Maastricht Treaty defines an excessive deficit in terms of the deficit and the debt ratio, it is quite surprising that the Pact does not specify sanctions in case the debt ratio is too high. Breaching the debt criterion never leads to sanctions! There is one additional serious problem with the sanctions: they do not alleviate the problem at hand. On the contrary, the most severe sanctions (fines) cause both the government deficit and the debt to rise. Deposits also raise the debt ratio, but do not influence the deficit.

Finally, changing the Regulations requires unanimity. It will therefore prove to be very difficult to change the procedures.

Coming back to Figure 4.2, we can conclude that the budget rule is *ex post*, override is only possible by unanimity, and amendment is very difficult. With respect to the enforcement we can conclude that access is almost closed, the enforcer is partisan, but that penalties are quite heavy. So it seems that the European rules perform reasonably well in comparison to those of US states. Still, a well-known drawback of numerical targets is the incentives they introduce for one-off accounting measures in an attempt to satisfy the criteria. This entails a serious loss of information about the government's true budgetary situation. However, empirical evidence for the US states shows that although accounting devices make up a non-negligible part of fiscal adjustment in the short run, they do not appear to be the primary source of deficit reduction in the long run. Over longer time horizons, both taxes and spending tend to adjust (Poterba 1996).

4.2.3 Life without the Stability Pact

Although the Stability and Growth Pact improves the excessive deficit procedure of the Maastricht Treaty, it is questionable whether these fiscal rules will be adhered to

Box 20 Effective Budgetary Adjustments

Putting public finances in order is difficult. Increasing taxes and cutting expenditure will generally hurt various groups in society and may even bring economic hardship. Fiscal retrenchment will probably not increase a government's popularity. So it is important for politicians if they decide for fiscal austerity to take the right measures. There is after all a fair chance that the electorate may reward them if they succeed in making the public finances healthy. The worst situation they may get into is a (politically costly) fiscal adjustment programme that fails in the end. So what should a government do? Recent research has shed some light on the factors determining the likelihood of success. Two features of budgetary adjustments seem in particular to be important in ensuring a successful outcome: scale and composition. The larger the magnitude of the budgetary cuts, the more likely their impact on government debt. In fact, large adjustment packages may increase confidence, thereby offsetting (or perhaps even reversing) the direct reduction in aggregate demand (Giavazzi and Pagano 1990). There is also evidence that deficit reductions through expenditure cuts have a much higher probability of reducing the government debt-to-GDP ratio. Especially cutting social expenditure and the wages component of government consumption will lead to more persistent improvements (Alesina and Perotti 1995*b*).

if a large number of member states would get into serious fiscal problems. As long as there are 'good guys', who are willing to exert peer pressure on the 'bad guys', the functioning of the Stability and Growth Pact is secured. However, this is less certain when (1) the number of 'bad guys' is large, (2) there is common interest to lay aside the stipulations laid down in the Pact (for instance, if all EU countries are not able to comply with the Treaty reference values with respect to the fiscal deficit and the public debt), or (3) a country is not willing to comply with the sanctions of the Ecofin Council, knowing that there is no ultimate penalty, like exclusion from the EU. The Council does not have the competence directly to intervene in national fiscal policy-making, for instance by cutting expenditures or increasing tax rates.

What about alternatives? As explained in section 4.1, one reason for imposing rules on national fiscal policy is to stave off a banking crisis which may result from fiscal distress of a member state. The vulnerability of banks to sharp movements in the government debt markets depends on two conditions: (1) the degree of government debt diversification by banks and (2) the degree of correlation between government default risks (Lemmen 1998*a*). Thus, if banks are not diversified in their government bond holding and all government default risk is systemic, banks are more likely to fail. Arnold and Lemmen (1999) have estimated the cross-country correlation co-efficients of government default risk between 10 EU countries. These calculations suggest that the diversification gains from investing in a European-wide portfolio of governments bonds is considerable, notably for Finland, Ireland, Portugal, and Italy. If banks would not voluntarily increase their diversification, adjusting current super-vision regulations might be an alternative. For instance, at present the *large exposure directive* (see Box 18), which states that a bank cannot lend more than 25 per cent of its

Box 21 Cracks in the Stability and Growth Pact?

The following news report illustrates some of the worries about the Stability and Growth Pact.

The first cracks in the economic 'stability pact' that underpins the euro opened yesterday when Guiliano Amato, Italy's newly appointed Treasury minister, forced European Union colleagues to change his country's budget deficit target. In a move that privately appalled European Commission officials, the finance ministers agreed to allow Italy to overshoot a budget deficit target of 2 per cent of gross domestic product this year in the event of a serious economic downturn. They gave Italy leeway to increase its 1999 deficit to 2.4 per cent of GDP. Yesterday's decision to give ground under pressure from Mr Amato raised fears that the EU system of 'peer group pressure' and stability programmes to discipline member states may be failing within six months of the euro's launch. It comes after the Commission and the European Central bank have expressed worries that other large euro member states, such as Germany and France, have been less than rigorous in pursuing deficit targets. At first, ministers insisted Italy stick to a deficit 'as targeted' of 2 per cent, but following what one official described as an emotional intervention by Mr Amato at lunch, the 15 ministers accepted that Italy's deficit could increase to 2.4 per cent of GDP if adverse economic conditions prevailed. Italy was strongly criticised by the European Commission for its lax budgetary policy earlier this year and was urged to correct its targets. Italy is expected to keep its budget deficit well below 3 per cent of gross domestic product, the ceiling permitted by the stability pact. But economic analysts say the country is only able to do this because the downswing in European interest rates has reduced service payments on its debt.

Source: Financial Times (26 May 1999).

capital to a single borrower, does not apply to government debt. Furthermore, under the *solvency ratio directive* Treasury bills and the long-term central government debt of OECD countries is currently placed in the 0 per cent risk category. If it were placed in the 20 per cent risk category, say, that would induce banks to hold more capital against government debt, and seek recovery of the additional cost by raising the interest on government loans. The implied higher interest burden for government provides a further incentive for reducing budget deficits. In short, by adjusting regulations financial market discipline may be enhanced.

There are, however, some problems with this view. First, changing only European regulation would imply a competitive loss for the European banking sector. Second, Gros and Thygesen (1998) argue that even if the solvency ratio and the large exposure directives were to be changed, government debt would mainly be held domestically in the early life of the euro, thus implying that a government funding crisis could yet endanger the stability of the financial system. Third, as pointed out before, financial markets may be disciplining governments not enough and/or too slowly. However, the disciplining effect of the bond market may be strengthened due to the Stability and Growth Pact. If the credit rating of member countries will depend on the approval of their stability programmes by the Council, they will have an additional incentive to keep their public finances in order.

Another suggested alternative for the Stability and Growth Pact is to introduce a system of *tradeable deficit permits*, similar to tradeable pollution permits (Casella 1999). In a market for pollution permits the regulatory authority sets the overall pollution limit, while the market ensures that all pollution sources will act to equalize their marginal costs of pollution reduction. Such a system leads to better outcomes than imposing the same pollution limit on all sources. In a system of tradeable deficit permits, each country is allocated a number of deficit permits equivalent, for example, to 3 per cent of its GDP. These permits are freely tradeable. Each country must have a sufficient number of permits to cover the year's deficit. When a government surpasses its allocation it has to buy additional permits. Buying a permit is buying the right to issue a unit of debt. In contrast to the Stability and Growth Pact, the additional expenses for exceeding the deficit threshold are not fixed but instead determined by the market. If other countries have enough permits, the price will be low and vice versa. Proponents of such a scheme see here an important advantage. If a country is hit by an asymmetric shock it can use fiscal policy to counteract the shock at relatively low cost. Another advantage is that good behaviour is rewarded as permits that are not needed may be sold. The current Stability and Growth Pact is all stick and no carrot.

4.3 Harmonization of Taxes

APART from affecting national budget deficits, the European integration process has also shaped tax policies of the member states. Taxes may seriously distort the functioning of the common market. Differences in tax regimes can alter the direction of trade and factor flows. Furthermore, national governments have little incentive to take into account the cross-border spill-over effects of their tax policies. The scale of the spill-over effects depends on the extent to which member states' tax systems differ and the degree of market integration. The potential for spill-over effects is highest in the case of taxation of goods and some services and capital taxation (Hoeller, Louppe, and Vergriete 1996). Although this view is widely shared, the appropriate response to the problem is not easily found. One approach could be to harmonize those taxes that most seriously undermine the common market. Especially the value added tax (VAT) has been focused upon. VAT is a general sales tax, levied on all stages of business activity, from production through to sales to final consumers. During the chain of production and distribution, tax payments accumulate on the basis of the value added. Business may credit tax paid on their purchases of inputs against the tax due on their sales.

VAT in the EU is levied on an invoice basis. Invoices (bills issued by a firm to its consumers, demanding payment for deliveries) govern the timing of VAT liabilities, and provide an audit trail for enforcement (Keen and Smith 1996). Most member states apply lower rates to a range of items, like food and some services. Some items are untaxed. A firm with sales of zero-rated goods receives a net refund from the tax authorities corresponding to any tax paid at earlier stages of the production and distribution process.

The EC-wide introduction of VAT in the early 1970s replaced the previous sales taxes of member states. As part of the progress towards the creation of the single European market in 1992 an attempt was made to harmonize VAT rates. In 1991 it was decided to have a 15 per cent minimum standard VAT rate by 1 January 1993 for a 'transitional period' up to the end of 1996. Until then, VAT rates differed widely across member states (see Table 4.3). The member states, however, enjoy the option of applying, alongside the normal rate, one (or two) reduced rates, equal to or higher than 5 per cent, applicable only to certain goods and services of a social or cultural nature. Examples include foodstuffs, books, newspapers, and periodicals.

In principle, the VAT is based on the destination principle (taxes are levied where the good is consumed; see also Box 22). This ensures that even if tax rates differ across countries, the tax does not discriminate between foreign and domestic producers. However, it requires the monitoring of cross-border flows of goods and services and involves a heavy administrative burden (Hoeller, Louppe, and Vergriete 1996). Before the 'transitional' system was introduced, goods and services moving within a member state were taxed differently from those that were exported. On exportation the product benefited from full tax rebate and was in return subject to the VAT of the country of import. That system depended on the frontier controls to check whether

Table 4.3 VAT Rates in 1991 (%) and Rates at 1 January 1998 (in parentheses)

Country	Reduced rate	Standard rate	Higher rate
Belgium	1/6 (0/1/6/12)	17/19 (21)	25/33 (–)
Denmark	– (–)	22 (25)	– (–)
Germany	7 (7)	14 (16)	– (–)
Greece	4/8 (4/8)	18 (18)	36 (–)
Spain	6 (4/7)	12 (16)	33 (–)
France	2.1/5.5/13 (21./5.5)	18.6 (20.6)	22 (–)
Ireland	0/2.3/10/12.5 (0/3.3/10/12.5)	21 (21)	– (–)
Italy	4/9 (4/10)	19 (20)	38 (–)
Luxembourg	3/6 (3/6/12)	15 (15)	– (–)
Netherlands	6 (6)	17 (17.5)	30 (–)
Portugal	0/8 (5/12)	17 (17)	30 (–)
UK	0 (0/2.5/5)	17.5 (17.5)	– (–)
Austria	(10/12)	(20)	(–)
Finland	(8/17)	(22)	(–)
Sweden	(0/6/12)	(25)	(–)

Source: Data provided by OECD Secretariat.

Note: As in some countries various tax rates are employed, there may be various entries, e.g. Belgium had in 1998 four reduced tax rates: 0%, 1%, 6%, and 12%.

the goods, which were the subject of an application for the reimbursement of tax, had actually been exported. To remove fiscal frontiers, it was vital that cross-border trade be treated in the same way as purchase and sales within a state. For transactions between firms, little of economic substance has changed under the 'transitional' regime. Exports are zero-rated, just as before. What has changed is the implementation. There are no fiscal frontiers any more. This, of course, also affects cross-border shopping by consumers. They can buy products abroad and pay the VAT rate as applied there. Some special schemes exist to limit the scope for this type of tax arbitrage. For instance, mail order firms must charge and remit VAT according to the jurisdiction in which final consumption occurs once their turnover exceeds certain thresholds. Cars are also fully taxed on the basis of the destination principle (Keen and Smith 1996).

Although it was initially foreseen that the current system would be replaced by a 'definitive' system in 1997 (see below), the discussion about the future of VAT still continues. The delay reflects both the importance of VAT—making up about 18 per cent of member states' tax revenues—and the technical difficulties involved (Keen and Smith 1996). The challenge in designing a VAT regime is to accommodate two objectives:

- Preserving the maximum degree of autonomy for the member states in setting their tax rates.
- Ensuring that VAT structures and administrative procedures do not impede the single market.

These two objectives contain a trade-off. Preserving national autonomy risks

Box 22 Destination versus Origin Principle

Three aspects of the tax treatment of an international transaction are of interest:

- which country's tax rate determines the final burden of taxation?
- revenue allocation: which country receives the revenue?
- administration: which country collects the tax?

In the current VAT system all three coincide. In other systems the answers to these questions may differ. Following Keen and Smith (1996), we mean by the destination principle that the only tax rates affecting the tax burden on goods sold to consumers are those of the jurisdiction in which the final consumption occurs. Under the origin principle the tax paid depends, at least in part, on the tax rates of the jurisdiction in which the good was produced. Under the destination principle for indirect taxes commodity exports are exempt from the exporting country's tax and are instead subjected to the tax of the country of import. The destination principle ensures that firms compete on the basis of 'producer' prices (that is, prices net of taxes). Despite international tax rate differences, there is a tendency to equate the producer price ratios of any two commodities in all the countries that participate in the market. Under competitive conditions this implies efficient international specialization (Sinn 1990).

non-co-operative tax setting, with adverse effects on other member states revenues and resource allocation (Huizinga and Nielsen 1997).

The European Commission seeks to replace the 'transitional' regime by a 'definitive regime' under which exports by registered traders would be subject to the VAT of the country of production, but a tax credit for an equivalent amount would be granted to the registered importer by the country of destination. Some EU-wide form of clearing mechanism would be required for settling VAT balances of member states that are net importers. The basic idea of this approach is simply to extend the invoice method, which is currently applied within the countries of the European Union, to cross-border sales. For example, a German firm buying a French product will reclaim the French VAT contained in the price from the German revenue office and pay the German VAT on its sales instead. Since the importing rather than the exporting country gives a credit for the prepaid VAT, a clearing mechanism is necessary to redistribute the tax revenue between the jurisdictions involved.

Excise duties generate between 5 and 16 per cent of total tax revenues in EU countries and usually apply to goods with a low price elasticity. As part of the internal market programme, the European Commission proposed completely to harmonize excise duty rates on mineral oils, tobacco products, and alcoholic beverages. Ultimately, however, a system of minimum rates was adopted, which member states had to respect from 1 January 1993. Even after the progress towards harmonization, the dispersion of excise rates remains substantial. Differences are particularly marked for duties on alcoholic beverages (Hoeller, Louppe, and Vergriete 1996).

Given the high mobility of capital, taxes levied on capital income are more vulnerable to tax competition and tax evasion than most other taxes. Corporate tax systems differ markedly across EU countries and are far from ensuring export and import neutrality. *Capital import neutrality* prevails if effective tax rates are the same, irrespective of whether the recipient of capital income is a resident or non-resident. *Capital export neutrality* aims at ensuring that taxation does not interfere with decisions on where to invest and that investors face the same tax rates on investment, irrespective of where they invest (ibid). Despite the absence of the EC directives on corporate taxation, reductions in statutory tax rates coupled with base broadening (for example, by reducing tax deductions) have occurred in various EU member states (see Table 4.4). Corporate tax rates have converged to a rate of between 30 and 40 per cent.

The tax treatment of cross-border income flows varies also across EU member states. The latter concern the methods and extent of relief of double taxation for the recipient of capital income, as well as the imposition of withholding taxes at the source. A number of European Commission directives limiting the extent of double taxation were adopted, but attempts to harmonize corporate tax bases and rates in the mid-1970s were not successful. In the early 1990s, the recommendations of the Ruding Committee for a move towards harmonization were only partially endorsed by the Council. In the Council's view, action by the EU on business taxation should be limited to the minimum necessary (ibid.).

The risk of tax competition is very relevant in the case of withholding taxes on

Table 4.4 Corporate Tax Rates in the European Union

Countries	Tax rate in 1989 (%)	Corporate taxes as % GDP, 1989	Tax rate in 1997 (%)	Corporate taxes as % GDP, 1997
Austria	30.0	1.61	34.0	2.18
Belgium	41.0	2.77	39.0	3.13[a]
Denmark	40.0	2.10	34.0	2.42[a]
Finland	42.0	1.58	28.0	3.23
France	37.0	2.41	33.3	2.09
Germany	50.0	2.11	45.0	1.76
Greece	46.0	1.54	35.0	2.71
Ireland	43.0	1.18	36.0	3.48
Italy	36.0	3.81	37.0	2.17
Luxembourg	34.0	7.23	32.0	8.62
Netherlands	35.0	3.23	35.0	4.58
Portugal	36.5	1.37	36.0	3.76
Spain	35.0	2.96	35.0	2.64
Sweden	30.0	1.87[b]	28.0	3.34
UK	34.0	3.27[b]	31.0	3.95

Source: Coopers & Lybrand and OECD.

Notes
[a] 1996
[b] 1991

cross-border flows of interest from bank deposits and portfolio investments. In case of a *withholding tax* part of the interest payment is not paid to the investor, but is directly transferred to the government. The issue of a withholding tax on interest payments has been discussed for quite some time. Interest payments are taxed differently in the EU. To counter the risks of distortion and evasion in the present system, the European Commission proposed in May 1989 to introduce a minimum EU-wide withholding tax on interest payments made to all Union residents. The minimum tax rate should be 15 per cent. Many economists were critical of the proposal. First, the proposal did not take third countries into account. However, it seems vital to incorporate tax evasion opportunities arising outside the Union. Second, a minimum withholding tax is very difficult to enforce properly in practice. Third, a minimum withholding tax may not be the most appropriate solution to the problem of tax evasion. Some kind of 'reporting system', as in use in various EU countries, is perhaps a better solution. The reporting system entails that domestic banks and other financial institutions automatically report to tax authorities the amount of interest that has been paid out, and to whom. However, such a system on a EU-wide basis, runs counter to the bank secrecy and blocking laws prevailing in many EU countries (Huizinga and Nielsen 1997). Recently, the European Commission has put forward a proposal for the taxation of savings income of non-residents. It is based on a co-existence or 'hybrid' model, whereby each member state would have to either apply a withholding tax of least 20 per cent or provide information to other member states on interest income from savings. The proposal does not seek total harmonization of interest income within the EU, but covers only the taxation of cross-border savings, and it does not cover income paid to residents of third countries.

4.4 Tax Competition

TAXES across EU member states may also become more similar due to *tax competition*. Suppose, for instance, that one country imposes taxes on consumption that are much higher than those imposed by neighbouring countries. The individuals living in that country would then be encouraged to shop in other member states, thus contributing to the tax revenues of those states. Similarly, when a member state imposes much higher taxes on labour income than other countries, some individuals might be tempted to move to the other states unless the higher public expenditure in the former compensates them for higher taxes. This may especially apply to those segments of the labour market with a relatively high level of mobility, like managers of firms. Also, if taxes on capital income were higher, savers would have an incentive to invest their savings in member states with lower taxes. Relatively high taxes on enterprises may encourage enterprises to establish themselves in member states with lower tax unless the country concerned offers advantages in terms of social, physical, and legal environment, public services, amenities, quality of the work force (Tanzi and Zee 1998).

While tax differences are important, it is easy to exaggerate their impact. For one thing, individuals usually have a *preferred habitat*, which is often the place they have been living in and to which they have got accustomed. Small tax differences may not be sufficient to induce behavioural changes, as mobility may impose various costs, including psychological and social costs. Further economic integration and new technologies may, however, create opportunities that can be exploited at particularly low costs (ibid.). This seems to be relevant for the taxation of financial capital and the taxation of consumption (for example, shopping via Internet).

Figure 4.3 shows that, despite harmonization, current VAT rates in the EU still differ considerably across countries. The same is true for other taxes. An important question is how much divergence in taxes will be possible in a monetary union. Will tax competition lead to more similar tax systems in Europe? The experience of the United States could perhaps shed light on this issue (ibid.). The United States has no border controls and has been a monetary union for quite some time. Table 4.5 presents some figures on US state taxes, notably top marginal regular rates of individual and corporate income taxes as well as the rates of the retail sales tax imposed by the different states in 1994. The table suggests that there are significant differences across the US states. For instance, individual income tax differences are as large as 12 percentage points. The average tax rates, expressed as a percentage of personal income,

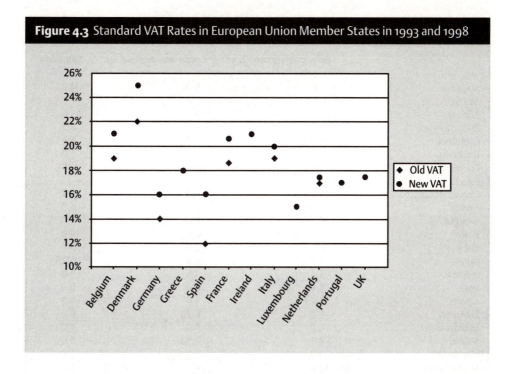

Figure 4.3 Standard VAT Rates in European Union Member States in 1993 and 1998

ranged from zero to 4.5 per cent, with a national average of 2.4 per cent.[10] The differences are also significant for the top marginal income taxes on corporations, ranging from zero to 10 per cent or more. Finally, differences in rates on sales taxes are the lowest of the taxes considered here. Still, it is clear that also in this case tax rates are definitely not the same across states.

There is clearly no consensus in the literature whether intensified tax competition is beneficial or not. Those who regard the state as a facility to maximize its citizens' welfare are more inclined to reject tax competition, as it will cause important allocative distortions. Those who consider the state as a Leviathan that pursues the interests of politicians and bureaucrats see tax competition as a means to stop public sector growth. In this line of reasoning, public production and services are provided at too high a cost and governments have insufficient incentives to care for the preferences of the population. If governments are judged to be inefficient, tax competition will be welcomed, as it would act as a brake on a government's capacity to appropriate and waste resources. So, it depends on the size of the economic and political distortions whether tax competition is beneficial or not (see Figure 4.4).

In both lines of reasoning, tax competition will lower government spending. We may illustrate this on the basis of a simplified model without political distortions in which it is assumed that only (physical) capital is taxed, while there is capital mobility.[11]

[10] Because state and local income taxes are deductible from income in the determination of federal income tax, effective marginal tax rates are somewhat lower than reported in Table 4.5 (Tanzi and Zee 1998).

[11] We are grateful to Harry Huizinga for his assistance with the model.

Table 4.5 United States: Rates of State Income and Sales Taxes, 1994

	Individual Income Tax[a]	Corporate Income Tax[b]	Sales Tax
Alabama	5.0	5.0	4.0
Alaska	—	9.4	—
Arizona	6.9	9.0	5.0
Arkansas	7.0	6.5	4.5
California	11.0	9.3	6.0
Colorado	5.0	5.1	3.0
Connecticut	4.5	11.5	6.0
Delaware	7.7	8.7	—
District of Columbia	9.5	10.0	5.75
Florida	—	5.5	6.0
Georgia	6.0	6.0	4.0
Hawaii	10.0	7.92	4.0
Idaho	8.2	8.0	5.0
Illinois	3.0	4.8	6.25
Indiana	3.4	4.5	5.0
Iowa	9.98	12.0	5.0
Kansas	7.75	4.0	4.9
Kentucky	6.0	8.25	6.0
Louisiana	6.0	8.0	4.0
Maine	8.5	8.93	6.0
Maryland	6.0	7.0	5.0
Massachusetts	12.0	—[c]	5.0
Michigan	4.4	—[c]	6.0
Minnesota	8.5	9.8	6.0
Mississippi	5.0	5.0	7.0
Missouri	6.0	6.5	4.225
Montana	11.0	6.75	—
Nebraska	6.99	7.81	5.0
Nevada	—	—	6.5
New Hampshire	5.0	7.5	—
New Jersey	6.65	9.0	6.0
New Mexico	8.5	7.6	5.0
New York	7.875	9.0	4.0
North Carolina	7.75	7.75	4.0
North Dakota	5.544	10.5	5.0
Ohio	7.5	8.9	5.0
Oklahoma	7.0	6.0	4.5
Oregon	9.0	6.6	—
Pennsylvania	2.8	11.99	6.0
Rhode Island	10.89	9.0	7.0
South Carolina	7.0	5.0	5.0
South Dakota	—	—	4.0
Tennessee	6.0	6.0	6.0
Texas	—	—	6.25
Utah	7.2	5.0	5.0
Vermont	9.9	8.25	5.0
Virginia	5.75	6.0	3.5
Washington	—	—	6.5
West Virginia	6.5	9.0	6.0
Wisconsin	6.93	7.9	5.0
Wyoming	—	—	4.0

Unweighted average	6.1	6.9	4.7
Standard deviation	3.2	3.0	1.8
Coefficient of variation	51.5	43.7	38.2

Source: ACIR 1995.

Notes
[a] Top marginal regular rates on residents, excludes local taxes.
[b] Top marginal regular rate, excludes local taxes.
[c] Taxes on corporation assessed on an alternative basis.

Figure 4.4 Allocative versus Political Decision-making Distortions

		Political decision-making distortion	
		small	large
Economic allocative distortion	small	do nothing	tax competition
	large	harmonization	??

Source: Frey 1998.

Suppose, first, that the economy is closed and that government tries to maximize the following utility function (which is concave in G):

$$U = C + V(G) \tag{4.6}$$

with $V' > 0$ and $V'' < 0$ and where U = utility, C = private consumption, and G = government spending on public goods. The production function is given as:

$$F = F(K) \tag{4.7}$$

with $F' > 0$ and $F'' < 0$ and where F = production and K = (physical) capital.

Suppose that we have only a tax on (physical) capital:

$$T = t.K = G \tag{4.8}$$

where T = total tax revenue, t = tax rate per unit (physical) capital, and total tax revenue equals total spending on public goods (government budget constraint).

The consumption function for the private sector is as follows:

$$C = F - t.K \tag{4.9}$$

that is, consumption equals production minus total tax revenue. The optimal tax problem for government is to maximize equation (4.6), subject to the government budget constraint. The resulting first order condition is: $V' = 1$ (that is, the marginal utility of government spending equals one). The next step in the analysis is to assume a second country that is similar to the one described above. So, we have for this country:

$$U^* = C^* + V^*(G^*) \tag{4.6'}$$

$$F^* = F^*(K^*) \tag{4.7'}$$

$$T^* = t^*.K^* = G^* \tag{4.8'}$$

$$C^* = F^* - t.^* K^* \tag{4.9'}$$

where * denotes that the variables refer to the other country. In addition, we now need an equation for the allocation of capital. Assuming that the after-tax marginal productivity determines the allocation, we can write:

$$F' - t = F^{*'} - t^* \tag{4.10}$$

where F' denotes marginal productivity of capital. In the equilibrium in case of Nash bargaining $V' > 1$. So, the open-economy tax rate is lower than the closed-economy rate. Thus government spending will also be lower. A higher domestic tax rate will cause a capital outflow to the other country. So every country has an incentive to lower its tax rate. Therefore, tax competition will result in a 'race to the bottom' (see also Box 23). Proponents of restricting tax competition point out that EU member states are using special tax schemes to compete with each other to attract investment and capital. According to European Commissioner Monti (1998),

Unbridled tax competition between member states has caused average tax rates on mobile factors of production, notably capital, to fall from 45.5 per cent to less than 35 per cent in the last fifteen years. In the same period, the average tax rate on labour has increased from 34.9 per cent to more than 42 per cent. A growing body of evidence now points to a strong negative effect of high labour taxes on the level of employment and growth in Europe. Without some form of co-ordination, not only will labour continue to be penalised for being less mobile than capital but the levels of tax revenue are liable to decrease.

Apart from the arguments discussed so far, other considerations have been put forward in the debate about tax competition. One empirical argument that has been raised by some proponents of tax competition is that in some federalist countries (United States, Switzerland) sub-national tax systems differ, while they work well (Frey and Eichenberger 1996). Opponents of tax competition point out that certain groups in society may be harmed excessively by tax competition. According to Sinn (1990), the losers of tax competition will be those who cannot escape and those who benefit from a large government sector. The first group includes immobile workers and landowners, while the second group consists of the poor. Those who see redistribution policy as the greed of Leviathan, will welcome the latter. However, Sinn (1990) argues that redistribution can be seen as an efficiency enhancing government activity, which compensates for a lack of risk markets.

The approach followed in the EU is to limit what is called 'harmful tax competition'. At 1 December 1997 the Ecofin reached an agreement on a package against harmful tax competition which had been proposed by the European Commission. The three measures agreed upon were a resolution on a code of conduct for business taxation and agreement that Directives should be brought forward to deal with the taxation of income of non-residents from savings, and to eliminate withholding taxes on cross border interest and royalty payments between companies.

Box 23 Tax Competition and the Tiebout Hypothesis

According to a survey by Wilson (1999), the main message of the literature on *tax competition* is that independent governments engage in wasteful competition for scarce capital through reductions in tax rates and public expenditure levels. Oates (1972) stated that the result of tax competition may well be a tendency towards less than efficient levels of output of local services. In an attempt to keep taxes low to attract business investment, local officials may hold spending below those levels for which marginal benefits equal marginal costs. So, local officials will add to the conventional measures of marginal costs the costs arising from the negative impact of taxation on business investment, such as lower wages and employment levels, capital losses on real estate and other assets, and reduced tax bases. Oates concluded that, when all governments behave this way, none gains a competitive advantage and, consequently, local communities are all worse off than they would have been if local officials had simply used the conventional measures of marginal costs. Stimulated by the many cases in the United States where states and municipalities have engaged in tax competition (for example, by large subsidies to attract foreign and domestic automobile companies), the research on tax competition has expanded rapidly since the mid-1980s.

However, the view that tax competition between governments is wasteful is contrary to the so-called *Tiebout hypothesis.* Tiebout (1956) provided in his seminal article a theory of local public good provision and argued that competition for mobile households is welfare enhancing. Subsequent work has applied similar ideas to competition for mobile firms. The Tiebout hypothesis supports policies that allow free capital and labour mobility and enable national governments to function independently in most policy areas. On the contrary, the tax competition literature focuses on the potentially adverse effects of this policy independence. These adverse effects are also reflected in Sinn's (1997) *selection principle* which indentifies a fundamental selection bias towards government activities that have proved to be unsuitable for private markets. Sinn argues that if private markets fail efficiently to provide particular goods and services, then introducing competition among governments that seek to provide them will result in similar problems.

Wilson (1999) concluded that the political approach to model (tax) competition between governments takes a middle ground. On the one hand, it follows the Tiebout approach by recognizing that this competition introduces efficiency-enhancing incentives similar to profit motives facing competitive firms. On the other hand, it departs from the Tiebout approach by recognizing that such incentives operate in an environment characterized by market failures that make a fully efficient equilibrium unattainable. Therefore, competition among governments has both good and bad aspects depending on the attributes of the goods and services that the governments provide.

4.5 Conclusion

THE philosophy underlying the Stability and Growth Pact is that in a monetary union restrictions on national fiscal policy are required. The most compelling argument for such restrictions is that they offer extra protection for the ECB from pressure for an inflationary debt bail-out. Excessive borrowing by a member country may also drive up interest rates in the union and affect the exchange rate of the euro. Because of these external effects, it will be in the interest of the other countries that a control mechanism exists restricting the size of budget deficits in member countries. It was shown that three issues are crucial in evaluating the need for fiscal rules in a monetary union: the disciplinary influence of financial markets, the credibility of the no-bail-out clause and the independence of the ECB. Even if heavy borrowers have to pay some risk premium, it seems doubtful that this will discipline governments (sufficiently). Only if financial markets are no longer willing to provide additional credit, governments will have to give in. But then it may be too late. Furthermore, the no-bail-out clause provided for by the Maastricht Treaty may not be entirely credible. Finally, the Statute of the ECB give the bank a very independent position. But again, one should be careful here as the ECB has not, as yet, a clear reputation similar, for instance, to that of the Bundesbank. The ECB will have to earn its credibility and under those circumstances it may be better not to give some member countries any reason to put the ECB to the test. So, from a political economy point of view it can be concluded that under the current circumstances a safety-first strategy with respect to fiscal policies of member countries may be beneficial.

It is also concluded that many—but not all—of the defects of the Maastricht Treaty (vague criteria, long procedures, no specific and deterrent sanctions, too much discretion) are (at least partly) repaired by the Stability and Growth Pact. In comparison to budget rules that proved to be effective for US states, the Stability and Growth Pact scores quite reasonably. However, there are a number of caveats: the sanctions do not alleviate the problem at hand and refer only to breaches of the deficit criterion. Finally, it is questionable whether the fiscal rules laid down in the Stability and Growth Pact will be adhered to if a large number of member states ever get into serious fiscal problems.

The chapter ended with a discussion of issues in tax harmonization and tax competition. The basic lesson from the theory of optimal taxation is that a country cannot, and should not, impose high taxes on activities whose supply and demand are price elastic. Elastic activities can escape taxation and thus imply a high excess burden relative to the tax collected. Whether tax competition or tax harmonization is the best answer to diverging tax systems in Europe is highly debated. So far, member states remain responsible for their tax systems, although some harmonization at the European level has been realized, notably so with respect to VAT.

Chapter 5
European Fiscal Policy

Introduction

THE budget of the EU is quite different from national budgets, both in terms of its size and composition. In absolute terms the EU budget is large. In 1999 EU spending amounted to more than 86 mrd euro. However, the size of a budget is normally related to the size of GDP. Seen in this way, the EU budget is small in relation to the budgets of the member states. It accounts for just over 1 per cent of the Union's GDP; a small amount compared with the budgets of national governments (including social security funds) that generally make up some 50 per cent of GDP. Many areas of EU policy are regulatory in nature and require no spending, except for administration. In contrast to national budgets, expenditure on social security, law and order, and education are largely absent at the EU budget. According to the Maastricht Treaty, for areas that do not fall under the exclusive competence of the EU the *subsidiarity principle* should be applied. Only if a policy objective can be better attained at the EU-wide level, should the Union be involved.

Section 5.1 discusses the EU budget and how it is financed in more detail. Section 5.2 discusses the EU budget until 2007. Reform of the EU budget is necessary in the light of future EU membership of a number of Central and Eastern European countries. The proposal on the future EU budget and new member countries is known as *Agenda 2000*.

As has been explained in Chapter 1, monetary union implies that one potentially useful adjustment mechanism (that is exchange rate adjustments) is no longer available. Various authors have therefore suggested that in EMU a similar kind of stabilization mechanism may be needed as currently exists in federal states like Canada, Germany, and the US. Section 5.3 presents the arguments for this view. Section 5.4 concludes.

5.1 The Budget of the European Union

Unlike the budget of national governments, the EU budget is circumscribed by a prohibition on borrowing. Revenue estimates must be equal to payment appropriations. Any shortfall in revenue must be made up by a supplementary or amending budget (Laffan 1998). Consequently, the financial resources available (subsection 5.1.1) have been of central importance in determining the scale of EU activities (subsection 5.1.2). The EU budgetary arrangements imply that there are both winners and losers in terms of *net payments* (that is, the difference between contributions to and receipts from the EU budget). This has led to a long-running debate about the extent to which net positive and negative balances of member states are satisfactory (subsection 5.1.3).

A number of the Union's financial instruments do not constitute part of the budget. For instance, the European Development Fund (EDF) for aid to developing countries in Africa, the Caribbean, and the Pacific has never been part of the budget. It is mainly financed by contributions from the member states. Also, the borrowing and lending activities of the Union do not appear in the budget. Subsection 5.1.4 deals with the latter.

5.1.1 Resources

During the first twelve years of what is now called the EU, the budget was funded entirely by direct contributions from the member states. Since 1970, however, the budget has been financed through so-called *own resources*, that is, by revenues that the member states have agreed should be the resources of the EU by right. Initially, there were three own resources: (1) custom duties on goods imported from outside the Union (2) agricultural levies (taxes on agricultural imports and levies on sugar production), and (3) a share of the VAT revenue raised in each country. The VAT revenues consisted of a rate of 1 per cent applied to a harmonized base (see Box 24).

Receipts from the traditional own resources (that is, custom duties and agricultural levies) have fallen gradually since the 1970s. Custom duties declined as a consequence of progress made in worldwide dismantling of tariffs. Owing to the trade liberalization the total yield of this resource failed to increase in line with the expansion of world trade. The rapid increase in agricultural production in the Union largely explains the downward trend in agricultural levies as a source of revenue. In absolute terms, traditional own resources have remained in the range of 12 to 14 mrd euro, resulting in the observed reduction in the share of total resources.

In the period 1975–84 revenue growth was eroded by a diminishing yield from traditional own resources, while revenues from VAT were adversely affected by the generally weak economic growth prevailing during this period. At the same time,

Box 24   The Evolution of the European Union's Own Resources

Own Resource System 1970	1. Customs duties
	2. Agricultural levies
	3. VAT contribution up to a ceiling of 1 per cent
Fontainebleau 1984	1. and 2. as above
	3. VAT rate raised to 1.4 per cent
Brussels (Delors I) 1988–92	1. and 2. as above
	3. Maximum VAT rate maintained at 1.4 per cent but capped at 55 per cent of GNP for all member states
	4. Topping up resources calculated on the basis of GNP
	5. Revenue limited to ceiling of 1.2 per cent of EU GNP in 1999
Edinburgh (Delors II) 1993–9	1. and 2. as above
	3. Maximum VAT rate reduced to 1 per cent and capped at 50 per cent for cohesion states from 1996 and for other member states in 1999
	4. Topping up based on GNP
	5. Revenue limited to 1.27 of EU GNP
Berlin (Agenda 2000) 2000–6	1. and 2. as above (but higher share for member states)
	3. Maximum VAT rate reduced to 0.5 per cent
	4. Topping up based on GNP
	5. Revenue limited to 1.27 of EU GNP

Source: Laffan (1998) and Berlin European Council, Presidency Conclusions.

spending increased owing to the launching of new policies, the inability to contain spending on the Common Agricultural Policy and expenditure growth associated with the two enlargements. Persistent complaints on the part of the UK concerning its financial contribution also became a feature of the budget disputes that were prominent during this period. A temporary resolution of the budget difficulties was secured at the Fontainebleau European Council. The maximum rate for the VAT resource was increased to 1.4 per cent. This decision took effect from January 1986. The VAT revenues at the time amounted to 56 per cent of total revenues. The Fontainebleau meeting has also established a correction mechanism for budgetary imbalances, which applied only to the UK.

The modifications proved insufficient, as they failed to generate sufficient revenues. In addition, the VAT resource was felt to contain a significant regressive element, because the contributions of member states with a low income per capita were, in relative terms, higher than those of more affluent EU countries. In February

1987 the European Commission presented comprehensive reform proposals, which came to be known as the *Delors I Package*. The reform, as agreed upon during the June 1988 Brussels European Council, maintained the traditional own resources derived from customs duties and agricultural levies. Also VAT revenues (with a rate of 1.4 per cent) remained in place. However, the VAT base was capped at 55 per cent of GNP in all member states. The most important novelty was that the Council accepted a new *fourth resource*. This was a variable, 'topping-up' resource, which would provide the revenue required to cover expenditure in excess of proceeds from the other resources, subject to an overall ceiling for the total of all own resources of 1.2 per cent of GNP.[1] The fourth resource reflects the principle of the ability to pay as it is based on member states' relative GNP. Being a residual source of financing, its magnitude shows some fluctuation.

The next important transformation of the budget arose out of the Edinburgh European Council of 1992. Based on proposals put forward by the European Commission, called the *Delors II Package*, the Edinburgh Agreement limited the role of VAT and put more emphasis on the fourth resource. The European Commission proposed a further increase in the budget to 1.37 per cent of EU GNP by 1997. More than half of the total increase would go to the Structural Funds, including the new Cohesion Fund (see below). The proposals met with considerable criticism. It was finally agreed that the own resources would rise less than proposed by the Commission. Between 1993 and 1999 the budget was assigned a maximum of own resources rising to 1.27 per cent of the Union's GNP. Total spending on structural policies should not increase to more than 0.46 per cent of EU GNP. The common VAT base was limited to 50 per cent of GNP in all countries in 1999 and the VAT rate was reduced to 1 per cent in 1999.[2]

The share of the various own resources changed significantly over time, as Figure 5.1 shows.[3] It is clear that the relative importance of the fourth resource increased considerably. In 1998 its share amounted to 43 per cent of total revenues. At the same time the share of VAT has declined, which primarily reflects policy reforms introduced by the 1988 and 1994 Own Resources Decisions. Contributions based on GNP are regarded as being more acceptable than those based on VAT, because they relate to a country's relative affluence. This is due to the fact that the VAT base forms a higher proportion of GNP in the poorer member states than in the more affluent ones.

In March 1999 at its meeting in Berlin the European Council reached an agreement about the EU budget for the period 2000–6 (see section 5.2). As part of the package, it was decided to reduce the maximum rate of the VAT resource to 0.75 per cent in 2002 and to 0.50 per cent in 2004. The traditional own resources will be maintained, with the percentage retained by the member states in the form of collection costs increasing from 10 to 25 per cent with effect from 2001.

[1] Actual own resources were generally below the ceilings agreed upon. In 1992 they amounted to 1.13 per cent of GNP.

[2] The modification of the system of own resources agreed in the Edinburgh meeting of the European Council in December 1992 was transformed into a formal decision in October 1994 and came into force, retroactively, on 1 January 1995.

[3] The 'rest' category in Figure 5.1 consists of fines, revenues accruing from the administrative operations of the Community institutions, contributions related to activities on the European Economic Area, interest on late payments, taxes on the salaries of employees of the European Institutions, income from borrowing and lending operations, and other miscellaneous revenues.

5.1.2 **Expenditure**

Table 5.1 presents the development of the European budget, whereas Figure 5.2 shows the shares of the most important spending categories.[4] Table 5.1 demonstrates that, although EU spending has increased over time, its share in European GDP is quite low. Also, in comparison with spending by national governments, the EU budget is rather small. EU spending per capita amounted to only 228 euro in 1998.

Figure 5.2 shows that the *Common Agricultural Policy* (CAP) still absorbs the largest part of the budget. Appropriations for the CAP contained in the 1998 budget, for example, accounted for some 48 per cent of total spending, a proportion that has fallen significantly from the peak values obtained in the early and mid-1970s, when agricultural spending frequently represented over 70 per cent of expenditure. As part of the Delors I Package it was decided in 1988 to limit the expansion of agricultural spending to 74 per cent of the rate of growth of EU real GNP. Owing to various reform measures (see below), the share of CAP spending has slowly been cut back.

The CAP has shaped the direction and structure of European agriculture by means of an elaborate regime of financial rewards and penalties. However, government involvement in agriculture is not unique to the EU. Many countries intervene at markets for agricultural products. The reason is that agricultural markets have more difficulty in getting to equilibrium than other markets, and the social consequences of disequilibria of agricultural markets are considered unacceptable. The causes for possible disequilibria are the following. On the demand side, agricultural products have a very low price elasticity. On the supply side, the vagaries of the weather may cause large fluctuations in production volume. Coupled with inelastic demand, this

Table 5.1 Spending by the European Union, 1960–1998

	1960	1965	1970	1975	1980	1985	1990	1995	1998
Mrd euro (prices 1998)	476	2,218	18,395	19,649	34,138	43,088	56,247	73,737	85,656
As percentage of national government spending	0.10	0.30	2.00	1.20	1.70	1.90	2.00	2.10	2.40
As percentage of EU GDP	0.03	0.11	0.74	0.54	0.80	0.93	0.95	1.06	1.15
Per capita in euro (prices 1998)	2.80	12.20	97.70	76.10	130.70	158.70	172.00	198.20	228.20

Source: European Commission 1998*a*.

---

[4] In the EU budget a distinction is made between *commitment appropriations* and *payment appropriations*. The implementation of the budget involves a time-lag between the commitment of resources and actual payments. Table 5.1 and Figure 5.2 show actual payments. Included are also the operating budget of the ECSC (which expires in 2002) and the EDF, which are not part of the EU budget.

Figure 5.1 Shares of Own Resources of the European Union, 1971–1999

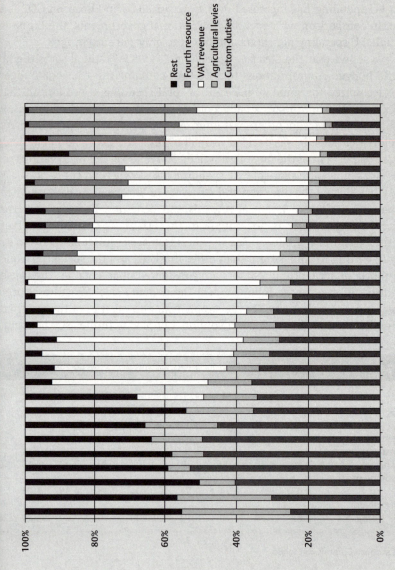

Rest
Fourth resource
VAT revenue
Agricultural levies
Custom duties

71 72 73 74 75 76 77 78 79 80 81 82 83 84 85 86 87 88 89 90 91 92 93 94 95 96 97 98 99

100%
80%
60%
40%
20%
0%

Source: European Commission 1998*a.*

Box 25 New Own Resources?

The 1992 proposal of the European Commission (Delors II) advocated a new *fifth own resource* to supplement the existing four resources, but did not specify what this resource might be. The issue was not central during the negotiations about Delors II. In 1993 a report of an independent group of economists (Stable money—sound finances) was published in which the issue was raised again (European Commission 1993). The experts argued that in EMU the budget should be financed in a different way. ECB profits were considered a convincing candidate for new own resources. Other well-suited candidates according to the experts are a tax on CO_2 emissions and corporate taxes. This conclusion was based on an assessment of various possible new resources based on three main criteria:

- If tax revenues are difficult or impossible to allocate between member states allocation to the EU budget is appropriate (for example, ECB profits).
- If the tax base is highly mobile, implying that a low rate in one member state erodes the tax base of other member states, a common tax is appropriate (for example, capital income tax).
- Whether the tax is effective in achieving agreed EU policy objectives (for example, CO_2 tax).

The Own Resources Decision of Edinburgh required the Commission to report on the feasibility of creating a new own resource as well as on the arrangements for the possible introduction of a fixed uniform rate levied on the VAT base. In its report the European Commission (1998*b*) concluded that the present own resources system performed satisfactorily as far as the criteria of resource adequacy and fair sharing of the burden are concerned. According to the Commission, the present arrangements have generated sufficient revenue to finance expenditure plans. Equity of gross contributions of the member states has improved, due to replacement of the VAT resource with the GNP resource. Still, the European Commission argued that the present system shows shortcomings in terms of financial autonomy, cost effectiveness, and transparency. The dominant part of EU resources derives from national contributions thereby reducing the financial autonomy of the EU. The collection of traditional own resources is very cumbersome and results in a substantial amount of administrative work. Furthermore, the calculation and financing arrangements of the UK rebate are so complex as to impair the transparency of this mechanism. Despite these criticisms, the Berlin meeting of the European Council decided to keep the basic system intact. Still, the European Council has asked the Commission to undertake a general review of the own resources system before 1 January 2006. As part of this review, the question of creating new autonomous own resources should also be addressed.

leads to large price fluctuations. The very many suppliers, by reacting simultaneously to price signals, may boost fluctuations even further (Molle 1994).

What were the aims of government intervention in agricultural markets in the EU? The Treaty of Rome formulates the following objectives of the CAP (Tracy 1989):

- to increase agricultural productivity;
- to ensure a fair standard of living for the agricultural community;
- to stabilize agricultural markets;
- to assure the availability of supplies;
- to ensure that supplies reach consumers at reasonable prices.

The three most important types of market control as originally envisaged by the CAP are (Molle 1994):

- A guarantee scheme and intervention prices, combined with levies on imports and subsidies on exports. This method of intervention applies to products like cereals, sugar, and dairy products. It guarantees a minimum price at which intervention agencies will buy up any excess domestic supply.

- Limited free price formation, separated from world market prices. This type of intervention has been introduced for certain kinds of fruit and vegetables, flowers, eggs, and poultry meat. Prices are not guaranteed, but imports are constrained by levies and restrictions.

- Bonuses based on the quantity produced. For some other products, for instance those for which international agreements allow no protection at the border, a system of subsidies on the value of the produce is sometimes applied.

To achieve these objectives, the *European Agricultural Guidance and Guarantee Fund* (EAGGF) was set up. It has two sections. Through the Guarantee Section intervention prices are financed. It also funds export subsidies when the price of EU farm goods set by the CAP is higher than world market prices. The Guidance Section of the EAGGF is directed towards structural policy for agriculture.

The CAP resulted in price levels for agricultural products that were significantly higher than those prevailing in most member states before its introduction. It is not surprising therefore that since the early 1960s there has been a steady increase in European agricultural production. In time, Europe went beyond self-sufficiency in many sectors and created an export potential. For dairy products this had already happened in the sixties; for cereals around 1980. This implied that CAP spending increased, while import levies on agricultural products decreased and did not suffice to compensate for the cost of export subsidies. Moreover, as every additional exported unit tends to have a negative effect on world market prices, the restitution needed per unit increased accordingly. This was especially the case for products where the EU has a large market share in world exports (dairy products and, to a lesser extent, cereals). The costs of stockholding also steadily mounted (Molle 1994). So it became clear that measures had to be taken.

An important reform of the CAP took place in 1984 when production quotas were introduced to curb milk production. Other policies were introduced in the late 1980s

Figure 5.2 Shares of Expenditure Categories in the European Union Budget, 1971–1999

Rest
Structural funds
CAP

71 72 73 74 75 76 77 78 79 80 81 82 83 84 85 86 87 88 89 90 91 92 93 94 95 96 97 98 99

100% 90% 80% 70% 60% 50% 40% 30%

Source: European Commission 1998a.

such as price cuts and the 'set-aside' policy whereby farmers are given direct area compensation payments to leave land fallow.

Another impetus for changing the CAP came from the international negotiations to liberalize trade. Agriculture was an important issue during the Uruguay round. Previous GATT rounds achieved multilateral tariff cuts for industrial products, but were less successful in dealing with agricultural goods. From 1986, when the Uruguay Round began, the United States and some important agricultural exporters sought to change international levels of agricultural support. Attention focused particularly on the high subsidies given to European farmers, especially on cereals, which were regarded as unfair competition.

In January 1991, in response to the long-term pressures for change and the necessity to bring the CAP in line with the results of the GATT round, the European Commission approved the so-called *MacSharry Plan*, named after the Commissioner who was responsible for Agriculture at the time. The MacSharry Plan proposed radical cuts to agricultural subsidies and substantial reductions in quotas. The plan was for the most part accepted by the Council of Ministers in May 1992. Its main emphasis was on cereals. This is not astonishing as cereals played a key role in the GATT negotiations. Measures included are:

- A 30 per cent reduction in three years in the support prices of cereals. This should assist livestock farmers by reducing the cost of feed. In turn, this would permit the lowering of beef support prices. Farmers are partly compensated by direct income aid.
- The further development of the set-aside system.
- Aid to farmers who adopted more environmentally friendly methods, and who were involved in countryside preservation and the conservation of natural resources.
- An early retirement scheme, particularly aimed at farmers who operated on non-viable holdings.
- Fixation of import levies.

The reforms have drastically changed the CAP. Owing to the abolition of variable tariffs world market price changes are now in principle reflected in EU prices. Furthermore, these tariffs have been substantially reduced, while export subsidies have been lowered, both in terms of volume and amounts of money concerned. For many products, notably cereals and beef, EU prices have declined substantially.

The proposed extension of the EU to include Hungary, Poland, the Czech Republic, Estonia, and Slovenia will have significant implications for the CAP. This enlargement would lead to a 50 per cent increase in the cultivated area of the EU and it would double the size of the agricultural labour force (European Commission 1997). In Agenda 2000 the European Commission argued for the continued reform of the CAP to prevent serious problems that would arise if the present CAP system were to be extended to cover the proposed new member states (see section 5.2).

Spending on structural operations is the second largest category at the EU budget.

Four funds are mainly responsible for this category: the European Regional Development Fund (ERDF), the European Social Fund (ESF), the Guidance section of the EAGGF, and the Cohesion Fund. The latter was introduced in the Maastricht Treaty. It provides additional funding for infrastructure and environmental projects in member states with a per capita income of less than 90 per cent of the EU average. Spain, Portugal, Greece, and Ireland were entitled to support from this facility. The projects supported by the Structural Funds are co-financed (that is, national/regional authorities also have to bear part of the expenditure). In the case of the Cohesion Fund, funding can cover up to 85 per cent of the total project costs.

During the early years of what is now the EU, funds for structural policies were negligible. The founding members were a fairly homogeneous group of countries. The only region with a low per capita income and high unemployment was the southern part of Italy. The successive enlargements of the Union increased regional disparities. Consequently, structural policies became more important.

In the recent past, the structural policies were arranged on the basis of various objectives and designation criteria (see Box 26).

In Agenda 2000 the European Commission also proposed important changes in structural policies, again necessitated by the accession of some Central and Eastern European Countries (see section 5.2).

Box 26 European Regional Policy Objectives, 1994–1999

1. Development and structural adjustment of backward regions.
2. Conversion of regions or parts of regions seriously affected by industrial decline.
3. Combating long-term unemployment and occupational integration of young people.
4. Facilitating structural change, promoting the adaptation of workers to changes in industry and systems of production.
5a. Speeding up the adjustment of agricultural and fisheries structures.
5b. Development and structural adjustment of rural areas.
6. Support for areas with low population density (Nordic regions).

Objectives 1, 2, 5b, and 6 are regional in nature, whereas objectives 3, 4, and 5a cover the entire EU. Objective 6 was added as a result of the 1995 enlargement of the EU. To be eligible for Objective 1 support, per capita income in the region concerned must be less than 75 per cent of the EU average for at least three consecutive years. In the period 1994–9 more than two-thirds of the available resources have been allocated to objective 1 regions. These include the whole of Greece, Ireland, Portugal, most of Spain, the Mezzogiorno, Northern Ireland, as well as Corsica and the overseas territories of France. After unification, the Eastern part of Germany was added as well. In order to qualify for the Objective 2 status, regions must have a greater unemployment rate and a higher share of industrial employment than the EU average.

5.1.3 Net Balances

The redistribution through the EU budget between member states has attracted a great deal of public attention, which is disproportionate to its real economic significance. No doubt, this is owing to the fact that gains and losses through the budget are thought to be more easily identifiable than, for example, the welfare effects of the CAP. In the past, debates about the net contribution of the UK hindered progress on other issues on the European integration agenda. The UK made continuous complaints about its net contributions (as the former prime minister Mrs Thatcher put it: 'we want our money back'). As the UK only has a small agricultural sector, it benefited very little from the EC's agricultural spending. Furthermore, the VAT base accounted for a very large proportion of the country's GNP. Consequently, the UK's net balance vis-à-vis the EU budget was negative. The matter was largely resolved following the Fontainebleau summit in June 1984. Ever since, the EU budget has contained provisions for bringing the UK contribution more closely in line with EU expenditures in the UK. This reduction in the UK contribution was financed by additional payments made by all other member states, except Germany, that only pays two-thirds of its normal share of the compensation. The balance is divided among the remaining countries. The size of the budgetary imbalance of the UK, and therefore that of its compensation, has fluctuated substantially since 1985 at around half a point of GNP for the imbalance and 0.3 per cent of GNP for the *rebate*. However, even after the rebate the UK remains a large net contributor to the EU budget (European Commission 1998*b*).

Table 5.2 shows net balances from the EU budget for the member states. It follows that various countries have benefited from the EU budget during the entire period considered (Greece, Ireland, Portugal, Spain, Denmark, Belgium, Luxembourg), whereas others were net-contributors (Germany, Italy, Netherlands, UK).

However, the estimates in Table 5.2 may be criticized for various reasons. First, calculating national contributions in relation to the customs duties poses difficulties as the point of collection is not necessarily the point of consumption. This is known as the *Rotterdam effect*. This is where customs duties are collected on entry into the EU, but the goods may be destined for another member state. Second, there are also difficulties associated with the identification of the ultimate beneficiaries of EU expenditure policies. CAP export restitutions, for instance, do not necessarily benefit the residents of the country where they are paid (European Commission 1998*b*). Third, the definition of budgetary balances is fraught with significant conceptual and accounting problems. To compute budgetary balances it is necessary to make various choices. Depending on the choices made, it is possible to obtain numerous, equally valid, definitions of budgetary balances which in some cases produce significantly different results. Finally, the distribution of net balances gives a restricted and partial view of the benefits of EU membership as they fail to account for the positive externalities arising from EU policies.

Nevertheless, the issue of net contributions is a thorny one. Germany, the Netherlands, Austria, and Sweden considered their negative budgetary positions as

Table 5.2 Net Transfers from the European Union Budget, 1992–1997 (Receipts Minus Contributions Expressed as Percentage of National GDP)

	1992	1993	1994	1995	1996	1997
Austria	—	—	—	−0.49	−0.12	−0.40
Belgium	0.71	0.72	0.58	0.81	0.66	0.50
Denmark	0.29	0.33	0.20	0.27	0.19	0.05
Finland	—	—	—	−0.14	0.09	0.06
France	−0.13	−0.10	−0.22	−0.13	−0.01	−0.06
Germany	−0.62	−0.71	−0.78	−0.72	−0.57	−0.60
Greece	4.66	5.17	4.62	3.99	4.20	4.13
Ireland	5.88	6.58	4.45	4.48	4.86	4.84
Italy	−0.03	−0.14	−0.28	−0.08	−0.12	−0.01
Luxembourg	5.24	5.91	4.55	4.88	5.49	4.89
Netherlands	−0.33	−0.48	−0.62	−0.64	−0.75	−0.71
Portugal	2.93	3.44	2.50	3.08	3.41	3.12
Spain	0.61	0.74	0.79	1.70	1.34	1.28
Sweden	—	—	—	−0.53	−0.35	−0.59
UK	−0.28	−0.37	−0.13	−0.55	−0.23	−0.16

Source: European Commission 1998*b*.

excessive 'relative to their prosperity'. They argued for a correction under the Fontainebleau agreement. In addition, these countries underlined their dissatisfaction that other member states with a similar capacity to contribute to the EU budget showed much smaller negative balances or even positive ones. Germany has had a large negative budgetary position for many years. Up to 1990, Germany had one of the highest per capita incomes in the EU. However, it fell to sixth place in the prosperity league after unification, yet it remains the highest contributor to the EU on a per capita basis (Laffan 1998). The Netherlands has gradually become a net contributor to the EU budget as it receives low returns from both the Structural Funds and on direct aid from agricultural expenditure (European Commission 1998*b*).

During the negotiations about Agenda 2000 the issue of net budgetary balances played an important role (see section 5.2). The countries which will join the European Union on the occasion of the next enlargement have a level of prosperity well below that of all the current members and will therefore become large net beneficiaries. This implies that the budgetary positions of the present member states will undergo a corresponding deterioration, estimated at around 0.15 per cent of their GNP by 2006 by the European Commission (1998*b*).

5.1.4 Lending and Borrowing Activities

As pointed out before, the EU budget does not contain the lending and borrowing activities of the EU. The economic rationale for the use of the loan instrument hinges on capital market imperfections. Private lending institutions may, for example, not be willing to lend to projects that involve initial high costs with returns spread over a long period. By acting as an intermediary, passing on the benefits of its AAA credit rating (that is, the highest degree of creditworthiness), the EU can circumvent the problem of unduly high borrowing costs or credit rationing. However, the improvement of financial conditions for the ultimate borrower comes at some costs (Kuhlmann 1993). It entails a financial and administrative burden for the EU and—given its size—may distort capital markets.

There exist five different loan instruments. The Treaty of Paris empowers the European Commission to provide loans to support restructuring in the coal and steel industry. Under the Euratom Treaty, the Union can borrow to finance research and investment in nuclear energy. The Union can also provide support in the form of conditional loans to member states with balance of payments difficulties. For instance, in 1993 Italy received an 8-milliard euro loan for balance of payments assistance. New Community Instrument (NCI) loans are geared to support investment by small and medium-sized enterprises. As can be seen from Table 5.3 the *European Investment Bank* (EIB) plays by far the most important role in the EU's borrowing and lending activities.

The EIB is the Union's bank for economic development. The EIB was established through the Rome Treaty. Its members are the EU member states. Despite this link, the EIB has operational and institutional autonomy, but there is a close working relationship with the European Commission. The EIB is, for example, involved with monitoring projects. Viability of projects proposed under the Cohesion Fund is also assessed by the EIB (Laffan 1998).

From a slow start in the early 1960s when it financed about three projects each year, the Bank is now the world's largest development Bank, lending more than the World Bank (ibid). Regional development is the central focus of EIB activity, underpinned by the provision in the Maastricht Treaty that the EIB 'should continue to devote the majority of its resources to the promotion of economic and social cohesion'. Over the period 1994–8 40 per cent of financing was spent on regional development projects (EIB, Annual Report 1998). All Europe's major infrastructural

Table 5.3 Borrowing and Lending Activities in the European Union, 1980–1997 (Mln Euro)

	1980		1990		1997	
	Borrowing	Lending	Borrowing	Lending	Borrowing	Lending
ECSC	1,004	1,031	1,086	993	474	541
Euratom	181	181	—	—	—	—
Balance of payments	—	—	350	350	195	195
NCI	305	197	76	24	—	—
EIB	2,384	2,724	10,996	12,605	23,025	26,148

Source: European Commission 1998*a*.

developments—the Channel Tunnel, the Alpine crossings, the Great Belt link in Denmark, high-speed train networks—have benefited from EIB financing (Laffan 1998). As follows from Table 5.4, in the period 1994–8 Italy was the main beneficiary of EIB loans. Since the unification, Germany is also a significant borrower from the EIB.

In 1994 the European Investment Fund was created. It is a mixed public/private organization, involving the EU, the EIB, and the private banking sector. The Fund is concerned with infrastructure projects in transport, energy, and telecommunications and projects for small and medium-sized enterprises. The Fund is not a lending agency, but guarantees private-sector loans in these areas with an aim to enhance availability of private-sector capital.

Finally, it should be mentioned that the EU is involved in the European Bank for Reconstruction and Development (EBRD). Although the latter is not a Union institution, both the European Commission and the EIB are shareholders of the EBRD.

Table 5.4 Signed European Investment Bank Credit Agreements, 1994–1998 (Mln Euro and Percentage)

	Amount	Share (%)
Austria	1,645	1.6
Belgium	3,935	3.7
Denmark	3,845	3.7
Finland	1,434	1.4
France	12,750	12.1
Germany	16,831	16.0
Greece	3,246	3.1
Ireland	1,278	1.2
Italy	18,559	17.6
Luxembourg	289	0.3
Netherlands	2,309	2.2
Portugal	6,490	6.2
Spain	14,252	13.5
Sweden	2,060	2.1
UK	13,924	13.2
Outside EU	1,812	1.7
Total	105,309	100.0

Source: European Investment Bank, Annual Report 1998.

5.2 Agenda 2000: Reform and New Member States

BASED on a proposal from the European Commission, the European Council decided in December 1997 to enter negotiations with five Central and Eastern European countries (CEEC) (that is, the Czech Republic, Estonia, Hungary, Poland, and Slovenia), about EU membership. At an earlier date, it was already decided to start similar negotiations with Cyprus. Entry of these countries is only possible after reform of the EU budget. In the same document in which the Commission presented its assessment of the political and economic situation in the various countries applying for EU membership, it also proposed significant reforms of the EU budget. This section summarizes the proposals of the European Commission (1997), known as Agenda 2000, and the decisions of the European Council meeting of March 1999 in Berlin.

5.2.1 Membership Applications

The European Commission assessed the applications for EU membership of ten CEEC on the basis of criteria determined by the European Council at its Copenhagen (1993) meeting. Apart from the five countries mentioned above, also Bulgaria, Latvia, Lithuania, Romania, and Slovakia applied for membership. The Copenhagen conditions were:

■ Stable and democratic institutions with the rule of law and respect and protection for minorities.
■ The establishment of a functioning market economy with the capacity to compete within the EU.
■ The ability to adhere to the obligations of membership including economic and monetary union.

The first criterion should be fulfilled at the start of the negotiations. According to the European Commission, Slovakia did not yet meet this criterion. As to the second criterion, Hungary and Poland came closest, while the Czech Republic and Slovenia were also near. Estonia has a functioning market economy, but has to make more progress in its ability to compete within the EU. Slovakia is judged not to have a functioning market economy.

The third criterion—that is, whether the country concerned is able to implement the *acquis communaitaire*—is clearly the most difficult one. None of the countries is considered to be able to join the Monetary Union on accession to the EU. According to the European Commission, Hungary, Poland, and the Czech Republic should be able to implement the *acquis* in the medium term, provided they strengthen their current policies. The other countries were considered to require significant further changes before they can meet these obligations (see Box 27 for a further discussion).

5.2.2 The EU Budget

Agenda 2000 also contains the European Commission proposals for the EU budget for the period 2000–6. It is assumed that annual real economic growth in the EU-15 will average 2½ per cent. From a historical perspective, this figure seems rather high. The future member states are expected to realize a growth rate of 4 per cent around 2006.

The European Commission argues that it should be possible to realize future policy targets without changing the maximum of own resources of 1.27 per cent of the Union's GNP. The European Council agreed with this view. Table 5.5 presents the financial perspective for the period 2000–6. It is drawn up on the basis of the working assumption of the accession of new member states starting from 2002. Expenditure for the pre-accession instruments enters in a new heading 7 in the financial perspective. The Presidency conclusions of the Berlin European Council meeting also contains an indicative financial framework for EU-21. This includes additional own resources resulting from the accession of six new member states. In an additional heading 8 (enlargement) it sets out the total cost of enlargement for each of the years 2002–6, divided into appropriations for agriculture, structural operations, internal policies, and administration. They are also shown in Table 5.5. Upon enlargement the financial perspective for the EU-15 should be adjusted, taking into account the actual number of acceding countries and the maximum amounts set out in heading 8. This decision will be taken by qualified majority.

Expenditure reserved for EU-15 (headings 1 to 6) cannot at any time be used for pre-accession assistance (heading 7) and, conversely, expenditure reserved for pre-accession assistance cannot be used by EU-15. Amounts available for accession can only be used in order to cover expenditure arising as a direct consequence of enlargement, and cannot cover unforeseen expenditure arising for EU-15 or pre-accession expenditure.

As pointed out before, the issue of net balances was a thorny one, because Austria, Germany, the Netherlands, and Sweden considered their positions unfair. At the same time, the UK wanted its abatement to remain intact. Eventually it was decided that the financing of the UK abatement by other member states will be modified to allow Austria, Germany, the Netherlands, and Sweden a reduction in their financing share to 25 per cent of the normal share. The agreement about Agenda 2000 and the decision to nominate Romano Prodi, former Italian prime minister, as president of the European Commission came after twenty hours of negotiations. Motivated by the political developments in Eastern Europe, the Helsinki European Council of December 1999 decided to enter negotiations with Bulgaria, Latvia, Lithuania, Malta, Romania, and Slovakia about entry conditions. The Council recalled that compliance

Box 27 Freedom Indicators in Central and Eastern European Countries

As follows from the main text, two important criteria for deciding about future membership of Central and Eastern European countries are their democratic character and whether they have a market economy. These issues can be assessed on the basis of indicators for political and economic freedom (Table B27.1). The Freedom House publishes information on political and civil liberties. *Political liberty* is present when citizens are free to participate in the political process (vote, lobby, and choose among candidates), elections are fair and competitive, and alternative parties are allowed to participate freely. *Civil liberty* encompasses the freedom of the press and the rights of individuals to assemble, hold alternative religious views, receive a fair trial, and express their views without fear of physical retaliation. The scores (in principle ranging between 1 (highest level of freedom) to 7) for the ten countries that applied for membership are shown below.

Table B27.1 also shows the scores for two *economic freedom* indicators for these countries. They can be seen as proxies for the existence of a market economy. The indicator of the Heritage Foundation/Wall Street Journal (Holmes, Johnson, and Kirkpatrick 1998) takes 10 elements into account: trade policy, taxation, government intervention in the economy, monetary policy, foreign investment, banking, wage and price controls, property rights, and black market activity. A score—running from 1 (most free) to 5 (least free)—is given and the unweighted average of all 10 elements constitutes the economic freedom rating of that country. Gwartney, Lawson, and Block (1996) choose 17 measures and rate countries on each of these measures on a scale of 0–10, in which zero means that a country is completely unfree and ten means it is completely free. In Table B27.1 the scores are inverted to make them comparable to the other indicators. The measures are in four broad areas: Money and inflation; government operations and regulations; 'takings' and discriminatory taxation; and international exchange.

Table B27.1 Liberties in Central and Eastern European Countries, 1997

	Political rights	Civil liberties	Economic freedom (Holmes, *et al.*)	Economic freedom (Gwartney, *et al.*)
Bulgaria	7	7	3.60 (10)	4.1 (9)
Czech Republic	1	2	2.05 (1)	3.4 (3)
Estonia	1	2	2.35 (2)	3.3 (2)
Hungary	1	2	2.90 (3)	2.8 (1)
Latvia	1	2	2.95 (4)	3.9 (6)
Lithuania	1	2	3.10 (6)	3.5 (4)
Poland	1	2	3.15 (8)	3.8 (5)
Romania	2	2	3.40 (9)	5.8 (10)
Slovakia	2	4	3.05 (5)	3.9 (6)
Slovenia	1	2	3.10 (6)	4.1 (8)

Source: Freedom House; Holmes, Johnson, and Kirkpatrick 1998; Gwartney, Lawson, and Block 1996.

The countries that have entered negotiations for future EU membership on the basis of the decision of the Berlin Council are indicated in italic. It follows that in terms of political rights and civil liberties most countries have a high score, except for Bulgaria and Slovakia. The rankings of the scores for the economic freedom indicators is shown in parentheses. They are in broad agreement with the conclusions of the European Commission as presented in Agenda 2000, with the possible exceptions of Latvia and Lithuania.

Table 5.5 Financial Perspective of the European Union, 2000–2006 (Mln Euro, 1999 Prices)

Appropriations for commitments	2000	2001	2002	2003	2004	2005	2006
1. Agriculture	40920	42800	43900	43770	42760	41930	41660
Cap expenditure (excluding rural development)	36620	38480	39570	39430	38410	37570	37290
Rural development and accompanying measures	4300	4320	4330	4340	4350	4360	4370
2. Structural operations	32045	31455	30865	30285	29595	29595	29170
Structural funds	29430	28840	28250	27670	27080	27080	26660
Cohesion fund	2615	2615	2615	2615	2515	2515	2510
3. Internal policies	5900	5950	6000	6050	6100	6150	6200
4. External action	4550	4560	4570	4580	4590	4600	4610
5. Administration	4560	4600	4700	4800	4900	5000	5100
6. Reserves	900	900	650	400	400	400	400
7. Pre-accession aid	3120	3120	3120	3120	3120	3120	3120
Total appropriations for commitments	91995	93385	93805	93005	91465	90795	90260
Total appropriations for payments	89590	91070	94130	94740	91720	89910	89310
Available for accession (appropriations for payments)			4140	6710	8890	11440	14220
Ceiling on appropriations for payments	89590	91070	98270	101450	100610	101350	103530
8. Enlargement of which			6450	9030	11610	14200	16780
agriculture structural			1600	2030	2450	2930	3400
operations			3750	5830	7920	10000	12080
Own resources ceiling (percentage GNP)	1.27	1.27	1.27	1.27	1.27	1.27	1.27

Source: Berlin European Council, Presidency Conclusions

with the Copenhagen criteria is a prerequisite for entering the Union. Turkey was not invited for entry negotiations, although the Council stated that Turkey is a 'candidate state destined to enter the EU'.

5.2.3 EU Policies

According to Agenda 2000, further reform of the CAP must improve the competitiveness of the Union's agricultural sector in both domestic and external markets. The European Commission proposed to deepen and extend the 1992 reform through further shifts from price support to direct payments, and by developing a coherent rural policy to accompany this process. The proposals by the European Commission provoked serious protests by farmers. Also, some member states, notably France, were critical about the Commission views. The decisions by the European Council therefore diverged considerably from the Commission proposals. In fact, many decisions were not taken. As a consequence, a further round of negotiations is needed before the former communist states can enter the EU. It is also questionable whether the decisions taken are sufficient for a successful next round of WTO negotiations.

The European Council aims for stabilization of spending on agriculture in real terms. In order to achieve this, the following decisions have been taken. For the crop sector, the European Council decided that the intervention price for cereals shall be reduced by 15 per cent in two equal steps of 7.5 per cent. The area payments shall be increased in two equal steps from 54 to 63 euro per ton average yield (the yield differs per region). The compulsory set-aside is fixed at 10 per cent for the period 2000–6. This percentage can be changed on the basis of a proposal by the European Commission. For beef, the European Council endorsed the agreement reached by the Council of ministers of Agriculture to reduce beef intervention prices by 20 per cent. In case of overproduction, the European Commission is asked to come up with proposals for necessary actions. There will be no dairy reform before 2005/6.

In Agenda 2000 the European Commission proposed to increase spending on structural operations. Despite the increase in absolute terms, the Commission aimed at keeping the total costs of structural policies below the threshold of 0.46 per cent of the GDP of the EU. With the extra resources generated by growth and a more efficient use of the resources available, the Commission thought it possible to finance both structural policies in the EU 15 and the gradual integration of new member states from the moment of their accession. The European Commission proposed to apply a maximum of 4 per cent of GDP of a member state for its total transfers received from the Structural Funds and the Cohesion Fund.

The Commission also proposed to reduce the number of objectives to three: two regional objectives and a horizontal objective for human resources. The previous Objective 1 would remain more or less intact. The total amount of funds to be allocated to Objective 1 regions should—as in the recent past—cover about two-thirds of the Structural Funds. This high priority is necessary, according to the Commission, as the level of unemployment in lagging regions is 60 per cent higher than the EU average. In some regions even more than one-quarter of the labour force is unemployed. Still, the threshold of a per capita income of 75 per cent of the Union average should be more strictly applied. For those regions, which as a consequence would no longer be eligible for Objective 1 transfers, a phasing out period will be required.

A new Objective 2 devoted to economic and social restructuring will bring together measures for other regions suffering from structural problems. The percentage of the population of the EU 15 covered by Objectives 1 and 2 should be reduced from 51 per cent to 35–40 per cent. The new Objective 2 would encompass not only the previous Objective 2, but also declining rural areas (the previous 5*b* Objective), regions that are heavily dependent on fishing and, finally, urban areas experiencing socio-economic difficulties.

The newly designed Objective 3 is supposed to focus on the development of human resources and encompasses old Objectives 3, 4, and 5*a*. It aims at regions not covered by Objectives 1 and 2. Objective 3 will promote activities in areas like lifelong education and training systems and active labour market policies.

The European Council accepted most of the reform proposals of the Commission. It decided that over the entire period 213 mrd euro will be available for structural operations. The Council also decided on a detailed breakdown over the various objectives:

- 69.7 per cent of the structural funds will be allocated to Objective 1.
- 11.5 per cent of the structural funds will be allocated to Objective 2.
- 12.3 per cent of the structural funds will be allocated to Objective 3.

Apart from these general decisions, the Council decided on a whole range of specific measures, to take into account special interests of various member states.

Finally, the European Council endorsed the proposal by the Commission to maintain the Cohesion Fund. It was also decided that a review of eligibility based on the 90 per cent income criterion will be undertaken at mid-term in 2003. The assistance rate granted by the Cohesion Fund shall remain unchanged at between 80 and 85 per cent.

5.3 A European Stabilization Policy?

WHEN business cycles in two or more countries in a monetary union are not synchronized, the need for stabilization policies will differ accordingly. Countries may be in different phases of the business cycle for various reasons, including the occurrence of asymmetric shocks as discussed in section 1.3. Countries experiencing excess demand prefer restrictive policies and those experiencing excess supply prefer expansionary policies. However, monetary policy of the ECB cannot solve the problems of both countries at the same time. And exchange rate policy, of course, can also not be employed.

The budget of the federal government may provide some kind of equalization if business cycles of member states of a monetary union are not in sync. With reference to the experience of the United States, this can be explained as follows. Whenever economic activity falls in a particular state in the United States, the taxes paid to the federal government decline as well, while the citizens in the state concerned receive more transfer payments from the federal government. The opposite occurs in booming states. So, a federal budget has a stabilizing effect. Here one has to distinguish between *insurance* proper (that is, an increase in transfers to one state, financed by all others) and the *stabilizing* effect that may occur due to an increase in the federal budget deficit to finance higher transfers (Fatás 1998). The crucial distinction between stabilization and insurance is that the former rests on intertemporal transfers, whereas the latter depends on interregional transfers.

In the US the role of net transfers to states in contributing to regional stabilization is double. There is insurance through interregional transfers and—to the extent that the federal government runs a deficit to finance the net transfers to a particular region—the state is sharing in the aggregate stabilization at the federal level. Sala-i-Martin and Sachs (1992) found that a region's tax payments to the federal government fall by about 34 cents when its per capita income declines by a dollar. Federal transfers to the region rise by about 6 cents, so that the federal budget offsets about 40 per cent of every decline in a region's income. This finding has sparked a lively discussion, which developed in two directions. First, the findings of Sala-i-Martin and Sachs have been criticized and extended (see Box 28). Second, the issue was raised whether a similar system was needed once EMU was in place, and, if so, how it could be arranged for. Should the EU budget be increased to similar levels as those of the federal government in the US or are alternative stabilizing mechanisms available?

One way of smoothing diverging business cycles would be to increase EU-wide fiscal transfers: for instance, a European unemployment benefits scheme. Then, if Spain were booming while Germany was in recession, Brussels would tax Spanish workers to help pay for Germany's unemployment benefits, limiting Spanish growth and stimulating that of Germany. Such a scheme implies an enormous increase in the EU budget and is therefore rather unlikely. Still, there are various proposals for an EU stabilization mechanism, which would imply a smaller increase in the EU budget.

For instance, Italianer and Vanheukelen (1993) analyse a scheme that works as follows. If the monthly increase in unemployment in a member state exceeds the EU average, the member state concerned automatically receives a transfer of α per cent of $^1/_{12}$ of the country's GDP for every percentage point that its unemployment rate increases more than the EU average. Assuming α to be 1 per cent, simulations for the period 1984–91 suggest that the system would lead to an average stabilization of 18 per cent (calculated as in Box 28). Such a scheme would imply an increase of the EU budget of about 0.2 per cent of GDP.

The Committee on Economic and Monetary Affairs and Industrial Policy of the European Parliament has suggested the creation of a stabilization fund. The Maastricht Treaty allows the Council to grant financial assistance if a member state is in difficulties or is seriously threatened with severe difficulties caused by exceptional occurrences beyond its control. According to the Committee such a fund should

Box 28 The Stabilizing Impact of the US Federal Budget

Following Sala-i-Martin and Sachs (1992), a number of other studies have examined the stabilizing effect of the US federal budget. The general methodology used is to measure the reaction of regional taxes and transfers to income fluctuations. The question addressed by all these studies is: if income in a region goes down by 1 per cent relative to the national average, what is the change in that region's taxes and transfers? The original findings of Sala-i-Martin and Sachs that the federal budget offsets about 40 per cent of every decline in a state's income have been criticized, as the authors estimated their regressions in levels. Thereby they mainly captured interregional transfers in response to differences in income per capita (redistribution). Bayoumi and Masson (1995) therefore ran regressions in growth rates. Despite the difference in approach, the estimated stabilizing impact that Bayoumi and Masson found is very close to that of Sala-i-Martin and Sachs: around 30 per cent.

In contrast, von Hagen (1992) presents estimates of the benefits of the US federal budget which are much smaller than those of Sala-i-Martin and Sachs or Bayoumi and Masson. According to his estimates, the federal budget absorbs only 10 per cent of a change in state income. Von Hagen's empirical specification takes into account the effect that changes in state income have on the overall federal budget. This is important since if a state's income falls, total tax revenues will decrease unless other regions' tax revenues exactly offset the initial fall. The fall in tax revenues will create a deficit that will have to be paid through future taxes by all states, including the depressed state. Therefore, the amount of insurance that the depressed state receives is less than what the change in this period's state disposable income indicates (Fatás 1998).

The estimates by Fatás (1998) (11 per cent stabilization) are almost identical to those of von Hagen (1992). Various other authors find similar or somewhat higher effects. In sum, most empirical studies confirm that there is a significant fiscal insurance against asymmetric shocks provided by the federal fiscal system in the US. There is still some disagreement about the exact size of the insurance, but it seems safe to conclude that the federal fiscal system does not offset much more than 10 cents on a dollar change in state income caused by an asymmetric shock.

provide two facilities: one for macroeconomic assistance and one for assistance in the event of a natural disaster. The assistance should take the form of loans.[5]

Whether a European stabilization scheme is necessary depends—apart from its effectiveness—upon the following issues:

- divergence in business cycles across the member states of the monetary union
- the effectiveness of alternative adjustment mechanisms
- the effect of a European stabilization scheme on these alternative adjustment mechanisms.

We will discuss these issues in turn.

[5] Committee on Economic and Monetary Affairs and Industrial Policy of the European Parliament, Report on the Adjustment Mechanism in Cases of Asymmetric Shocks, 11 Nov. 1998, A4-0422/98.

Before discussing business-cycle synchronization in EMU, it is important to point out that most evidence put forward on this issue suffers from the so-called *Lucas Critique*. Since the formation of a currency union is in itself a regime change, key behavioural relationships could change (see section 1.3) thereby reducing the relevance of evidence from the past. Observing what happens in existing currency unions like the United States may help to interpret the evidence. However, this evidence may itself be ambiguous. Is the observed behaviour in a currency union induced by membership or is the sustainability of the currency union a result of the observed behaviour?

We have already discussed in Chapter 1 the various shocks that may hit an EMU country and cause its business cycle to diverge from that of others. It is clear that at least policy-induced shocks diminished after the launch of the euro. Although monetary policy of the ECB may affect economies differently, because some are more responsive to interest-rate changes than others (see Chapter 6), national monetary policies will no longer differ and devaluations will no longer create or amplify (or cushion) shocks. Still, asymmetric shocks may occur in EMU. As the US experience shows, business cycles in the euro area may not be synchronized.

How serious is this problem? The evidence suggests that a significant degree of synchronization of the business cycle existed among various EMU countries over the past 30 or so years (Table 5.6). There are remarkably high correlations in cyclical output components across several member states, most particularly between Belgium, Luxembourg, France, Germany, and the Netherlands. The correlation of real output growth in individual member states and the EC aggregate is—except for Denmark—generally around 0.70. This is quite similar to the correlation of state income growth rates to the average US growth rate over the period 1969–90 as reported by Fatás (1998).

Cross-country output correlations could rise over time, as a consequence of three factors. First, owing to increasing trade interdependence and monetary integration business cycles may move more in tandem (section 1.3). Second, owing to increasing integration of financial markets (Chapter 6) country-specific shocks may be amplified across national borders. Third, policy convergence in the EU reduces the probability of country-specific policy shocks as a source of demand-induced business cycles. If business cycles become more synchronized, there is less need for a European fiscal insurance scheme. However, more business cycle synchronization may lead to higher amplitudes of the common business cycles. This can be seen as follows. If two countries are in different phases of the business cycle, this has a certain dampening effect. The country in recession faces buoyant export demand from the booming country. If both countries are in a similar phase of the business cycle, this dampening effect no longer works. This issue has been neglected in the literature on fiscal stabilization in a monetary union, which focuses almost entirely on asymmetric shocks and the resulting divergence of business cycles.[6]

---

[6] A similar issue is the impact of a regional stabilization mechanism on aggregate fluctuations. If regions react differently to a fiscal impulse, the fiscal transfer mechanism translates purely relative fluctuations into aggregate fluctuations. The transfer lowers (raises) demand in one region by less than it raises (lowers) demand in the other, raising or lowering national aggregate demand as a result (von Hagen 1999).

Table 5.6 Percentage Standard Deviations and Contemporaneous Cross-correlations for Real Output across European Union Member States (Real Output Deviation from Trend, Annual Data, 1960–1990)

	Standard deviation	Belgium	Denmark	France	Germany	Greece	Ireland	Italy	Luxembourg	Netherlands	Portugal	Spain	UK	EU
Belgium	1.71	1.00	0.06	0.83	0.74	0.45	0.42	0.44	0.72	0.65	0.70	0.67	0.38	0.80
Denmark	1.79		1.00	0.01	0.41	0.38	-0.28	0.02	0.43	0.33	-0.01	0.15	0.54	0.22
France	1.20			1.00	0.78	0.57	0.58	0.51	0.60	0.67	0.79	0.52	0.45	0.91
Germany	1.84				1.00	0.71	0.41	0.43	0.66	0.73	0.60	0.43	0.50	0.84
Greece	2.20					1.00	0.31	0.21	0.42	0.45	0.44	0.22	0.51	0.62
Ireland	2.14						1.00	0.43	0.18	0.40	0.38	0.26	0.06	0.53
Italy	1.83							1.00	0.27	0.34	0.52	0.29	0.23	0.59
Luxembourg	2.82								1.00	0.60	0.47	0.64	0.68	0.71
Netherlands	1.76									1.00	0.43	0.42	0.50	0.78
Portugal	2.75										1.00	0.41	0.43	0.73
Spain	2.44											1.00	0.56	0.62
UK	1.88												1.00	0.68
EU	1.34													1.00

Source: Christodoulakis, Dimelis, and Kollintzas 1995.

The effectiveness of alternative stabilization mechanisms is also relevant in the discussion on the need for a European insurance/stabilization scheme. As pointed out in Section 1.3, in a monetary union labour mobility may be an important adjustment mechanism in case of lack of business-cycle synchronization. Americans readily move to where the jobs have shifted, even if this means crossing state lines. In contrast, in the EU labour mobility is low. Even within national boundaries European labour mobility is low and not capable of erasing regional disparities. The OECD (1990) notes that 3 per cent of Americans change their region of residence annually. The same is true for only 0.6 per cent of Italians and 1.1 per cent of Britons and Germans. One explanation for this low level of regional mobility could be that it reflects absence of asymmetric, region-specific shocks (Eichengreen 1998). However, some studies cast doubt on this explanation. Viñals and Jimeno (1996), for instance, report that two-thirds of variance of regional unemployment rates within European regions is caused by region-specific factors. European labour is probably less responsive to wage and unemployment differentials than labour in the United States. Estimates of labour mobility for Europe by Decressin and Fatás (1995) indicate that European regions tend to adjust to adverse employment shocks via changes in labour force participation as opposed to residence.

Yet factor mobility in a monetary union is by no means restricted to labour, and under conditions of constant returns one must be indifferent whether the capital migrates to labour or labour migrates to capital (Burda 1999).[7] Table 5.7 shows the evolution of intra-EU foreign direct investment (FDI) flows. It follows that FDI has risen markedly in the last two decades.

As pointed out in section 1.3, wage flexibility could also function as an adjustment mechanism in the case of asymmetric shocks or asynchronous business cycles in the euro zone. Real wage flexibility is generally considered to be higher in the United States than in Europe. One explanation is that the large role of centralized collective bargaining, the use of indexation, and its high degree of openness made Europe more prone to translate demand disturbances into inflation more quickly than the United States (Burda 1999). It is also widely believed that regulation and a generous social security system also contribute to the lack of flexibility of European labour markets, thereby hampering employment growth. Despite the popularity of this view, the role of regulation in explaining differences in employment growth in Europe is not overwhelmingly strong (see Box 30).

Will EMU affect wage flexibility? Wage flexibility may increase because exchange rates are fixed. It is conceivable that European workers will recognize that, with devaluation no longer an option, wage demands have to be more flexible. Indeed, Alogoskoufis and Smith (1991) report greater nominal wage flexibility when exchange rates are fixed than when they are flexible. Similarly, the authors of a number of country case studies report evidence of greater wage and price flexibility with the hardening of the exchange rate commitment. For instance, it is often claimed that in

---

[7] Product market integration may also reduce the need for labour mobility. The factor price equalization theorem of Heckscher-Ohlin trade theory states that under the conditions of classical trade theory and incomplete specialization, convergence of product prices in traded output produced with the same technology leads to equal wages. In doing so, the need for labour to migrate is eliminated (Burda 1999).

Table 5.7 Intra European Union Foreign Direct Investment Flows, 1985–1994 (Percentage of GDP)

	Direct investment inflows from EU countries	
	1985–1989	1990–1994
Austria	0.24	0.35
Belgium/Luxembourg	1.64	3.05
Denmark	0.39	1.05
Finland	0.23	0.47
France	0.42	0.67
Germany	0.17	0.11
Greece	0.21	0.53
Ireland	(0.32)	(0.13)
Italy	0.24	0.19
Netherlands	0.91	1.29
Portugal	1.01	1.72
Spain	1.02	1.54
Sweden	0.26	1.11
UK	0.84	0.69

Source: Burda 1999.

Box 29 Insurance through Financial Markets

Insurance against divergent income patterns in the member states of a monetary union owing to fiscal federalism could also be provided through capital markets. Atkeson and Bayoumi (1993) used US state data for 1966–86 to estimate the extent to which state incomes are insured against state-specific risks through the US capital market. They regressed changes in per capita income earned from capital located in a state on changes in per capita income earned from capital located in the rest of the country, state labour incomes, and state capital products. They find that a decline in state labour income is offset by a small but significant increase in capital incomes. Asdrubali, Sørensen, and Yosha (1996) report that capital markets smooth 39 per cent of cross-sate fluctuations in gross state product. Credit markets smooth another 23 per cent of the fluctuations. Athanasoulis and van Wincoop (1998) estimate the reduction of the standard deviation of state income owing to financial markets at about 30 per cent at short-term horizons and somewhat higher for long-term horizons.

Austria the pegging of the schilling to the German mark affected trade union behaviour (Hochreiter and Winckler 1995). But it is also possible that nothing will change. After all, the French have hardly embraced flexible labour markets, even after years of pegging their currency to the German mark and despite very high unemployment. Anderton and Barrell (1995) report for their sample of ten European

Box 30 Labour Market Regulation and Employment Growth

It is widely believed that labour market regulation leads to less flexible labour markets, which in turn would lead to high levels of unemployment. However, the results of certain recent studies cast some doubt on this view. Figure B30.1 shows the index of Koedijk and Kremers (1996) on *labour market regulation* for a number of EU member states. The index includes issues like regulation on work time, irregular hours, temporary employment, dismissal protection, and minimum wage. A higher score indicates more regulation. The vertical axis of the figure shows employment growth. It follows from the figure that there is quite some variation between countries, both in terms of employment growth and in terms of regulation providing an interesting opportunity to examine whether there is evidence for a systematic link. In line with Winston's (1993) results for the United States, Figure B30.1 does not suggest a negative relationship between labour market regulation and employment growth (see also OECD 1998*b*).

Fig. B30.1 Employment Growth (1981–1993) and Ranking of Labour Market Regulation

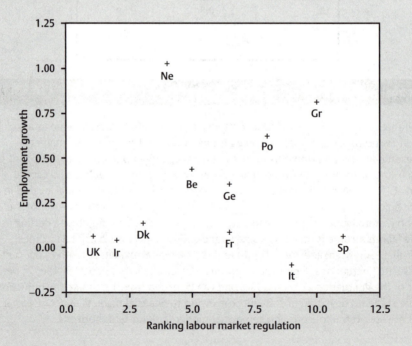

Source: Koedijk and Kremers (1996).

countries that, with the exception of Italy, there is not much evidence of an ERM-related structural shift in the wage-determination process.

Neither does theory provide a definite answer whether EMU membership will lead to more nominal wage flexibility. One explanation for nominal wage inflexibility is that wages are set for fixed contract periods. Theories of contract length emphasize the costs of wage negotiations that consume scarce time and may upset labour-management relations (Calmfors 1998a). There is a trade-off between these costs and the costs in terms of additional variations in output, employment, and profits if wages are not adjusted to unforeseen events during the contract period. The marginal costs of long-term wage contracts increase with variability in aggregate demand. So, if EMU membership affects variability in demand it would also affect optimal contract length. One argument as to why contract length could be reduced in EMU is that country-specific disturbances can no longer be stabilized by national monetary policy (ibid.). However, as pointed out before, these country-specific shocks may also be reduced due to EMU. And even if demand shocks would increase nominal wage flexibility, the quantitative effect may be limited.

There are also reasons why money wages may become less flexible in EMU. For instance, low inflation implies an incentive for concluding wage contracts of longer duration, because nominal wages then have to be adjusted less frequently (ibid.).

As pointed out before, one of the reasons for wage inflexibility is labour market regulation. Labour market reform could enhance the flexibility of the labour market, thereby (possibly) reducing unemployment and making adjustments to economic shocks easier.[8] However, deregulating the labour market is politically difficult. Labour market reform would include reductions in the level and duration of unemployment benefits, more effective labour market policy, lower minimum wages, and possibly also reductions in employment protection (ibid.). Such reforms may not be implemented because of political constraints. Politicians are highly reluctant to pursue policies that in the short run may harm large groups of voters and special interest groups. People who are employed are likely to oppose reform that lowers their real wages. They also have an interest in job protection legislation and high unemployment benefits to mitigate the consequences of job loss. The already unemployed have, of course, an even greater interest in generous benefits. EMU might affect the incentives for government for labour market reform. Although it is often argued that EMU may reinforce the incentives for labour market reform, this need not be true. A modified version of the model first presented in Chapter 2 (see also Sibert and Sutherland 1997; Calmfors 1998b; Berthold and Fehn 1998) may illustrate this. First, we modify the loss function of government by introducing the costs of labour market reform:

$$L = \tfrac{1}{2}\pi_t^2 + \frac{\gamma}{2}(u_t - u^*)^2 + \frac{\tau}{2}r_t^2 \tag{5.1}$$

where π_t denotes inflation; u_t is actual unemployment; u^* is the target rate of unemployment (which is lower than the natural rate of unemployment u_n); r denotes the level of labour market reform.

---

[8] This view is widely subscribed to, despite the warnings raised in Box 30.

Next, we write an expectations-augmented Phillips curve, instead of the Lucas supply function presented in Chapter 2:

$$u_t = u_{wr} - \lambda r - (\pi_t - \pi_t^e) + \varepsilon_t \tag{5.2}$$

where u_{wr} is unemployment without reform, π^e is expected inflation, and ε_t is a random shock.

It is easy to see how EMU can affect the incentives for labour market reform. If there is no credibility problem (that is, there is full commitment), the optimum level of labour market reform (r^*) is simply:

$$r^* = \frac{\gamma\lambda}{\tau + \lambda^2\gamma}(u_{wr} - u^*) \tag{5.3}$$

The marginal benefits of reform owing to lower unemployment are equal to the marginal political costs of this reform. Under discretion (that is, with a time inconsistency problem), the solution is:

$$r^* = \frac{\gamma\lambda(1 + \gamma)}{\tau + \lambda^2\gamma}(u_{wr} - u^*) \tag{5.4}$$

The value for r^* in equation (5.4) is higher than in (5.3). In other words, there will be more labour market reform under a discretionary regime than under a rule-based monetary regime. The intuition for this result is that the inflationary bias introduced by the policy-maker's time inconsistency problem raises the marginal benefits of regulatory reform. In addition to a reduction in structural unemployment, deregulation also lowers the incentive for surprise inflation. If the ECB-led policy reduces the inflationary bias in comparison with the situation before EMU, there will be less labour market reform than before EMU.

But even if the ECB suffers from the same inflation bias as national central banks before EMU started, there may be less labour market reform (Calmfors 1998a). This is owing to the fact that labour market reform in an individual country has only a small effect on aggregate unemployment in the monetary union. So each member state internalizes only a fraction of the benefits of labour market reform. Thus, the incentive to undertake reform is weakened by EMU membership. This effect is strongest in small countries, because the effects of their labour market reforms on aggregate unemployment in the euro zone will be the smallest.

The previous analysis leads to the conclusion that EMU will reduce the incentive for labour market reform. There is, however, also an argument why the incentive for reform could be stronger due to EMU (ibid.). Suppose that variations in unemployment levels are regarded as more serious, the higher the average equilibrium rate of unemployment around which these variations occur. If EMU leads to greater variations in employment because national monetary policy can no longer be used to stabilize country-specific shocks, there is a precautionary motive for more reform inside than outside EMU. Policy-makers may prefer labour market reform to lower the equilibrium unemployment rate, thereby reducing the utility costs of employment fluctuations. As will be clear, this argument hinges on the assumption that EMU will not lead to less country-specific shocks. As pointed out in section 1.3, there are some reasons to expect that country-specific shocks may become less important due to EMU.

Apart from wage flexibility and factor mobility, national budgetary policy could function as a stabilization mechanism. Bayoumi and Masson (1995) have demonstrated that national stabilization in EU countries amounts to some 30 per cent. This evidence suggests that automatic fiscal stabilization by EU member states roughly offsets the same share of local income shocks as neutralized by fiscal federalism within the US. This implies that there is no need for a European system of fiscal federalism as long as member states' automatic stabilizers are allowed to operate (Eichengreen 1998). A crucial condition is that the necessary room for manoeuvre has been created within the limits imposed by the Stability and Growth Pact.

Finally, let us turn to the question of whether a European insurance/stabilization scheme would affect the alternative adjustment mechanisms outlined above. As with every insurance scheme, there are moral hazard problems inherent to a European fiscal insurance system. There are two aspects that deserve further scrutiny in this regard. First, the insurance scheme may provide governments and trade unions wrong incentives. If, for instance, the costs of rising unemployment owing to excessive wage claims or misguided government policies can at least partly be shifted onto others, the likelihood of such behaviour will increase. Courchene (1993) points to the example of Quebec that maintained a higher minimum wage than other Canadian provinces in the 1970s and was able to shift the cost of higher unemployment on to the federal budget. The presence of a fiscal insurance mechanism might also lead to a lack of fiscal discipline in the knowledge that there will be a bail-out from the insurance mechanism.

Second, the effectiveness of other adjustment mechanisms may be reduced owing to some insurance scheme. For instance, individuals who receive transfer incomes when their country fares badly, may see less reason to accept wage cuts or to move to other industries or other countries (von Hagen 1999).

So, what should we conclude from the foregoing analysis? In our view, the arguments that have been raised against some kind of European insurance/stabilization scheme outweigh the arguments in favour. It is also unlikely that such a scheme would be politically acceptable to the EU member states.

5.4 Conclusion

THE EU budget is small in relation to the budgets of the member states, accounting for just over 1 per cent of EU GDP. Compared with the budgets of national governments this is a small amount. Although its share in total EU expenditure is declining, agricultural policy still accounts for the largest share of the EU budget, followed by spending on structural policies. Since 1970 the EU budget is financed through so-called own resources. Initially, there were three own resources: custom duties on goods imported from outside the Union, agricultural levies, and a share of the VAT revenue raised in each country. Since 1988 the EU budget is partly financed by a fourth resource, which better reflects the principle of the ability to pay as it is based on member states' relative GNP. Its share in the financing of the budget has been rising; this trend will continue.

Negotiations with five Central and Eastern European countries (Estonia, the Czech Republic, Hungary, Poland, and Slovenia) and with Cyprus about future EU membership are under way. Recently, it was decided also to start negotiations with Bulgaria, Latvia, Lithuania, Malta, Romania, and Slovakia. Entry of these countries requires reform of the EU budget. Although the European Council has taken a number of decisions on Agenda 2000, further reforms are necessary, notably of the CAP.

The final part of this chapter dealt with the need for some kind of European stabilization/insurance scheme. The most compelling argument for such a scheme is that a common monetary policy cannot be used to synchronize diverging business cycles in the member states. Whether a European stabilization scheme is necessary depends—apart from its effectiveness—primarily upon the effectiveness of alternative adjustment mechanisms. It is argued that these alternative adjustments may deliver similar levels of stabilization to the US system of fiscal federalism. So, based on this analysis, our conclusion is that there is no need for a European stabilization/insurance scheme.

Chapter 6

Financial Integration and Financial Market Structure

Introduction

THIS chapter deals with financial market integration in the EU after the start of the EMS in March 1979 and in addition reviews differences in financial structure in the EU member states. As to the first issue, the key question is whether the step-by-step liberalization of short-term capital movements, in preparing for the EMU, has resulted in greater financial market integration in the EU. Differences between financial structure in the euro zone countries may affect the transmission mechanism of the monetary policy of the ECB. This is easy to understand. If, for instance, household mortgages have a flexible interest rate, a change in central bank interest rates will quickly affect spending by households. If, in contrast, mortgages are on a fixed-rate basis monetary policy actions will have substantially less impact on the level of consumer spending. The questions that we try to answer are how important are these differences in financial structures and whether they are likely to remain.

This chapter is organized as follows. Section 6.1 first specifies two alternative criteria for financial market integration, that is, covered nominal interest parity and *ex ante* uncovered nominal interest parity. Subsequently, we introduce the decomposition method of Frankel and MacArthur (1988) to identify the main components of these interest parity conditions. Then, the discussion focuses on the integration of European financial markets, in terms of the size and variability of deviations from interest parity of various European countries vis-à-vis Germany. In section 6.2 the structure of European financial markets and its consequences for the monetary transmission mechanism in euroland will be discussed. Section 6.3 offers a perspective on recent and future developments in the European financial landscape. As usual, the chapter ends with conclusions.

6.1 The Integration of European Financial Markets

6.1.1 Interest Parities

Quantifying the degree of financial market integration implies measuring the degree to which capital flows equalize expected and realized returns on comparable assets denominated in different currencies.[1] Following Frankel and MacArthur (1988), Table 6.1 summarizes an ascending order of two alternative criteria for financial integration according to their cumulative assumptions. The criteria rely on the dispersion of prices (that is, short-term interest rates) of comparable European financial assets.

Covered interest parity (CIP) holds if the forward premium (discount), $f_t^{t+k} - s_t$, equals the difference between the domestic and foreign nominal interest rates, $i_{t,\,t+k} - i_{t,\,t+k}^*$, at the appropriate maturity:

$$i_{t,\,t+k} - i_{t,\,t+k}^* = f_t^{t+k} - s_t \tag{6.1}$$

A forward premium (discount) on foreign currency means that the forward price of foreign currency delivered and paid for some time in the future expressed in domestic currency is higher (lower) than the current spot price. If the current domestic nominal interest rate is higher (lower) than the foreign nominal interest, the lower (higher) foreign nominal interest rate is compensated by a forward premium (discount) on foreign currency. Investors will buy (sell) foreign currency spot to sell (buy) it forward. A premium (discount) on the foreign currency corresponds with an expected future rise (fall) in the spot exchange rate. It implies a zero-covered nominal interest differential or, in other words, a zero country premium. Deviations from CIP reflect barriers to the integration of financial markets across national boundaries such as transaction costs, capital controls, information costs, tax laws that discriminate by country of residence, default risk, and risk of capital controls introduced in the future.

Ex ante *uncovered interest parity* (UIP) examines capital mobility of a higher degree. Replacement of the forward exchange rate, f_t^{t+k}, by the expected future spot exchange rate, $E_t\,s_{t+k}$, yields UIP. UIP holds if the expected nominal exchange rate change,

---

[1] Interest parity conditions are not the only tests for the degree of financial market integration. For example, Feldstein and Horioka (1980) apply savings–investment correlations. Alternatively, Obstfeld (1986) proposes another test based upon the Euler equation for inter-temporal consumption behaviour. In particular, the Feldstein–Horioka approach has been severely criticized. See, amongst others, Lemmen (1998*b*).

$E_t(s_{t+k} - s_t)$, equals the nominal interest differential, $i_{t,\,t+k} - i^*_{t,\,t+k}$, at the appropriate maturity:

$$i_{t,\,t+k} - i^*_{t,\,t+k} = E_t(s_{t+k} - s_t) \tag{6.2}$$

Investors expect a depreciation of the exchange rate when the domestic nominal interest rate exceeds the foreign nominal interest rate. *Ex ante* UIP requires a zero country premium, $i_{t,\,t+k} - i^*_{t,\,t+k} - (f_t^{t+k} - s_t) = 0$, and a zero exchange risk premium, $(f_t^{t+k} - s_t) - E_t(s_{t+k} - s_t) = 0$.

CIP and *ex ante*-UIP measure two important aspects of financial integration: capital mobility and substitutability among assets denominated in different currencies. CIP is an *arbitrage* condition with covered positions (that is, without any exchange rate risk). The degree of substitutability between domestic and foreign bonds based on exchange rate risk and the degree of risk aversion of the investors are therefore completely irrelevant. Since the absence of CIP suggests that there exist arbitrage opportunities, CIP should indeed hold in integrated markets (without transaction costs). Absence of UIP implies the existence of a risk premium in the exchange rate.

Table 6.1 Interest Parity Conditions

I. Covered nominal interest parity (CIP)

Assumption:

$$i_{t,\,t+k} - i^*_{t,\,t+k} = f_t^{t+k} - s_t$$

Yields:

$$i_{t,\,t+k} - i^*_{t,\,t+k} = f_t^{t+k} - s_t$$

II. *Ex ante* uncovered nominal interest parity (UIP)

Assumptions:

$$i_{t,\,t+k} - i^*_{t,\,t+k} = f_t^{t+k} - s_t$$

$$E_t s_{t+k} = f_t^{t+k}$$

Yield:

$$i_{t,\,t+k} - i^*_{t,\,t+k} = E_t(s_{t+k} - s_t)$$

Source: Frankel and MacArthur 1988; Frankel 1989.

6.1.2 The Degree of European Money Market Integration

The CIP condition is the least stringent criterion for money market integration. A negative country premium is indicative of capital export restrictions, the domestic return is artificially low to the German return, and capital export restrictions exist. On the other hand, a positive country premium indicates capital import restrictions.

Figure 6.1 shows the deviations from covered interest parity (CIP) relative to Germany for six EU countries during the period March 1979 to June 1993. The deviations are given in percentages per year for Belgium, the Netherlands, and the UK (upper part), and for France, Italy, and Spain (lower part). The process of European money market integration can be split in two sub-periods by the break of the Basle-Nyborg agreement (see also section 1.2). According to Figure 6.1, the size and variability of the country premium was already limited for Belgium, the Netherlands, and the UK and declined significantly for France, Italy, and Spain after the Basle-Nyborg agreement. An important explanation for these results was the directive of 24 June 1988, when the European Commission stated that as from 1 July 1990 all *short- and long-term* capital movements in Europe are to be free of restrictions. However, Greece, Ireland, Portugal, and Spain did not have to fulfil this directive until 31 December 1992. Moreover, Portugal and Greece had the possibility of postponing implementation of this directive until 31 December 1995.

6.1.3 The Trade-off between the Speed and Degree of Money Market Integration

After discussing the degree of European money market integration, it would be interesting to see whether or not we may observe a difference in the speed of money market integration (in terms of CIP) as well. And if so, is there a trade-off between the speed and degree of money market integration?

We measure the *degree* of money market integration by regressing mean absolute deviations of CIP vis-à-vis Germany against a constant. Our sample period is from March 1979 to August 1992. The European countries considered are Belgium, Denmark, France, Ireland, Italy, The Netherlands, Portugal, Spain, and the UK. The data used are monthly observations of three-month domestic money market interest rates, spot exchange rates vis-à-vis the German mark, and forward exchange rates vis-à-vis the German mark of the same three-month maturity. The *speed* of money market integration is measured by regressing absolute deviations from CIP vis-à-vis Germany against a constant (coefficient β_0) and a time trend (coefficient β_1) (analogous to Frankel, Phillips, and Chinn, 1993).

Figure 6.2 summarizes the results. The speed of money market integration is on the

Figure 6.1 Deviations from Covered Interest Parity Relative to Germany (Percentages per Year)

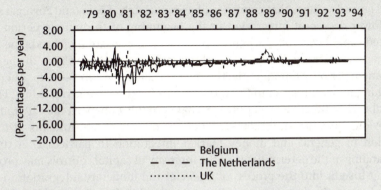

Deviations from CIP relative to Germany (March 1979–June 1993)

'79 '80 '81 '82 '83 '84 '85 '86 '87 '88 '89 '90 '91 '92 '93 '94

——— Belgium
– – – The Netherlands
·········· UK

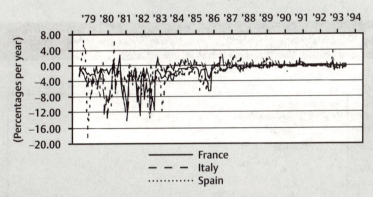

Deviations from CIP relative to Germany (March 1979–June 1993)

'79 '80 '81 '82 '83 '84 '85 '86 '87 '88 '89 '90 '91 '92 '93 '94

——— France
– – – Italy
·········· Spain

vertical axis and the degree of integration (deviations from CIP) on the horizontal axis. The speed is captured by the negative trend coefficient reflecting the downward trend in mean absolute deviations from CIP. Or, in other words, the trend coefficient β_1 captures the monthly change in the degree of money market integration. For example, the monthly decline of absolute CIP differentials with respect to Belgium amounts to 0.013 per cent per year over the period from March 1979 to August 1992. All nine European countries show significant negative trend coefficients with respect to absolute deviations from CIP. Regarding absolute deviations from CIP, we may list the countries in ascending order of money market integration: the UK, the Netherlands, Ireland, Belgium, Denmark, France, Italy, Spain, and Portugal. The relatively low speed of integration of the Netherlands and the UK may be explained by the already high degree of integration at the start of the sample period. Portugal and Spain had a much larger gap to bridge in terms of CIP integration.

It follows from Figure 6.2 that a negative trade-off between the degree and speed of money market integration does exist. Countries with a relatively low degree of integration show a relatively high speed of integration, and vice versa. The trade-off may be motivated by the political will to form an Economic and Monetary Union in Europe. Figure 6.1 shows that countries like France, Italy, Spain, and Portugal starting from a lower degree of integration in the beginning of the sample period rapidly eliminated capital controls during the remainder of the sample period. The UK and the Netherlands already showed small absolute deviations from CIP in the beginning of the sample period. Consequently, the speed of CIP integration—or, in other words, the catching up with respect to CIP integration—for those countries is low. The capital liberalization directive of 24 June 1988 has certainly enhanced the CIP trade-off.

An obvious question is, of course, what are the main determinants of financial integration in general and money market integration in particular? A thorough understanding of the determinants of the intensity of capital controls may provide an important insight into the process of financial and monetary integration in Europe and may help in the formulation of European fiscal and monetary policy. This question is briefly discussed in Box 31.

Figure 6.2 The Trade-off between the Degree and Speed of Money Market Integration over the Period from March 1979 to August 1992

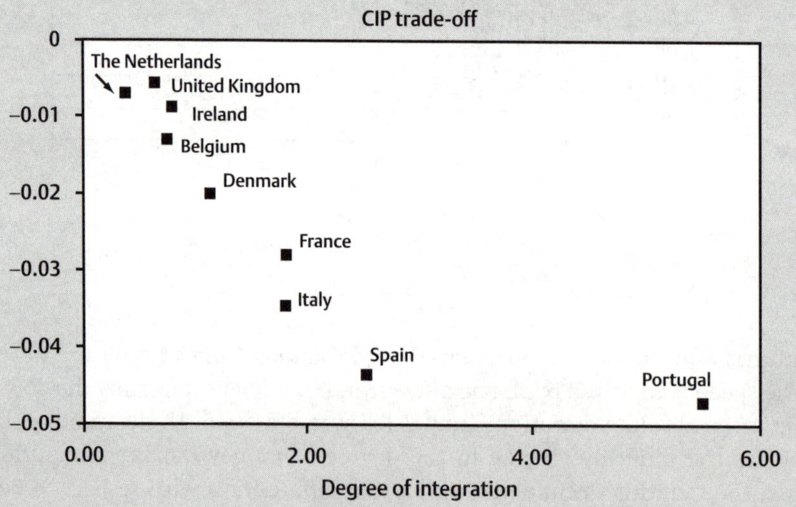

Source: Lemmen 1998b.

Note: The degree of integration (horizontal axis) is measured as the coefficient β_0 of $|y_t| = \beta_0 + e_t$. The speed of integration (vertical axis) is measured as the coefficient β_1 of $|y_t| = \beta_0 + \beta_1 + xt\,\varepsilon_t$

Box 31 The Determinants of Capital Controls

The analysis of the determinants of the intensity of capital controls started with Epstein and Schor (1992) and Alesina, Grilli, and Milesi-Ferretti (1994). These authors typically constructed dummy variables or capital control indices to measure the degree of financial integration. For example, Alesina, *et al.* use dummy variables—taking the value 1 when capital controls are in place and 0 otherwise—to measure capital controls. Unfortunately, dummy variables cannot explain different degrees of intensity of capital controls over time. The binary nature of dummy variables is not capable of capturing the actual intensity of capital controls. Alesina, *et al.* analyse the financial markets of twenty OECD countries and find that capital export controls are more likely in countries with high inflation rates and significant government changes. Grilli and Milesi-Ferretti (1995) and Milesi-Ferretti (1998) extend this analysis to sixty-one developed and less-developed countries.

Epstein and Schor (1992) construct an annual capital control index compiled from the summary table in the IMF's *Annual Reports on Exchange Arrangements and Exchange Restrictions*. This index is composed of restrictions on payments for capital transactions (capital controls) and the use of separate exchange rate(s) for some or all capital transactions and/or some or all invisibles (exchange controls). If both restrictions are in place, the index takes the value of 2, if one restriction applies the index takes the value of 1, and 0 otherwise. Capital control indices are better capable of explaining different degrees of intensity of capital controls than dummy variables. However, the IMF and, thus, Epstein and Schor do not distinguish between restrictions to limit capital outflows and those on capital inflows (so, the direction of capital flows), and between restrictions on short-term and long-term capital flows (so, the maturity of these flows).

In order to account for the intensity and direction of capital controls, Lemmen and Eijffinger (1996) have measured differentials between domestic onshore and offshore nominal interest rates, which reflect existing and expected capital controls. Resulting negative (positive) deviations are associated with capital export (import) restrictions. Their analysis covers the period 1974–93. They conclude that realized inflation, government instability, and gross fixed capital formation provide a reasonable explanation of interest rate differentials and, thereby, capital controls in the EU.

6.2 Financial Market Structure and Monetary Transmission

6.2.1 Introduction

The impact of policy decisions by the ECB may differ across euro zone countries. It is often thought that differences in monetary policy transmission depend on diverging financial structures. This section will therefore discuss three issues: 1. how much evidence is there to suggest that EMU countries react differently to monetary policy actions? 2. how is financial structure related to monetary policy? 3. will existing differences in the financial system across countries disappear over time?

6.2.2 Do EMU Countries have Different Transmission Mechanisms?

Although there seem to be differences in the existing monetary transmission mechanism across EMU countries, empirical evidence does not give a clear picture on how important these differences actually are. This may be owing to the fact that different methodologies have been employed. At least four modelling strategies have been attempted (OECD 1999):

- simulating existing macroeconomic (single or multi-country) models
- small structural models
- reduced form equations
- structural Vector Autoregression (VAR) models.

Table 6.2 provides, for illustrative purposes, the main conclusions of some representative studies, each an example of the distinguished modelling strategies. The table shows the estimated impact of a 1 per cent increase in short-term interest rates on real GDP 4 to 8 quarters after the policy shock. It follows that the various studies do not give a clear picture. Even those studies which identify an uneven response to monetary policy actions, do not agree on a single country as being more sensitive to interest rate changes.

6.2.3 The Importance of Financial Structure

To answer the second question (why may differences in financial structure matter for monetary policy transmission?), it may be useful to first briefly summarize the main transmission channels of monetary policy. Following Mishkin (1996), we can distinguish at least seven *transmission channels* (see Figure 6.3).

The first row of Figure 6.3 shows the traditional Keynesian view of monetary policy. A restrictive monetary policy leads to a rise in real interest rates (r_r), which causes a decline in investment (I) and (durable) consumption spending (C). If the expected price level (P^e) drops in view of restrictive monetary policy and hence expected inflation (π^e) decreases, the real interest rate may go up, thereby hampering investment and consumption (row 2 in Figure 6.3). Although the *interest rate channel* is often considered to be the main channel of monetary policy actions, various researchers had great difficulty in identifying significant effects of interest rates through the cost of capital (see, for example, Bernanke and Gertler 1995).

Monetary policy may also work through asset prices (exchange rate, price of equity). A higher interest rate may affect the exchange rate(s), which in turn will have an impact on net exports (NX). Equity prices (P_e) may also play a role in the transmission mechanism, be it through Tobin's q or through wealth effects. Tobin's q is defined as the market value of firms divided by the replacement cost of capital. A high q indicates that new plant and equipment are relatively cheap. Firms can then easily issue equity. Thus investment will rise (decline) if q goes up (down). Monetary policy may affect q in the following way. A reduction of the money stock will stimulate the

Table 6.2 Empirical Assessments of the Impact of Monetary Policy on Output

Study	France	Germany	Italy	UK	Ranking of Germany, France, Italy, and UK
Single country macro models: BIS (1995)	−0.4	−0.4	−0.4	−0.9	G = F = I < UK
Fed's Multi-country macro model: BIS (1995)	−0.7	−0.7	−0.3	−1.2	I < G = F < UK
Small structural model: Britton and Whitley (1997)	−0.5	−0.5	—	−0.3	UK < G = F
Reduced form models: Dornbusch, *et al.* (1998);	−1.5	−1.4	−2.1	−0.9	UK < G = F < I
Cecchetti (1999)[a]	−1.3	−1.2	−0.6	−0.5	UK = I < G = F
Structural VAR model: (Gerlach and Smeth (1995)	−0.5	−1.0	−0.5	−0.7	F = I < UK < G

Source: OECD 1999; Cecchetti 1999.

Notes: [a] This row shows the maximum impact on output; for most countries this occurs in the fourth or fifth quarter after the policy change; for the UK the peak occurs only after thirteen quarters.

private sector to rebalance its portfolio. The smaller demand for stocks will drive down prices. Alternatively, one can think of a substitution from stocks to bonds, the latter having become more attractive owing to the higher interest rate after a monetary contraction. If the price of equity goes down, private sector wealth (W) will decrease. According to the life-cycle hypothesis of consumption this in turn will restrict consumption (row 5 in Figure 6.3).

During the past decade or so, a number of authors have developed alternative views of monetary policy transmission (see, for example, Bernanke and Gertler 1995). The theoretical foundation of this so-called *lending view* focuses on the intermediation role of banks and capital market imperfections. The lending view has two parts, one that focuses on the balance sheet of borrowers and a second that focuses on bank loans.

By dampening expected future sales, a deflationary monetary policy may decrease the firm's net worth. Or—as above—the monetary hike may reduce the price of equity. A third way in which restrictive monetary policy may affect the net worth of firms is through the general price level. An unanticipated decline in the price level increases the value of firms' liabilities in real terms. No matter what causes the decline in net worth, it will have important consequences. The lower the firm's net worth the more severe the adverse selection and moral hazard problems are in lending to this firm. This, in turn, will restrict external financing.

As far as the second part of the lending channel (bank loans) is concerned, it has been pointed out that some firms (notably small ones) are dependent on banks for finance. A reduction in the quantity of reserves forces a reduction in the level of deposits, which should be matched by a fall in loans (Cecchetti 1999).[2] When loans and bonds are imperfect substitutes on the balance sheets of banks, a rise of the interest rate resulting in a liquidity squeeze may reduce the amount of bank loans.

Figure 6.3 Monetary Transmission Mechanisms

Monetary policy action	Transmission mechanism	Effect on output
1. $M \downarrow \Rightarrow$	$r_r \uparrow \Rightarrow I, C \downarrow \Rightarrow$	$Y \downarrow$
2. $M \downarrow \Rightarrow$	$P^e \downarrow \Rightarrow \pi^e \downarrow \Rightarrow r_r \uparrow \Rightarrow I, C \downarrow \Rightarrow$	$Y \downarrow$
3. $M \downarrow \Rightarrow$	$P_e \downarrow \Rightarrow q \downarrow \Rightarrow I \downarrow \Rightarrow$	$Y \downarrow$
4. $M \downarrow \Rightarrow$	$r_r \uparrow \Rightarrow s \uparrow \Rightarrow NX \downarrow \Rightarrow$	$Y \downarrow$
5. $M \downarrow \Rightarrow$	$P_e \downarrow \Rightarrow W \downarrow \Rightarrow C \downarrow \Rightarrow$	$Y \downarrow$
6. $M \downarrow \Rightarrow$	firm's net worth $\downarrow \Rightarrow$ adverse selection/moral hazard $\uparrow \Rightarrow$ lending $\downarrow \Rightarrow I \downarrow \Rightarrow$	$Y \downarrow$
7. $M \downarrow \Rightarrow$	bank deposits $\downarrow \Rightarrow$ bank loans $\downarrow \Rightarrow I \downarrow \Rightarrow$	$Y \downarrow$

Source: Mishkin 1996.

[2] Moreover, if bank lending to the firm depends on the availability of collateral, a decline of the interest rate could also raise the market value of collateral (for example, the value of real estate) affecting its access to bank lending even further (Kiyotaki and Moore 1997).

How does monetary transmission depend on financial structure? One factor that may be relevant is the extent to which private sector credit is on an *adjustable interest basis*. The quicker the interest rates on loans to the private sector are adjusted, the more a policy induced change of interest rates will affect aggregate demand.

Table 6.3 shows which part of bank lending to the private sector—households and firms—is at short-term or adjustable interest rates. Lending contracts included are of a short-term character, indexed to short-term interest rates, or adjustable in the short term (within 1 year). Evidently, the terms of bank lending both to households and firms differ considerably between EU countries. The large share of floating-rate bank lending in Italy and the UK probably reflects the long history of high and volatile inflation rates in these countries which has made fixed-rate lending unduly risky for banks. In Austria private sector loans consist largely of credit with an adjustable interest rate. The low share of floating-rate bank lending in Belgium, France, Germany, the Netherlands, and Sweden expresses a long-standing tradition of monetary stability. Consequently, an increase in the short-term inter-bank money market rate will lead very quickly to a rise in the bank lending rate in Austria, Italy, and the UK, with detrimental effects on output and employment. On the contrary, raising the money market rate will leave the bank lending rate in Belgium, France, Germany, and the Netherlands relatively unaffected.

Monetary policy actions affect the reserves of the banks, thereby determining their willingness to lend. How this will affect individual firms depends on the financing alternatives available to them. Firms that have the possibility of borrowing at the bond market or issue equity will be less affected by contractions in bank loans than firms that rely entirely on bank financing. Table 6.4 presents an international comparison of financial systems. It follows from this table that in euroland the banking sector accounts for over 50 per cent of financial intermediation. At the other end of

Table 6.3 Credit at Adjustable Interest Rates in the European Union

| Countries | Credit at adjustable interest rates (percentage of total credit) | | |
	All sectors	Households	Firms
Austria	74	—	—
Belgium	44	18	67
Germany	39	36	40
France	44	13	56
Italy	73	59/69*	77
Netherlands	25	8	37
Spain	43/64*	—	—
Sweden	35	—	—
UK	73	90	48

Source: BIS 1995.

Notes
* First percentage refers to indexed short-term rates and second percentage to adjustable within 1 year.

the spectrum is the US, where the banking sector represents only about one-fifth of the total. The UK occupies a middle position. These figures suggest that the lending channel in the euro zone may be quite important.

It also follows from Table 6.4 that as far as the importance of segments of the capital market is concerned the bond market in euroland is considerably smaller than in the United States (see below for further details).

Apart from the relative importance of bank lending, some other features of the banking system may be relevant for monetary transmission. Cecchetti (1999) argues that larger and healthier banks will be able to adjust to policy-induced reserve changes more easily than smaller and less-healthy banks. It is therefore expected that countries with less concentrated and less-healthy banking systems will be more sensitive to monetary policy actions by the ECB. Table 6.5 presents some indicators for the banking sector in EU member states. It clearly follows that there are considerable differences between the banking sectors of individual member states. Although the intermediation role of the banking sector in the euro zone is on average more important than in the US, within EMU there are substantial differences (second column of Table 6.5). Also, in terms of concentration and health, banking systems in EMU diverge to a considerable extent. So if monetary transmission depends on financial structure, ECB policy actions will have diverging impact in the various euro zone countries.

6.2.4 The Future of Financial Structure

What will happen with these differences in financial structure? Will, for instance, national banking systems, and the implied sensitivity of each country's real economy to monetary policy actions, change because of Economic and Monetary Union? Again, different answers have been put forward.

Table 6.4 International Comparison of Financial Systems

	EMU (%)	UK (%)	US (%)
Total intermediation (percentage GDP)	291	376	377
Of which:			
banks	54	32	20
markets	46	68	80
Of which:			
stocks	33	75	48
bonds	67	25	52

Source: Hurst, Perée, and Fischbach 1999.

Table 6.5 Indicators for the Banking System in the European Union, 1996				
	Ratio of bank loans to all other forms of finance	Banks per mln people	Concentration ratio (top 5 banks)	Net interest margin	Operating costs
Austria	65	126	48	1.67	2.45
Belgium	49	14	57	1.41	1.67
Denmark	25	22	17	1.28	0.97
Finland	39	68	78	2.07	3.05
France	49	24	40	1.43	1.84
Germany	55	43	17	1.24	2.19
Greece	48	2	71	1.98	2.77
Ireland	80	18	41	3.36	3.32
Italy	50	16	25	2.32	3.19
Netherlands	53	11	79	2.06	2.48
Portugal	62	5	76	2.60	3.80
Spain	58	8	44	2.20	2.69
Sweden	32	14	90	1.90	1.77
UK	37	8	28	2.15	2.42

Source: Cecchetti 1999.

According to Cecchetti (1999) the existing variation in financial intermediation across European countries is a consequence of their *dissimilar legal structures*. His view is based on an analysis of La Porta, *et al.* (1997; 1998). These authors argue that the structure of finance in a country depends on the legal rights of shareholders and creditors, as well as on the degree to which the relevant laws are enforced. This view is built on the premiss that investors provide capital to firms only if they have the ability to get their money back. For equity holders, this means that they must be able to vote out managers who do not perform according to expectations. For creditors, this means that they must have the authority to repossess collateral (Cecchetti 1999). As Table 6.6 shows, EU countries differ considerably in this respect. The second column reports an index that is higher when shareholders find it less costly and easier to outvote managers. The third column shows an index indicating creditors' rights to reorganize or liquidate a firm. The final columns provide information on enforcement and the origin of the legal system to which a country belongs. Enforcement is an assessment of countries' rigour in carrying out their laws. La Porta, *et al.* (1998) show that legal systems in the OECD countries belong to four families: English common law, French civil law, Scandinavian civil law, and German civil law. Evidence suggests that those countries with a common law system, such as the United States and the UK, provide greatest investor protection and also support the most developed equity markets. Countries governed by the French civil law system provide the weakest investor protection and support the smallest equity markets. Countries with German and Scandinavian legal systems are positioned between these extremes.

If Cecchetti's view is correct that the legal system determines the financial structure, this will have serious implications. For as long as the legal systems of the euro

Table 6.6 Differences in Legal Systems in the European Union

	Shareholders rights	Creditor rights	Enforcement	Origin of legal system
Austria	2	3	10.00	German
Belgium	0	2	10.00	French
Denmark	3	3	10.00	Scandinavian
Finland	2	1	10.00	Scandinavian
France	2	0	8.98	French
Germany	1	3	9.23	German
Greece	1	1	6.18	French
Ireland	3	1	7.80	English
Italy	0	2	8.33	French
Netherlands	2	2	10.00	French
Portugal	2	1	8.68	French
Spain	2	2	7.80	French
Sweden	2	2	10.00	Scandinavian
UK	4	4	8.57	English

Source: La Porta, *et al.* 1997.

zone countries remain distinct—as they probably will—the impact of ECB interest rate actions across EMU countries will differ.

Other views on the future of financial systems in EU member countries have also been put forward. The financial structure may, for instance, be changed as a consequence of the policies of the ECB. We have shown that the structure of European financial markets may affect the monetary transmission mechanism in the short to medium run. However, in the (very) long run, European financial market structures will be in turn influenced by policy-making of the ECB and its track record on price stability. This mutual interaction between financial market structure and monetary policy-making can be clarified with the following example which is related to the situation of the UK in the early 1990s (Eijffinger 1996).

During the ERM currency crisis of 1992 (see also section 1.2) it was almost impossible for the British minister of Finance to raise the short-term interest rate because both public and private debt were mainly of short maturity. A rise of the short-term interest rate would not only have brought about higher interest payments on the floating-rate government debt, but also higher interest payments by households with a mortgage debt (the so-called 'roll-overs').[3] With already double-digit short-term interest rates in the UK, this would have meant more-or-less 'political suicide' for the British government of the time. At that time, in many other EU countries the majority of home mortgages were at a fixed long-term interest rate. This difference reflected a

[3] According to *The Economist* (10 Apr. 1993), at the time of the 1992 currency crisis more than 90 per cent of all home mortgages in the UK were at floating interest rates compared with only 10 per cent or less in Germany and France. However, as from 1993 there is a tendency towards more fixed-rate loans in Britain. In the same period, the proportion of fixed-rate company debt was approximately 80 per cent in Germany, 60 per cent in France, and less than 50 per cent in the UK.

long-standing tradition in the UK of high and volatile inflation rates during the 1970s and 1980s that made financial institutions reluctant to lend on a fixed-rate basis. If monetary authorities implement a credible and time-consistent monetary policy directed on price stability, lending on a fixed-rate basis becomes less risky. Indeed, more recently UK citizens have shifted their mortgages to fixed rates. According to estimates by Bishop (1998) some 59 per cent of new mortgages have a fixed rate.

Apart from the impact of monetary policy on financial structure, EMU may also have other consequences. It is widely believed that the euro will act as a catalyst, speeding up the rate at which the financial system in Europe becomes more similar to that in the United States. McCauley and White (1997) suggest that the rate at which securities replace loans on the asset side of the balance sheet of banks will accelerate. In other words, the process of securitization will get stronger. *Securitization* is defined here in a broad sense. It means connecting the suppliers of funds directly with the users, via a securities market, rather than through an intermediary bank (Bishop 1998). The term is often applied to the specific process of turning small loans—for instance, on residential mortgages—into bonds that can be issued on the capital markets.

One reason why EMU may matter here is due to the *matching rules*. For example, European life insurance companies must match 80 per cent of their assets to the currency of their liabilities. As the vast majority of those liabilities are denominated in national currency, so are most of the assets. Now these institutions can diversify their portfolios across the euro zone (Bishop 1999).

Increasing securitization implies a less important role for banks as an intermediary. As a consequence, the lending channel may become less important. It is expected that the balance sheet of European financial institutions will become more similar to those in the United States. The share of credit extended by the banking system has remained essentially unchanged in the US over the past twenty years. But the striking feature of the US financial system is the rise of the bond market. Although the EU bond market has also expanded, bond markets in the United States show a much higher growth rate. Apart from size, there is another major difference between EMU and US bond markets. The bond market in euroland is much more skewed towards high-quality borrowers than the bond market in the United States. Investors in the United States can now extend credit directly to virtually all the sectors that were formerly the preserve of the banks (Bishop 1998).

The growth of the US bond market has not been driven by government deficits. Still, government played a crucial role as the securitization of mortgages was stimulated to sponsor home ownership. Various agencies, such as the Federal Home Loan Mortgage Corporation (Freddie Mac), which are shareholder-owned but sponsored and regulated by the federal government, have been founded for this purpose. It seems unlikely that public authorities in the EU will foster the development of similar agencies.[4]

---

[4] However, in the past mortgage banks in some European countries played a similar role. These banks issue Pfandbriefe (mortgage bonds) and lend to property owners. According to Bishop (1999) these banks may, however, find it difficult to ensure that there is a sufficiently similar legal basis in each EU member state for taking a mortgage on a property and putting it into a pan-European collateral pool.

Apart from this factor, there are some other reasons why financial markets in euroland will probably not become copies of those in the US. Schinasi and Smith (1998) identify six factors that appear to have been important to explain the (lack of) development of corporate debt securities in various advanced economies. The first factor is that a well-functioning money market (for example, the market for Commercial Paper; CP) appears to be a critical first step in developing corporate bond markets. Money markets are important for financing positions and for pricing liquidity. Second, regulatory policies have been an important influence historically in either encouraging or inhibiting the development of corporate fixed-income markets. Countries like France, Germany, and Italy have had strict regulation (including taxation) in corporate securities markets. Likewise, the underdevelopment of money markets in many European countries is attributable to the fact that CP issues have simply been precluded. Third, the market power of banks may impede the development of securities markets. Schinasi and Smith (1998) argue that emphasis in the US to ensure that market power in the financial industry was limited, may have contributed to the growth of securities markets. Still, there is no relationship between the concentration ratio in the EU banking sector and the importance of bank loans for the financing of firms as reported in Table 6.5. Fourth, issuing corporate securities involves investment banking expertise (advising, underwriting) which is time-consuming to develop and generally quite expensive to purchase. Another element of the primary market infrastructure that is better developed in the US than in euroland is credit ratings. Fifth, as far as the secondary market is concerned, it is quite remarkable that trading in corporate bonds is generally over-the-counter (OTC), which limits liquidity. The final factor that Schinasi and Smith point out to be important is the development of an international investor base for corporate securities. Foreign investors and large institutions increasingly hold government securities and corporate debt securities.

It follows from the foregoing analysis that although bond markets in euroland will become more similar to those in the US, they will probably continue to be different in some respects. For instance, government bonds will remain more important. Financial markets that have felt the impact of EMU most forcibly to date are the government bond markets. Now that EMU is operational, all new government debt of the 11 countries in the euro zone will be issued in euro. Furthermore, a considerable part of outstanding debt has been (or will be) re-denominated. As pointed out by Bishop (1998), government debt is also being securitized. At the end of 1998 on average 44 per cent of gross government debt of the EU member states consisted of bonds. This average conceals a wide variation between states—from a high of more than 90 per cent in Denmark to a low of 26 per cent in Austria. If this securitization continues, the size of the European government bond markets will further increase. Bishop (1998) estimates the effects of a move towards 75 per cent securitization. This would increase the market value of government debt from 2334 mrd euro in 1998 to 3876 mrd euro.

Interest rates on government bonds of EMU member states have converged. Removing the foreign exchange risk increased the substitutability and the correlations of returns between bonds markets of different governments (Brookes 1998).

This has reduced diversification opportunities for portfolio managers. Investors seeking new fixed-income investments to boost returns on bond portfolios (like pension funds; see section 6.3) may therefore turn to the corporate bond market. As pointed out by Brookes (1998), this has already happened to some extent, but the process is likely to accelerate. EMU will increase the scope to diversify away individual corporate credit risk by broadening the availability of domestic currency corporate bonds.

6.3 The New European Financial Landscape

APART from the trend of increased securitization as outlined in the previous section, at least three other trends may be discerned that will change the European financial landscape. First, owing to demographic developments, the role of pension funds becomes increasingly important as a result of the probable transition from unfunded or Pay-As-You-Go (PAYG) to at least partly funded social security systems. In most European countries state pensions are *unfunded*, that is pensions paid to the current generation of retired are financed from contributions made by current workers. In countries like the Netherlands and the UK, however, pensions are *funded*: pension funds use the contributions made by the workers to accumulate a stock of assets in order to finance pensions whose values might be only loosely linked to the returns generated over a specific period.[5]

Second, the national bias in equity markets will be reduced. These equity markets are likely to grow as more companies go public and more investors seek to invest funds in equity markets (Brookes 1998).

Third, pension funds and securities markets might be at the hub of the future European financial system, in stark contrast with the current situation. This will induce deep changes in the funding of companies and on their relationship with banks. As a consequence, competition in the banking sector will further increase, thereby fuelling mergers and acquisitions. These issues will be discussed in turn in this section.

6.3.1 Pension Fund Reform and European Financial Markets

With a view to the ageing of the population, combined with comprehensive unfunded pension systems, the introduction of changes in pension systems seems to be inevitable in many EU countries. These changes could take the form of raising

---

[5] Whereas funded pension systems have (a degree of) risk sharing between different generations, unfunded (PAYG) pension systems mainly depend on contributions raised from future workers. In other words, funded systems do have elements of intergenerational smoothing and unfunded systems do not.

retirement ages, raising contribution rates, and reducing pension benefits, or even imply a complete pension fund reform. It is often argued that when such reform involves funding of future pensions, this may have important implications for financial market structure and behaviour, which may impact on some long-established features of EU financial markets. Davis (1999) maintains that, taken together, the forces unleashed by EMU and pension funding may act to change the European financial landscape more radically than would be the case for each alone, and will have a final outcome close to the US model.

The EU countries face a sharp increase in the proportion of the population aged 65 and over. This 'greying' results mainly from a decline in fertility to below replacement in most EU countries. Furthermore, it is also related to an increase in average life expectancy and a low level of net migration. With an unchanged retirement age, such a demographic shift will naturally lead to higher transfers in the context of unfunded pension systems. The problem is, however, compounded by the scope and generosity of public pension systems in the EU. Combining these elements, sharp and unsustainable increases of pension expenditure are projected for a number of EU countries.

EMU enhances pressure for reform of public pension systems. First, owing to the Stability and Growth Pact there will be much less scope for governments to run large deficits when ageing becomes an acute burden on social security, even as part of pension system reforms. Contribution rates will have to be adjusted closely to match benefit payments at all times, thus forcing governments to look more closely at their social security obligations at an early stage. Second, financial markets, and rating agencies in particular, will increasingly focus on general government obligations, of which pension liabilities are the largest part. Those governments retaining generous unfunded social security systems in the face of a deteriorating demographic situation may face higher long-term interest rates, *ceteris paribus*. Third, in the context of EMU there will be price transparency in terms of differences in prices and costs. This will arguably tend to put countries imposing high taxes on employers for social security purposes under greater pressure to adapt their systems, as high taxes would otherwise lead firms to relocate their activities where such taxes are lower (Davis 1999).

Table 6.7 shows some features of European pension systems: only Ireland and the Netherlands have a basic type of pension system. Scandinavian countries and the UK have a mixed pension system, whereas the other European countries and the United States rely on insurance to finance pensions. In continental European countries state pensions make up 50 to 80 per cent of average earnings. In Ireland and the UK state pensions are less generous. The British replacement rate is now lower than 20 per cent and steadily declining because UK basic pensions are indexed to prices rather than to average earnings.

Table 6.8 presents information on replacement rates, support ratios, and estimated future contribution rates that would be needed to balance the pension budget. The replacement rate is the ratio between the state pension and average earnings. The support ratio is the ratio between the number of contributors to and beneficiaries of state pension systems. The projected fall of the support ratio requires a sharp rise of the equilibrium contribution rate in countries with unfunded pension systems, such

Table 6.7 Social Security Pension Systems in the European Union

Country and type of social security pension system	Gross social security replacement rate (Watson Wyatt 1997) at final salary of $20,000 and $50,000 (%)	Social security contributions (1997) as percentage of earnings (at a salary of $20,000 and $50,000)	Employers' social security contribution rate (1997) (at a salary of $20,000 and $50,000) (%)
Austria (insurance)	70–70	36–36	19–19
Belgium (insurance)	58–45	46–47	33–33
Denmark (mixed)	93–37	10–9	2–1
Finland (mixed)	60–59	31–32	24–24
France (insurance)	67–51	63–63	42–43
Germany (insurance)	45–43	42–42	21–21
Greece (insurance)	70–48	43–25	27–16
Ireland (basic)	53–21	18–16	12–11
Italy (insurance)	78–75	61–58	51–48
Luxembourg (insurance)	87–76	21–21	11–11
Netherlands (basic)	76–31	24–20	18–13
Portugal (insurance)	74–74	35–35	24–24
Spain (insurance)	94–63	37–27	31–23
Sweden (mixed)	63–50	37–37	32–32
UK (mixed)	35–14	18–17	10–10
US (insurance)	71–45	15–15	8–8

Source: Davis 1999, based on Watson Wyatt 1997.

Note: Final salary for married man. Tax treatment of benefits varies across countries. Notably German benefits are tax-free.

as France, Germany, and Italy. The equilibrium rate is the contribution rate (including net budget transfers as a percentage of the wage bill) that maintains year-by-year financial balance of the pension system. From Table 6.8 it is clear that the equilibrium contribution rates would need to increase considerably in France, Germany, and Italy to keep state pension systems in balance, but remains almost constant in the UK in the very long run.

Table 6.9 provides the stock of pension assets both in absolute terms and as a percentage of GDP for EU countries, Canada, Japan, and the United States. The Netherlands and the UK have a substantial stock of pension assets of 75 per cent or more of GDP. The European average is a little more than 20 per cent. The relatively generous (unfunded) state pensions in continental European countries have made funded pension systems there less important than in the Anglo-Saxon countries (Canada, Ireland, the UK, and the United States). The ageing population on the continent of Europe threatens the future viability of its unfunded state pension systems which is providing most of the income to the retired.

The main argument to move from unfunded or Pay-As-You-Go state pension systems to greater reliance on funded pension systems is to smooth the pension burden over generations. By moving in the direction of more funded systems, the projected

Table 6.8 Projections of Pension Replacement Rates, Support Ratios, and Contribution Rates

	2000	2010	2030	2050
France				
Replacement rate	59.4	59.5	59.8	59.5
Support ratio	2.6	2.4	1.6	1.4
Equilibrium rate	23.2	24.4	37.7	41.2
Projected rate	23.4	23.4	23.4	23.4
Germany				
Replacement rate	51.0	49.0	48.8	48.7
Support ratio	2.1	2.0	1.2	1.2
Equilibrium rate	25.0	24.7	41.1	41.6
Projected rate	22.8	22.9	22.9	22.9
Italy				
Replacement rate	55.8	55.6	53.7	50.8
Support ratio	1.2	1.4	0.9	0.7
Equilibrium rate	45.5	40.4	61.9	68.2
Projected rate	42.6	42.6	42.6	42.6
UK				
Replacement rate	17.4	16.8	14.4	10.6
Support ratio	2.7	2.5	2.1	2.1
Equilibrium rate	6.4	6.8	6.9	5.0
Projected rate	6.2	6.2	6.2	6.2

Source: IMF staff estimates reported in Chand and Jaeger 1996.

Note: The replacement rate is defined as the average pension benefit as a percentage of the average gross wage. The support ratio is defined as the ratio of contributors to beneficiaries. The equilibrium rate is the contribution rate including net budget transfers (as a percentage of the wage bill) that maintains year-by-year financial balance of the pension system. The projected rate is the projected contribution rate including net budget transfers (as a percentage of the wage bill).

future increase under a PAYG system will be lower at the cost of higher payments in the short to medium run. According to Miles and Timmermann (1999), a major problem with switching from an unfunded to a funded system is how to manage the transition process. They argue that, if contributions by current workers have to be accumulated in a pension fund to phase out the unfunded part of pensions, then these contributions will not be available to pay pensions to the current retired. Moreover, future retired (current) workers who had expected to receive relatively generous pensions financed from contributions of future workers will find insufficient time to accumulate a large enough funding for providing their own pension. Moreover, Miles and Timmermann argue that the proposition by some authors that, if the rate of return earned on funds would be very high relative to the increase in average wages, the transition could be handled easily without any losers is a false one. They state that, no matter how high the rate of return on assets, the transition from an unfunded to a funded system always makes some people (cohorts) worse off. Of course, allocating the burden of lower consumption across generations is a question of considerable political significance. Who the losers are and how much they lose

Table 6.9 Private Pension Financing in the European Union (to 1996)

	Private pension assets in US dollars (mrd)	Private pension assets as a percentage of GDP
Austria	3	1.1
Belgium	11	4.3
Denmark	38	22.2
Finland	18	14.4
France	69	4.5
Germany	137	5.8
Greece	4	2.8
Ireland	32	43.3
Italy	32	2.5
Luxembourg	0	0.2
Netherlands	349	88.9
Portugal	10	10.7
Spain	22	4.1
Sweden	38	32.7
UK	966	75.6
European Union	*1730*	*20.9*
Canada	213	45.4
Japan	943	21.8
United States	4763	62.4

Source: Davis 1999 based on European Federation for Retirement Provision 1996.

depends not only upon the rates of return but also upon labour productivity and demographic change. Miles and Timmermann conclude that the transition costs could well be considerable. They find that the scale of projected returns within a fully funded pension system relative to the growth in aggregate wages (being the key factor for an unfunded system) is critical to the transition costs from an unfunded to a funded system.

6.3.2 Equity Markets

There is considerable evidence that investors in equity markets have a strong domestic bias. A shift towards foreign funds would reduce the volatility of portfolio returns without reducing the level of returns. With EMU one of the barriers to such diversification (exchange rate risk) has been removed. Owing to the redefinition of the home market it is expected by various observers that portfolios will be more managed along sectoral lines. Others expect a continuing focus along national lines instead. The issue here is whether an investor should compare the share price of German banks, say, with the share price of other German companies or with those of banks in other European countries.

The question of whether investors will look at sectors or countries when making their investment decisions is an empirical issue. A survey by Goldman Sachs under their clients suggests that EMU will affect investment behaviour (Brookes 1998). Out of the fund managers surveyed, 70 per cent said that EMU would lead them to reconsider their approach to asset allocation. The fund managers were also asked whether they would organize their European equity portfolio on a country or a sector basis. Only 9 per cent answered that portfolios would be organized on a country basis, whereas 64 per cent said they would be organized on a sector basis. The remaining 27 per cent said 'other', probably indicating a mixture of country and sector factors. A final interesting feature of the survey was the speed with which changes are likely to be implemented. Almost 90 per cent of the respondents expected the transition to be finished three years after the start of EMU.

A final issue is how equity markets in Europe will develop. It is well known that the size of the stock market in continental Europe is small in comparison to the markets in the United States and the UK (see also Table 6.4). The ratio of market capitalization to GDP over the period 1982–91 averaged 76 per cent in the UK, while it was approximately 20 per cent in France and Germany. The average for the OECD countries as a whole was 30 per cent (Mayer 1999). It is often contended that the smaller size of equity markets in Europe reflects the difficulties of smaller and medium-sized firms in Europe gaining a listing. Some recent evidence provided by Brookes (1998) suggests that this may not be true. One simple way to test this view is to see whether the structure of the US equity market differs markedly from euroland equity markets. If it is true that small and medium-sized enterprises are restricted in their access to equity, one would find relatively few of this type of firm being listed in euroland than in the United States. Brookes (1998) compares the number of companies listed on the NYSE and NASDAQ with the aggregate of the EMU-11 countries. There do not appear to be any marked differences between the two markets from this comparison. This suggests that it is not a matter of scale that prevents firms from seeking a listing in euroland.

6.3.3 Bank Restructuring

It is widely believed that the introduction of the euro may change the process of banking restructuring already under way in Europe (as in many other countries of the world). As long as European countries maintained their monetary sovereignty, the scope for possible cross-border banking consolidation was limited (Hurst, Perée, and Fischbach 1999). This subsection analyses the process of mergers and acquisitions in some detail.

In the EU, the run-up to the single market ('Europe 1992') had large effects in many industries. For the banking sector, the Second Banking Directive has been very important. It introduced the concept of the *single passport* and the recognition of *home country control*. Banks that have been recognized and approved in their home country can freely offer banking services across the European Union. The supervisory function is allocated to the home country supervisor (ibid.).

In the period 1988–92, the EU bank markets have witnessed an unprecedented number of bank takeovers in the run-up to the single market. This is illustrated in Table 6.10. Three types of takeovers are distinguished. In majority *participations* the acquirer obtains decisive voting power (> 50 per cent) in the target bank but the institutions remain legally independent, retaining their own names, branch networks, and management teams. The second subsample involves full *acquisitions* and assembles the take-overs of a relatively small bank by a larger competitor, whereby the former is legally absorbed by the latter. The third group is *mergers* in which credit institutions of approximately equal size are effectively integrated.

An understanding of the determinants and consequences of merger and acquisition deals may help to assess the effect of a further consolidation on the performance and competitive viability of European banks. For regulators and supervisors it is important to know whether mergers lead to a more efficient banking system or simply increase market concentration. The recent wave of takeovers associated with the transition to the monetary union indicates that the restructuring of the European banking sector is far from finished.

Proponents of bank consolidation assert that bank mergers may have advantages owing to (1) scale and (2) scope effects, (3) elimination of inferior management leading to a more efficient banking system, and (4) a more diversified banking system. Sceptics argue that mergers may be primarily motivated by market power considerations and excessive growth strategies and that the promised efficiency improvements may often be elusive.

Table 6.10 Domestic Bank Takeovers in the European Union during 1988–1992

	Majority participations	Acquisitions	Mergers	Total
Belgium	4	5	2	11
Denmark	2	42	7	51
France	16	12	1	29
Germany	12	72	11	95
Ireland	2	1	—	3
Italy	25	79	24	128
Luxembourg	—	1	4	5
Netherlands	3	5	7	15
Portugal	2	—	—	2
Spain	10	42	16	68
UK	7	13	1	21
Total	83	272	73	428

Source: Vander Vennet 1999.

In an information and distribution-intensive industry with high fixed costs such as banking, there is ample potential for economies of scale, as well as potential for diseconomies of scale. The latter are attributable to disproportionate increases in administrative overheads, management of complexity, agency problems, and other cost factors once very large firm size is reached (Walter 1999). If economies of scale prevail, increased size will help create more efficiency and shareholder value. If diseconomies prevail, both will be destroyed. Many studies of economies of scale have been undertaken in the banking industry over the years. According to a survey by Berger, Demsetz, and Strahan (1998), there is no clear evidence of economies of scale among very large banks. Most recent studies have concluded that scale economies are exhausted at a size level between 3 and 25 mrd US dollar (Vander Vennet, 1999). Thus, it is expected that the smaller the combined size of the merging banks, the more probable are any merger benefits. So, for most banks in the euro zone, except the smallest among them, scale economies seem likely to have relatively little bearing on competitive performance (Walter 1999).

Most empirical studies—which mainly refer to the United States—have also failed to find economies of scope in the banking industry. Most of them conclude that some diseconomies of scope are encountered when firms in the financial services sector add new product-ranges to their portfolios (ibid.).

Various authors have found very large disparities in cost structures among banks of similar size, suggesting that the way banks are run is more important than their size or the selection of businesses that they pursue. A recent study by Wagenvoort and Schurer (1999) into 1974 European banks finds that costs are unnecessarily high in more than 80 per cent of the cases. The most important reason for inefficiencies in European banking is managerial inability to control costs, so-called X-inefficiency, that is whether banks use their available inputs efficiently. X-inefficiency may be caused by wasting of resources (for example, a bank which uses old-fashioned technology, has too many offices and too many people on the payroll, etc.) but may also stem from unprofitable purchase of these resources. The average level of X-inefficiency, computed for the European banking sector as a whole by taking into account the relative size of both its inefficient and efficient institutions, still exceeded 16 per cent in 1997, according to Wagenvoort and Schurer (Table 6.11). Although in some countries, such as the UK and the Netherlands, cost reductions were rapidly achieved, bankers in Austria, France, Germany, and Luxembourg did not improve their performance.

The takeover market is viewed as the ultimate disciplinary tool to align the potentially diverging interests of managers and shareholders. The hypothesis is that acquisitions eliminate bad management and turn poorly performing banks into well-managed ones. Target banks are expected to exhibit relatively inferior profitability and efficiency before their acquisition. If the takeover succeeds, we expect to observe a positive correlation between performance and the takeover dummy in the period following the takeover. Acquiring banks are expected to be relatively good performers, so that they will be able to upgrade the acquired institution.

Finance theory learns that the diversification of income sources should lower the earnings volatility of a bank and may lead to increased creditworthiness. In principle,

Table 6.11 Weighted Average of the Estimated X-inefficiencies in Banking in the European Union (Percentages)

	1993	1994	1995	1996	1997
EU 15 (1974)	20	19	19	20	16
Austria (50)	7	14	18	16	11
Belgium (69)	20	16	18	23	13
Denmark (82)	32	37	27	25	20
Finland (7)	32	28	11	17	10
France (295)	22	22	21	21	22
Germany (886)	10	14	14	19	16
Greece (17)	67	67	64	63	59
Ireland (7)	31	35	33	35	21
Italy (194)	24	22	26	18	14
Luxembourg (97)	20	11	19	20	22
Netherlands (35)	28	21	21	24	13
Portugal (24)	41	36	36	33	30
Spain (125)	29	23	25	24	22
Sweden (12)	39	35	23	30	28
UK (74)	20	13	10	8	−4

Source: Wagenvoort and Schurer 1999.

Note: The weight of each bank is obtained from its total asset amount. The number of banks in each country is given in parentheses.

the diversification motive is less applicable to horizontal takeovers between credit institutions. Nevertheless, banks do diversify their income streams, as evidenced by the growth of off-balance-sheet activity and fee-income business. Takeovers may also aid in the diversification of various banking risks by, for example, targeting a specific sectoral exposure or credit quality-lending segment.

As the major non-value maximization explanation, the management utility maximization theory states that managers may undertake acquisitions based on their own utility functions. Two possible sources of managerial utility are increased size and expense-preference behaviour. The size-maximization hypothesis states that managers seek rapid growth in an effort to increase their job security and compensation levels. Hence, takeovers may constitute a rapid way of increasing balance sheet totals. Non-pecuniary management utility such as power or prestige is perceived as being closely linked with firm size.

Vander Vennet (1999) has analysed the determinants of domestic EU bank takeovers as shown in Table 6.10. The evidence suggests that domestic majority participations and domestic acquisitions were primarily motivated by market power and growth considerations. Large universal banks with a solid market position tend to acquire credit institutions, which also have an established presence in their local deposit and loan markets. The target institutions exhibit inferior efficiency and profit levels and are thus candidates for performance upgrading. However, the expected improvements fail to materialize, at least in the short run. In the case of participations, the fact that the banks remain independent entities probably prevents the full exploitation of synergies and lowers the feasibility of drastic managerial action. In the case of acquisitions, the integration of a small competitor by a large bank seems to offer limited consolidation benefits. On the other hand, domestic mergers between equal-sized partners appear to supply tangible scope for efficiency improvements. Although market power and growth motivations may be part of the story, especially for the mega-mergers, there is evidence of real gains due to synergy. For the mergers among relatively small institutions scale economies are probably part of the explanation. In large mergers, it is hypothesized that focused rationalization exercises are the main cause for the observed performance improvement. These mergers also allow the rebalancing of various bank risks.

6.4 Conclusion

THIS chapter first analyses money market integration between various European countries and Germany, using the covered interest parity (CIP) condition. We find strong support for an increasing degree of money market integration in Europe. Our results indicate that the size and variability of the mean (absolute) country premium declined significantly after the Basle–Nyborg agreement of September 1987. The initial low degree of money market integration urged countries like France, Italy, Portugal, and Spain to catch up with the rest of the European countries during the 1980s. There seems to be a trade-off between the speed and degree of money market integration in Europe during the 1980s.

Furthermore, the chapter discusses the structure of financial markets and its consequences for the monetary transmission mechanism in euroland. There are still large differences in financial structure across EMU countries. It is not certain whether these will remain or not. There are some, albeit conflicting, indications that differences in financial structure cause asymmetries in the monetary transmission mechanism.

The final part of the chapter deals with various issues: securitization, pension fund reform, equity markets, and bank restructuring. It is concluded that owing to securitization the role of the so-called lending channel will probably be reduced. Pension fund reform is widely seen as essential in order to defuse the difficulties EU governments would otherwise face in respect of their social security pension systems in a context of population ageing. In the wake of this, European financial markets will be strongly affected by pension fund reform as well as by EMU, and there will be important interactions between the two. Among the key elements are that both funding and EMU would seem to favour an increased role for securities markets and a lesser role for traditional banking. EMU may also reduce the domestic bias in European equity markets. Restructuring of the banking sector, notably in terms of capacity and income sources, will be needed in order to ensure the associated adjustment in capacity occurs smoothly.

Chapter 7
EMU and International Policy Co-ordination

Introduction

WHILE EMU implies a new regime for the participating countries, it will also have important external implications. One interesting question is how important the euro will become as an international currency. A currency is an international currency when it is widely used by the governments and residents of other countries as a means of payment, a unit of account, and a store of value. So far, the US dollar has had a prominent role in this regard. Governments hold a considerable part of their foreign currency reserves in dollars. In major commodity markets (the oil market, for instance) the dollar is used to price and trade products. In foreign exchange markets prices of many currencies are quoted in dollars. Financial instruments are often denominated in dollars (Kenen 1995). Will EMU make the international monetary system more symmetric in this regard? And, if so, what consequences might this have for international economic relations? Section 7.1 deals with the first question, while section 7.2 looks at the second.

7.1 The International Role of the Euro

7.1.1 The European Union in the World Economy

With a share of world GDP of 15 per cent, the euro area is one of the largest economies in the world (see Table 7.1). In comparison, Germany only accounts for just over 4 per cent of world GDP. Being a large economy, the euro zone is much less open than individual member states. However, the EMU countries combined have a slightly higher export-to-GDP ratio than the United States and Japan. The share of the euro area in total world exports amounts to almost 16 per cent, which is well above the shares of the United States and Japan. In one respect the EMU member states differ substantially from the United States and Japan: their public sectors are substantially larger.

Although the dollar is still the dominant international currency, its role has diminished after the demise of the Bretton Woods system. The German mark and other European currencies have started to play an increasingly important role, along with the Japanese yen. Still, the pace of change has been uneven. Securities are issued in many currencies. For instance, the share of US dollar bonds in the international bond market has fallen from 62 per cent of the stock of bonds outstanding in 1985 to 38 per cent in 1996. Similarly, deposits are held in many currencies. Change has been slow in those domains where transaction costs are reduced by using a single currency as unit of account or medium of exchange, as in commodity and foreign exchange markets (Kenen 1995). In 1995 the dollar was used in 83 per cent of two-way transactions on foreign exchange markets, against 90 per cent in 1989 (see Table 7.2).

Will the introduction of the euro reinforce the relative decline of the dollar as an international currency, and will this also happen in those domains where the pace of change has been slowest? To answer these questions, we will first analyse the functions of international money. Then, we will discuss the benefits and costs of having an international currency.

Table 7.1 Economic Indicators: USA, Japan, EU11

	USA	Japan	EU11
Population (million, 1998)	270	127	292
Share of world GDP (%, 1997)	20.2	7.7	15.0
Exports-to-GDP ratio (%, 1997)	8.5	10.0	13.6
Exports (% world export, 1997)	12.6	7.7	15.7
Government spending (% GDP, 1998)	34.5	38.6	49.1

Source: ECB, Monthly Bulletin (Jan. 1999).

Table 7.2 Transactions on Foreign Exchange Markets (Percentage of Total Transactions)

	April 1989	April 1992	April 1995
US dollar	90	82	83
German mark	27	40	37
Japanese yen	27	23	24

Source: BIS, surveys on foreign exchange markets.

Note: Since any transaction on the foreign exchange market involves two currencies, the total involving all currencies is 200 per cent.

7.1.2 The Functions of International Money

A currency develops at the international level when its use for various purposes extends beyond the frontiers of the issuing country by both private and official operators. The three traditional functions that money has are: means of payment or a medium of exchange, a unit of account (numeraire), and a store of value. First, money is a medium through which people exchange a whole range of goods and services, as well as financial assets. Second, money is a store of value because it can be used to make purchases in the future. Third, money is a unit of account (that is, a unit in which prices are quoted and accounts are kept). Of course, these three functions of money are not independent. Any medium of exchange must be a store of value and also implies a unit of account. It is clear, for example, that if money is to be accepted as a medium of exchange, it also has to be a store of value. No one would accept money as payment for goods supplied today, if the money has become worthless at the time one wants to buy goods with it. However, many stores of value (for example, government bonds) do not circulate as a medium of exchange.

A functional definition of international money was first developed by Cohen (1971) and further elaborated by Hartmann (1998). Cohen (1971) defines the private and public functions of international currency starting from the three traditional functions of money. Hartmann (1998) uses the definition of the various private and public money functions to make a typology of the different functions of an international currency. Table 7.3 integrates Cohen's definition with Hartmann's typology.

Table 7.3 not only distinguishes the three traditional money functions but also differentiates between use by private and public agents. The latter refers to the use of international currency by monetary authorities. Governments and central banks may try to influence the exchange rates of their own currency against other currencies by intervening in the foreign exchange market. They determine the intervention currency (or currencies) by their decision in which market they want to intervene. Directly related to the intervention currency is the choice of the reserve currency, because monetary authorities can only intervene in those foreign currencies in which they hold some reserves or have a credit line, like the VSTF in the ERM. In case of an exchange rate arrangement, governments choose a currency to peg to with the aim of keeping the exchange rate at a some fixed level or within a certain specified band.

The private use of international currency and its money functions are a more complicated matter. According to Hartmann (1998), there are two types of vehicle currencies: *trade* vehicles, which serve as a medium of exchange in goods, and *forex* vehicles, which serve as a medium of exchange in currency.[1]

Hartmann defines trade vehicles by referring to a trade transaction between

---

[1] We may distinguish trade vehicles further in domestic and foreign trade vehicles. The first means that residents of the same country use a foreign currency as a medium of exchange for their local transaction, also known as *direct currency substitution*. In the latter case, a foreign currency is used by residents of two different countries to invoice (and settle) for trade contracts between both countries. For example, we speak of a foreign trade vehicle if the EU invoices imports from less-developed countries in US dollars.

Table 7.3 Private and Public Functions of International Currency

Money function	Private sector use	Public sector use
Means of payments or medium of exchange	*Vehicle currency* used to settle international trade and to discharge international financial obligations	*Intervention currency* used in foreign exchange markets and currency used for balance of payments financing
Unit of account (numeraire)	*Quotation currency* used to denominate international financial instruments and to invoice foreign trade transactions	*Pegging currency* used in expressing exchange rate relationships and as an anchor for other currencies
Store of value	*Investment currency* used to denominate deposits, loans, and bonds	*Reserve currency* used as international reserves by monetary authorities

Source: Hartmann 1998, based on Cohen 1971.

industrial countries, which is invoiced and settled in the exporter's currency. The importer mostly does not have balances in the exporter's currency available and has to convert domestic currency into foreign currency through a bank for settling the trade transaction. Therefore, the importer uses the exporter's currency as a medium of exchange implying its internationalization.

Since banks provide foreign currencies to the trading firms that do not exchange currencies among themselves, there is an *inter-bank* foreign exchange market for banks quickly to acquire the currencies needed by trading firms as well as by international borrowers and lenders. If there is only one (international) currency, for example, the US dollar, which has a liquid inter-bank market with the other currencies, while all the other cross-currency markets are illiquid, the US dollar will consequently be used on a wide scale. Of course, the existence of merely one forex vehicle is an extreme case not corresponding with the present situation in which one major forex vehicle (US dollar) exists as well as some minor forex vehicles.

Quotation currencies are the (foreign) currencies in whose units prices of goods or assets are expressed when they are different from respectively the supplier of the goods or the issuer of the assets. *Investment currencies* are those currencies in which asset contracts are settled.

According to Portes and Rey (1998), a currency will become an international vehicle currency if *transaction costs* (information costs, search costs, uncertainty, negotiation, and execution costs) are lower when that currency is used instead of the domestic currency. The lower the exchange-rate volatility of a certain currency against other currencies and the larger the volume of transactions in that currency, the lower the transaction costs are likely to be. Apparently, there exist (external) economies of scale or network externalities linked to the use of an international currency. If a currency is a vehicle currency, its diffusion increases and the transaction costs of that currency relative to other currencies decrease.

With respect to the functions of international money (see Table 7.3), Hartmann (1998) concludes that owing to the integration of goods and capital markets most currencies of industrial countries are nowadays internationalized to some extent. However, the degree of internationalization of these currencies differs considerably. Only a few currencies do really perform many private and public functions of international money and can be called *key currencies*. Owing to transaction costs and network externalities, there may be a single *dominant* key currency performing most of those functions to a larger extent than the other key currencies. Since the Second World War, the US dollar has been the dominant key currency in the world. The crucial question is, of course, whether the euro can compete with the dollar in this respect. Before discussing the possible international role of the euro in the future, we may ask what the benefits (advantages) and costs (responsibilities) are of having an international currency. This issue will be addressed in the next subsection.

7.1.3 The Benefits and Costs of an International Currency

Having a key currency might be compared with having a key language, like English or, to lesser extent, French, German, or Spanish. On the one hand, residents of these countries may be able to express themselves in their native language abroad and do not need to learn a foreign language, which saves them a lot of time and effort. On the other hand, those residents cannot talk in private with their countrymen when they feel the need to do this (except by using perhaps an unknown dialect). Although not an exact comparison, the same benefits and costs apply to a country with an international currency.

Having a dominant international currency offers the country concerned both political and economic benefits in the sense that it can take advantage of the international private and public use of its currency (Cohen 1997). Monetary supremacy has substantial political benefits. At home, the dominant country is insulated from foreign influence in forming and implementing economic and other policies. Abroad, that country is better able to pursue objectives in its foreign policy without constraints and may influence, or even coerce, other countries. Many political scientists believe that the political supremacy of the USA has been more than proportional (that is, bigger than its share in the world economy (see Table 7.1)), because of the dominance of the dollar since the Second World War.

Currency hegemony brings also considerable economic benefits to the dominant country. First, the issuer of the key currency can collect seigniorage. Monetary supremacy gives the possibility of obtaining real goods and services in exchange for costless notes and coins. The issuer of the international currency may therefore profit from its monopoly issue of notes and coins. Seigniorage from US dollars held abroad is estimated to be worth 0.1 per cent of American GDP (Alogoskoufis and Portes 1991).

Second, currency hegemony enables the dominant country to collect a liquidity discount. Owing to the depth and liquidity of its bond market, the interest rate on its debt is relatively low. Portes and Rey (1998) have estimated the value of this liquidity discount on US government debt between 0.25 and 0.5 per cent. Given that non-residents are estimated to hold 2 trillion dollars of US government debt, annual savings of 5 to 10 mrd dollar results as a consequence of the liquidity discount. This amount is similar to the benefits from seigniorage for the USA.

Third, monetary dominance gives a country the possibility of financing its current-account deficits in its own currency. When the country deliberately allows for larger current account deficits, like the United States did in the past, this financing of the current account could well be the biggest advantage. The former president of France, Charles de Gaulle, complained that the exorbitant privilege of the dollar 'enabled the United States to be indebted to foreign countries free of charge' (*The Economist*, 14 Nov. 1998). Although the United States does pay interest on all government debt, De Gaulle had a point in the sense that the United States would have had many more problems in financing its huge current account deficits if the dollar were not the dominant key currency in that period.

As the US experience in the 1970s has shown, there are also substantial costs (responsibilities) of having a dominant international currency. If these responsibilities are taken seriously, this may actually lead to a policy of active or passive discouragement of the internationalization of the currency by the responsible monetary authorities. This was, for example, the case with the suppressed international role of the German mark during the 1980s and 1990s. The Bundesbank was not prepared to accept all the responsibilities of having a major key currency.

First, as mentioned by Tavlas (1991) and Tavlas and Ozeki (1992), a precondition for the use of an international currency is trust in the political stability of the issuing country and, thereby, in the stability of the currency. Evidently, the value of an international currency has to be stable in order to ensure that its relative price in terms of other currencies (that is, the exchange rate), gives sufficient and relevant information about the development of the 'fundamentals' in the key country. Inflation (uncertainty) may not only disturb the relative prices and the efficient allocation of resources among countries, but also reduces the purchasing power of that currency which implies a degradation in the store of value function of money. Having an international currency requires that the monetary authorities pursue a stable and time-consistent monetary policy (and fiscal policy) to guarantee price stability and to maintain credibility in its role as a key currency in the medium and long run. However, price stability does not necessarily imply stability of the external value of the currency ('it takes two to tango').

Second, another responsibility of having a dominant international currency is that its issuer has to avoid a conflict between the provision of liquidity and the preservation of credibility. This conflict plagued the US dollar in the late 1960s and early 1970s until the breakdown of the Bretton Woods system in 1973 and has become known as the *Triffin dilemma* (see Triffin 1963). The United States had accepted a balance of payments deficit in order to provide liquidity to the world economy. This liquidity was supplied at the expense of the future convertibility of dollars in gold (because of the limited growth of the US gold reserves). However, if the US had conducted a policy of reducing the balance of payments deficit, it would have increased the credibility of the dollar as a key currency at the expense of the liquidity of the international monetary system. As the growth of international liquidity is a necessary condition for the development of world trade, such a policy would have hampered global economic growth seriously. So, a key currency has to be simultaneously scarce to preserve its credibility and abundant to provide liquidity. The Triffin dilemma is still relevant, because it emphasizes that when a national currency is used as a reserve currency in other countries, the responsible monetary authorities have to give up (at least partly) the control of their money supply. This is exactly the reason why the Bundesbank has resisted the use of the German mark as a reserve currency. The Bundesbank considered the costs of losing control of German money supply higher than the benefits of seigniorage or other advantages of a key currency.

Third, another responsibility of having an international currency, related to the former, is the readiness to act as a lender of last resort in international financial crises to bail out not only domestic but also foreign banks and other financial institutions.

Fourth, it is essential that the financial markets in the country or area issuing an international currency must be large, deep, and free of capital controls in order to reduce transaction costs as much as possible (Bergsten 1997).

7.1.4 The Role of the Euro as an International Currency

After discussing the functions of international money and the benefits and costs of having an international currency, we turn to the question whether or not the euro will become a dominant key currency on equal footing with the US dollar in the (near) future.

Let us start with the role of the euro as a reserve currency. Countries in Central and Eastern Europe and the CFA franc area (see Chapter 3) define their currencies in euro. However, Kenen (1995) expects that total reserve-currency holdings of euro may not be very big at first, compared with reserve holdings of the currencies, which are replaced by the euro. First, the share of various currencies in the total foreign exchange reserves of the developing countries has been fairly stable for many years and may not change (see Table 7.4). Second, the EMU countries will, of course, no

Table 7.4 Shares of Various Currencies in Total Foreign Exchange Reserves of Developing Countries (per cent)

	1981	1985	1989	1993	1997
US dollar	64.1	64.5	59.8	63.1	56.7
German mark	12.5	10.0	11.4	11.1	9.5
British pound	3.4	4.3	5.3	4.0	4.7
French franc	2.1	1.9	2.1	1.9	1.4
Japanese yen	4.9	6.9	6.6	7.6	4.4
Swiss franc	3.7	2.6	2.2	2.2	1.1

Source: International Monetary Fund, Annual Reports (1981–93).

longer need to hold other euro area currencies to support stable exchange rates. According to Kenen (1995), the excess reserves of EMU countries will eventually lead to financial instability in Europe. He argues that the ECB and its national central banks have three alternatives for eliminating the excess reserves, which will all cause financial instability since these reserves amount to about 4 per cent of European GDP. Changing the excess reserves into euros and allowing them to circulate in the European money markets would increase the money supply and, thus, the inflation in euroland. Sterilizing the excess reserves through open market operations by issuing bonds would raise the interest rate, strengthen the euro and, possibly, result in a recession. Changing the excess reserves into US dollars and keeping them with the E(S)CB, would depreciate the euro against the dollar and cause (imported) inflation.

Regarding the international role of the euro, we may distinguish two camps: the euro-enthusiasts and the euro-sceptics (*The Economist*, 14 Nov. 1998). On the one hand, we have the *euro-enthusiasts* (Bergsten, Hartmann, Portes, and Rey) arguing that the euro will be a stable and strong currency rapidly challenging the dominance of the dollar, because investors will diversify their portfolios from dollars into euros. These euro-enthusiasts envisage that this process of portfolio diversification will take place quickly in line with the speed in which the international financial markets develop. On the other hand, we have the *euro-sceptics* (Kenen, Feldstein, Summers, and other American economists) thinking that the euro will need to establish a track record before investors redress their portfolios and move into euros. The euro-sceptics believe that inertia in (reserve) diversification would spread this process over one or more decades. Analogous to the dominant position of the British pound as a key currency after the decline of Britain's economic hegemony, the US dollar could maintain its dominance for many years to come.

First, we turn to the euro-enthusiasts and discuss the reasons why the demand for euros might increase. Bergsten (1997) argues that European capital markets and financial systems will integrate rapidly for the following reasons: (1) the development of an efficient trans-border payment system (TARGET; see Box 15 in Chapter 3) connecting the existing financial centres; (2) the harmonization of European financial instruments inducing the most efficient means of financing; (3) the single monetary policy unifying European money markets and intensifying competition between banks and other financial institutions; (4) the increasing depth and liquidity of European financial markets; and (5) the elimination of exchange rate risk between EMU countries facilitating transactions and improving trade and investment. Bergsten expects the ECB to pursue a tight monetary policy and central banks and private investors to diversify their portfolios out of dollars and into euros. He predicts that ultimately 40 to 50 per cent of world financial assets will be denominated in US dollar, 30 to 40 per cent denominated in euro, and the remainder in Japanese yen and other currencies (British pound and Swiss franc). Bergsten expects a once-and-for-all portfolio shift of between 500 mrd and 1 trillion dollars into euros and, consequently, an appreciation of the euro against the dollar.

Portes and Rey (1998) are looking for a more solid theoretical and empirical basis for their analysis, which focuses on the means of payment and store of value functions of international money (see Table 7.4). Portes and Rey argue that the transaction costs of private and public use of the euro will be decisive for its role in international financial markets. Lower transaction costs in foreign exchange markets will increase the role of the euro as a currency for denominating trade (vehicle currency). Owing to the integration of European capital and securities markets, the depth and liquidity of these markets will increase leading to lower transaction costs and, thus, more investment in euros (investment currency). If further institutional changes in Europe's financial markets take place and if the UK—with its better developed capital markets—would adopt the euro, Portes and Rey reckon that the euro could challenge the US dollar sooner than expected. They analyse alternative steady-state scenarios for the role of the euro as an international means of payment and store of value: (1) the quasi status quo scenario in which the euro replaces the dollar as dominant currency for exchanges between the EU and Asian bloc but the dollar remains the vehicle currency on the foreign exchange markets; (2) the medium euro scenario in which the euro replaces the US dollar as the dominant currency for financial assets transactions except for transactions between the US and Asian bloc, but the dollar remains the vehicle currency on the foreign exchange market; and (3) the big euro scenario in which the euro takes on the role of vehicle currency for all transactions. Assessing the plausibility of those scenarios and the implications for economic efficiency and welfare, Portes and Rey conclude that the quasi status quo scenario is the most likely one for the euro.

Hartmann (1998) agrees with the predictions by Portes and Rey, but argues that existing theories of international money can only explain a small part of the functions of international money. He states that the most neglected function of international money is that of the forex vehicle currency. This and other mediums of exchange functions are characterized by the presence of network externalities driving towards concentration to one or a few dominant currencies. In contrast, investment currency theory predicts that optimal international portfolio choice will be geared to reaping the benefits of diversification. In this perspective, currency competition may therefore imply a friction between the medium of exchange and store of value functions. Hartmann tests the hypothesis of a long-run negative relationship between the volume of payments in a currency and its transaction costs which are measured by foreign exchange bid-ask spreads. A forex-dealer model integrating inventory and order processing costs is used to derive the long-run relationship between transaction costs, expected trading volume and expected exchange rate volatility. The latter variables are the two main determinants of costs in the foreign exchange market. Hartmann finds a negative relationship between the expected trading volume and transaction costs, but a positive one between expected exchange rate volatility and transaction costs.

Turning next to the euro-sceptics, we discuss the reasons why the demand for euros might not increase. Various American economists are quite sceptical about the international role of the euro. They point out that the euro has no proven track record as a stable currency, in particular in its function of a store of value. Apart from the arguments related to the use of the euro as reserve currency which were already outlined above, some additional arguments have been put forward to explain why the demand for euros will perhaps not increase very quickly.

First, major industrial countries, such as the United States and Japan, will swap their reserves denominated in EU currencies for euros. However, if the euro proves to be a strong and hence an expensive currency, they will not buy more euros than is necessary for portfolio diversification.

Second, because EMU currencies are withdrawn from circulation, risk-averse investors (central banks, firms, and individuals) will strive for keeping a sufficient degree of diversification requiring the holding of a variety of currencies. The reduction of the number of European currencies makes a switch to non-euro currencies likely in due time.

Box 32 Does EMU Lead to War?

Feldstein (1997) goes beyond the economic, financial, and monetary implications of the euro and discusses the political implications. EMU will change the political character of Europe in ways that could lead to conflicts in Europe and even to confrontations with the United States. According to Feldstein the most direct link between EMU and intra-European conflicts would be disagreement about the goals and methods of European monetary policy. The Maastricht Treaty transferred all responsibility for monetary policy-making from the national central banks to the ECB, which only controls the supply of euros and sets the short-term interest rate in euroland. The treaty made price stability the primary objective of the ECB, which is independent of all political control by the member states and European political institutions. These conditions, being very much what Germany wanted for the ECB, differ sharply from the opinions about monetary policy in France and other European countries. He predicts that when EMU proceeds, the independence of the ECB and the goals of monetary policy will become a source of serious conflict among member states. As EMU evolves into a more general political union, conflicts could arise from incompatible expectations about the sharing of power. France sees EMU and the resulting political union as a way of becoming a co-manager of Europe and an equal of Germany. The French may also hope that their natural Mediterranean allies, Italy and Spain, will give France a decisive influence on European policies. Feldstein even expects that 'skilful international French civil servants might come to dominate the administration of the European government' (Feldstein 1997; 5). It is clear that a French aspiration for equality and a German expectation of hegemony are not consistent and would lead to disagreements and conflicts when they could not be fulfilled. He sees war within Europe not as impossible because of conflicts over economic policies and interference with national sovereignty reinforcing long-standing animosities based on history, nationality, and religion. Germany's assertion that it should be contained within a European political union is itself a warning in this respect.

7.2 Co-ordination of Exchange Rate Policies

7.2.1 Instruments of Exchange Rate Policy

If the ECB wanted to conduct an exchange rate policy for the euro against any third currency, it could use the European money market interest rate to influence the nominal exchange rate of the euro given the foreign money market interest rate. For instance, the monetary authorities may be bound to an external or exchange rate policy as a consequence of exchange rate agreements on an international level, like the Plaza and Louvre agreements within the G5 and G7 respectively.[2] Central banks are then obliged to maintain some nominal exchange rates within an either implicitly or explicitly fixed band. Depending on the different degrees of commitment, they will realize this by (co-ordinated) foreign exchange market interventions and adjustment of the money market interest rates in the relevant countries. An increase (decrease) in the domestic money market interest rate relative to the foreign money market interest rate will result in an appreciation (depreciation) of its own currency against the foreign currency. However, the ECB uses its (inter-bank) money market interest rate also as an operational target of European monetary policy as well (see Table 3.5). Internal monetary policy implies that the central bank tries to influence money growth and (expected) inflation through an intermediary variable, namely: the (inter-bank) money market interest rate. The aim is to reduce (expand) the money supply by an increase (decrease) of the domestic money market interest rate. So there may arise a conflict between the internal and external monetary policy of the ECB. Depending on the desired direction within the framework of the internal and external track, four cases can be distinguished (see Table 7.5).

Table 7.5 Conflicts between the ECB's Internal and External Monetary Policies

Internal/external	ECB's exchange rate policy aimed at *appreciation* of Euro	ECB's exchange rate policy aimed at *depreciation* of Euro
ECB's *restrictive* money supply policy (*overshooting* of monetary target and/or expected inflation)	*No conflict*: internally and externally higher European money market interest rate	*Possible conflict*: internally higher, but externally lower European money market interest rate
ECB's *expansionary* money supply policy (*undershooting* of monetary target and/or expected inflation)	*Possible conflict*: internally lower, but externally higher European money market interest rate	*No conflict*: internally and externally lower European money market interest rate

[2] The possibility of these exchange rate agreements on a G3 level (euroland, Japan, and the United States), in particular target zones for G3 currencies, will be discussed in the next subsection.

Table 7.5 shows that there will only be a possible conflict between the ECB's money supply policy and its exchange rate policy in two out of the four cases distinguished there. It will be clear that the occurrence of a conflict between the internal and external track not only depends on the extent to which the ECB's exchange rate policy is bound to certain preconditions, but also on the openness and relative size of euroland's economy.

Evidently, the probability that the ECB's exchange rate policy will conflict with its ultimate objective of price stability is quite high. Then, the only remaining instrument of exchange rate policy will be the use of (co-ordinated) foreign exchange market intervention to influence the external value of the euro against third currencies.

7.2.2 Effectiveness of Foreign Exchange Intervention

A purchase (sale) of foreign exchange by a central bank leads, *ceteris paribus*, to an increase (decrease) in the reserve position of the private banking system as a whole. The induced loosening (tightening) of the domestic money market results in an increase (decrease) in the money stock. Depreciation (appreciation) of the domestic currency is the immediate consequence of the intervention in the forex market. To prevent the money stock from increasing (decreasing) monetary authorities can *sterilize* the effect of the exchange market intervention by selling (buying) short-term domestic assets to (from) the banking system, leaving the monetary base of the country unchanged.

Theoretically, sterilized purchases and sales of foreign exchange can have an impact on the exchange rate. Loopesko (1984) distinguishes three possible channels. According to the *portfolio-balance channel*, it is assumed that risk-averse wealth holders diversify their portfolios across assets denominated in different currencies. Suppose that wealth holders do not view otherwise identical government bonds denominated in currency A and currency B as perfect substitutes. A disturbance of the portfolio-balance caused by a sterilized purchase of currency B by the central bank of country A will, *ceteris paribus*, lead to a rise in the spot exchange rate (s_t) of currency B in terms of currency A.

The level of the risk premium on government bonds denominated in currency B (RP_t^B) can be defined as:

$$RP_t^B = (i_B - i_A)_t - (s_t - E_t s_{t+1}) \tag{7.1}$$

The sale of short-term government bonds denominated in currency A, necessary to leave the monetary base in country A unchanged, induces a rise in i_A and an excess demand for foreign securities by the investors who try to rebalance their portfolios. However, an inducement to switch their assets denominated in currency A for assets denominated in currency B is required. A depreciation of currency A in terms of currency B restores portfolio-balance by lowering the risk premium on government bonds denominated in currency B, and by increasing the value of government bonds denominated in currency B in terms of currency A.

Besides the portfolio-balance channel, two other channels exist through which sterilized interventions can affect the exchange rate. The *market-efficiency channel* implies that the central bank can '[focus] the attention of the public on neglected information that is germane to exchange rate determination' (ibid. 258). It must be noted that in our opinion it is very hard for the central bankers to pinpoint market inefficiencies with certainty. According to the *superior-information channel*, the central bank may provide the market with new information or a signal about the future course of the exchange rate or of monetary policy. The exchange rate can then be expected to change immediately after the intervention. Notably, supporters of the asset market view of exchange rates see this as the main channel through which interventions can affect the exchange rate (see, for example, Dominguez and Frankel 1993).

The effectiveness of interventions via the portfolio-balance channel has diminished owing to the enormous growth in financial market turnovers during the last decades. As argued before, the portfolio-balance channel can only be effective if the risk premium (RP_t^B) in equation (7.1) does not equal zero. Problems arise, however, when one wants to calculate the risk premium. Various attempts have been made using different kinds of expectations formations. Another complication lies in the fact that the effect of central bank interventions is absorbed in the movements of the exchange rate immediately. To get a clear view of the actual effectiveness one should be able to compare these movements with the fluctuations in the exchange rate that would have occurred in the absence of intervention. Furthermore, it can be argued that the estimations are rather partial as most of the time intervention will be accompanied by other measures of monetary policy (for instance, interest rate policy).

In general, no systematic effect of sterilized intervention via the portfolio-balance channel is found implying that interventions do not constitute an independent tool of monetary policy (for an overview see Edison 1993). Only official exchange market operations which create expectations of changes in monetary policy or which embody another sufficient 'news'-content appear to have a chance of affecting the exchange rate significantly. Several attempts have been made to detect the components of which the announcement effect is made up. In this context the effectiveness of interventions carried out after a certain period with no interventions and co-ordinated intervention is investigated. The results are rather mixed, indicating, perhaps, that whether or not market participants pay attention to the interventions also depends on the availability of other 'news'. Furthermore, statements of politicians and monetary authorities which accompany the intervention can lend support to or detract from its effectiveness (see also Eijffinger 1999).

The general conclusion is that the effectiveness of foreign exchange intervention is quite limited given the foreign exchange reserves of the central banks concerned. So one might wonder why central banks still intervene in the foreign exchange market. The answer has to do with the ownership of the foreign exchange account in the relevant countries. For example, the foreign exchange account in Japan is not owned by the Bank of Japan but by the Japanese Ministry of Finance. This can explain why the monetary authorities in Japan have intervened so often in foreign exchange markets. In the United States, both the Federal Reserve System (Board of Governors and the Federal Reserve Bank of New York) and the Treasury are owners of the foreign exchange account. Therefore, in case of foreign exchange intervention both monetary authorities have to agree. If they agree, the Federal Reserve Bank of New York will conduct the foreign exchange intervention. Until January 1999 the Deutsche Bundesbank was the sole owner of the foreign exchange account in Germany. The German central bank gave priority to its ultimate objective of price stability. This explained why the Bundesbank has always been very reluctant to intervene in the foreign exchange market. However, there were times when the Bundesbank was—despite its scepticism regarding foreign exchange intervention—towed along with other G3 and G7 central banks in co-ordinated interventions. The position of the European (System of) Central Bank(s) is rather comparable with that of the Bundesbank before January 1999. The E(S)CB has only price stability as its ultimate objective and gives, thus, priority to the internal track of monetary policy. Furthermore, the E(S)CB owns the foreign exchange account solely and is not obliged to agree with the Ecofin about decisions to intervene or not. This will make the E(S)CB probably quite restrictive in its intervention policy.

7.2.3 Target Zones for Exchange Rates

Under a system of target zones, governments set a level for the exchange rate between two currencies and a (maximum) fluctuation margin around this level. They promise to use money market interest rates and/or foreign exchange interventions to keep the exchange rate on track (that is, within the fluctuation margin agreed upon). If target zones are explicitly formulated, then they constitute a strong commitment of the respective governments to a target for the exchange rate and are subject to the possible conflicts with the internal monetary policy of the central banks involved. In case of an implicit target zone, the foreign exchange markets will certainly test the intervention limits informally set by the governments and will either become obsolete or explicit target zones, which have to be defended by their central banks.

Three objections can be raised against target zones. First, a conflict with the internal monetary policies of central banks may arise. Second, the limited effectiveness of central bank interventions in today's foreign exchange markets as described before undermines target zones. Finally, one could question whether governments are able to determine target (equilibrium) exchange rates anyhow. Given the divergent business cycles and/or political cycles in the respective countries, it seems hard, if not impossible, to determine target levels for exchange rates for a longer period of time.

These objections have not impeded some academics and politicians from advocating the establishment of target zones for G3 currencies (US dollar, German mark, and Japanese yen) in the past. One of the leading advocates of target zones over the years has been John Williamson (see, among others, Williamson 1994). He favours a system of a *crawling band (peg)*. Such systems use target zones that are relatively wide, that is allowing the exchange rate to vary by, for example, plus and minus 10 per cent around a central rate. More crucially, these crawling bands move according to rules announced in advance. They take account of differences in inflation between countries. If one country has higher inflation than its trading partners, its currency band should be lowered to facilitate a gradual depreciation of its currency. This would keep the real exchange rate steady despite the fluctuations of the nominal exchange rate within the band itself. A crawling band cannot bring inflation down if inflation is already high in a country, although it might cause a gradual real appreciation providing some restraint on inflation. The aim of a crawling band is, however, to avoid big misalignments between currencies which may jeopardize international trade between countries.

Very soon after the start of EMU, various politicians worried about the euro–dollar exchange rate (see also Box 9 in Chapter 1). Still, the ECB did not intervene in the exchange market as it did not share these worries. Was the ECB right?

Fig. 7.1 shows the development of the (synthetic) nominal euro–US dollar rate during the period January 1980 to June 1999. Of course, the euro came into existence at 1 January 1999 as a currency. Nevertheless, because one euro had to be equivalent in value to one ECU at the eve of 31 December 1998, one can calculate a *synthetic* exchange rate for the period before 1 January 1999. This can be done on the basis of the (fixed) amount of each EU currency participating in ERM I and the ECU basket and their bilateral (market) exchange rates vis-à-vis the US dollar. The fall of the dollar with interruptions from its maximum level of 3.47 German marks on 26 December 1985 to its minimum level of 1.58 German marks as a consequence of the *Plaza agreement* (Sept. 1985) is also clearly reflected in the synthetic euro–dollar rate. The same applies to the *Louvre agreement* of 22 February 1987 on closer co-operation between the monetary authorities of the G7 countries to foster stability of exchange rates.

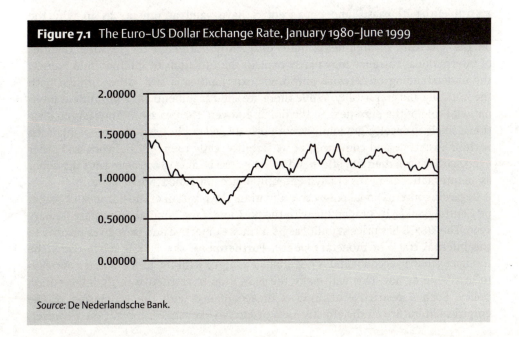

Figure 7.1 The Euro–US Dollar Exchange Rate, January 1980–June 1999

Source: De Nederlandsche Bank.

Looking to the most recent period, it becomes evident that the euro lost more than 10 per cent of its value vis-à-vis the dollar since its introduction and was at the time of writing almost approaching parity. Although the depreciation of the euro was unexpected by many, it was not unwelcome from the point of view of the business cycle situation in the euro area. The current weakness of the euro is certainly not unprecedented if considering the synthetic euro–dollar rate before January 1999. At the end of 1985 the synthetic euro was worth less than 0.7 US dollars. The recent decline in the external value of the euro can be mostly explained by conventional economic fundamentals, such as divergent cyclical developments between the US and the euro area. Other factors also played a role, like the ECB's policy response to the unexpected weakness of euro area economic activity (including the first formal interest rate cut by the ECB on 8 April 1999). Last but not least, squabbles in the first months of 1999 about possible 'exchange rate orientations' by the Council of Ministers to the ECB Governing Council perhaps also played some role in reducing the confidence of the financial markets in the euro (see Box 33). Despite an agreement to desist from exchange rate orientations except under 'exceptional circumstances', it is not clear who determines when circumstances are exceptional and there is still the possibility that this agreement, not being part of the Treaty, can be revoked at any moment by the Council of Ministers.

7.3 Conclusion

BOTH euro-enthusiasts and euro-sceptics have valid arguments as to why the demand for euros might or might not increase. It is clear that they put weight on the spectrum of arguments quite differently. Although the existing theories of international currency may partly explain the functions of international money, the understanding of network and other externalities is still rather limited both theoretically and empirically. While there are solid arguments for a prominent international role of the euro next to the dollar and yen, the process of internationalization is likely to develop gradually as both private and public users become acquainted with its existence and convinced of its stability. Only then will network and other externalities have their full effect and will the euro be able to compete with the dollar as an international means of payment, unit of account, and store of value.

Regarding international policy co-ordination, the position of the European (System of) Central Bank(s) is comparable with the position of the Bundesbank before January 1999. The E(S)CB has price stability as its ultimate objective and thus gives priority to the internal track of monetary policy. Furthermore, the E(S)CB solely owns the foreign exchange account and is not obliged to agree with the Ecofin about a decision to intervene or not. This will make the E(S)CB quite restrictive in its intervention policy. Such a restrictive attitude is in accordance with the conclusion of the empirical literature on the effectiveness of foreign exchange intervention. However,

Box 33 Target Zones for the Euro?

The idea of target zones, championed by Fred Bergsten and John Williamson of the Institute for International Economics in Washington, DC, is not new and comes up at least once every decade. At the end of 1998 it was the turn of Oskar Lafontaine, Germany's then new minister of Finance. Supported by his French colleague, Dominique Strauss-Kahn, he accused the ECB of not taking account of economic growth and employment in euroland. Furthermore, he proposed target zones for the G3 currencies and, in particular, between the euro and dollar. Apparently, his aim was to get a grip on European monetary policy through the back door of exchange rate arrangements, which are the prerogative of the *euro-11-council*, euroland's ministers of Finance. According to the Maastricht Treaty, 'In the absence of an exchange rate system in relation to one or more non-Community currencies . . . the Council, acting by a qualified majority either on a recommendation from the Commission and after consulting the ECB, or on a recommendation from the ECB, may formulate general orientations for exchange rate policy in relation to these currencies. These general orientations shall be without prejudice to the primary objective of the ESCB to maintain price stability'. This article may be considered to be the Achilles' heel of the Maastricht Treaty because it could very well conflict with the ECB's mandate to achieve price stability. A commitment for the ECB to stabilize the euro against the dollar (and yen) by formal target zones will certainly undermine its stability-oriented internal monetary policy. The idea was therefore immediately rejected by a chorus of leading central bankers on both sides of the Atlantic. Not only the president of the ECB, Wim Duisenberg, denounced such target zones, but also Alan Greenspan, the chairman of the Federal Reserve System. Eddie George, governor of the Bank of England, observed that narrow target zones break down and wide ones are useless. It is obvious that Lafontaine wanted to put the ECB under pressure by proposing target zones. However, under a target zone system both exchange rate policy and money supply policy are operationally indivisible: they are two sides of the same coin. Therefore, external and internal monetary policy should be in the hands of the ECB. Although the discussion about target zones is a repetition of the old arguments, it has uncovered a major design flaw in the Maastricht Treaty.

international monetary co-operation sometimes implies that policy-makers meet halfway and, thereby, cannot stick to their preferred habitat despite the soundness of their arguments. In years to come, the E(S)CB will probably find out that international policy co-ordination is a matter of second-best and third-best solutions.

References

Advisory Commission on Intergovernmental Relations (1997), *Significant Features of Fiscal Federalism*, ii (Washington, DC ACIR).

Alberola, E., and T. Tyrväinen (1998), 'Is There Scope for Inflation Differentials in EMU? An Empirical Evaluation of the Balassa–Samuelson Model in EMU Countries', *Bank of Finland Discussion Paper*, 15.

Alesina, A. (1989), 'Politics and Business Cycles in Industrial Democracies', *Economic Policy*, 8: 55–98.

—— V. Grilli, and G. M. Milesi-Ferretti (1994), 'The Political Economy of Capital Controls', in L. Leiderman and A. Razin (eds.), *Capital Mobility: The Impact on Consumption, Investment and Growth* (Cambridge, Cambridge University Press).

—— and R. Perotti (1995*a*), 'The Political Economy of Budget Deficits', *IMF Staff Papers*, 42: 1–31.

—— and —— (1995*b*), 'Fiscal Expansions and Adjustments in OECD Countries', *Economic Policy*, 21: 207–48.

Alogoskoufis, G., and R. Portes (1991), 'International Costs and Benefits from EMU', in European Commission, *European Economy*, Spec. Edn. 1.

—— and R. Smith (1991), 'The Phillips Curve, the Persistence of Inflation, and the Lucas Critique: Evidence from Exchange Rate Regimes', *American Economic Review*, 81: 1254–75.

Amtenbrink, F. (1999), *The Democratic Accountability of Central Banks* (London, Hart).

Anderton, R., and R. Barrell (1995), 'The ERM and Structural Change in European Labour Markets', *Weltwirtschaftliches Archiv*, 131: 47–66.

Angeloni, I. (1999), 'Comments on The Role of a Regional Bank in a System of Central Banks', *Carnegie-Rochester Conference Series on Public Policy*, forthcoming.

Arnold, I. (1994), 'The Myth of a Stable European Money Demand', *Open Economies Review*, 5: 245–59.

—— (1999), 'The Third Leg of the Stool. Financial Stability as a Prerequisite for EMU', *Weltwirtschaftliches Archiv*, 135(2): 280–305.

—— and J. J. G. Lemmen (1999) 'The Vulnerability of Banks to Government Default Risk in the EMU', FMG Special Paper 115.

Artis, M., and W. Zhang (1997), 'International Business Cycles and the ERM: Is There a European Business Cycle?', *International Journal of Finance and Economics*, 2: 1–16.

—— and —— (1999), 'Further Evidence on International Business Cycles and the ERM: Is There a European Business Cycle?', *Oxford Economic Papers*, 51: 120–32.

Asdrubali, P., B. E. Sørensen, and O. Yosha (1996), 'Channels of Interstate Risk Sharing: United States 1963-1990', *Quarterly Journal of Economics*, 111: 1081–110.

Athanasoulis, S., and E. van Wincoop (1998), 'Risksharing Within the United States: What Have Financial Markets and Fiscal Federalism Accomplished?', Research Paper 9808 (New York, Federal Reserve Bank of New York).

Atkeson, A., and T. Bayoumi (1993), 'Do Private Capital Markets Insure Regional Risk? Evidence from the United States and Europe', *Open Economies Review*, 4: 303–24.

Bade, R., and M. Parkin (1988), 'Central Bank Laws and Monetary Policy', unpub. MS, University of Western Ontario.

Bank for International Settlements (1995), *Financial Structure and the Monetary Policy Transmission Mechanism* (Basle, BIS).

Barro, R. J. (1997), *Determinants of Economic Growth* (Cambridge, Mass., MIT Press).

—— and D. Gordon (1983), 'Rules, Discretion, and Reputation in a Positive

Model of Monetary Policy', *Journal of Monetary Economics*, 12: 101–21.

Bayoumi, T., and B. Eichengreen (1994), 'One Money or Many? Analyzing the Prospects for Monetary Unification in Various Parts of the World', *Princeton Studies in International Finance*, 76.

—— and P. R. Masson (1995), 'Fiscal Flows in the United States and Canada: Lessons for Monetary Union in Europe', *European Economic Review*, 39: 253–74.

Berger, A. N., R. S. Demsetz, and P. E. Strahan (1998), 'The Consolidation of the Financial Services Industry: Causes, Consequences, and Implications for the Future' (New York, Federal Reserve Bank of New York).

Berger, H., and A. Ritschl (1995), 'Germany and the Political Economy of the Marshall Plan, 1947–51', in B. Eichengreen (ed.), *Europe's Post-War Recovery* (Cambridge, Cambridge University Press).

—— and J. de Haan, and S. C. W. Eijffinger (2000), 'Central Bank Independence: An Update of Theory and Evidence', *CEPR Discussion Paper*, 2353.

Bergin, P., and M. Moersch (1997), 'EMU and Outsiders: Fixed versus Flexible Exchange Rates', in P. J. J. Welfens (ed.), *European Monetary Union: Transition, International Impacts and Policy Options* (Berlin, Springer).

Bergsten, C. F. (1997), 'The Dollar and the Euro', *Foreign Affairs*, 76(4).

Bernanke, B., and M. Gertler (1995), 'Inside the Black Box: The Credit Channel of Monetary Transmission Mechanism', *Journal of Economic Perspectives*, 9: 27–49.

—— T. Laubach, F. Mishkin, and A. Posen (1998), *Inflation Targeting* (Princeton, NJ, Princeton University Press).

Berthold, N., and R. Fehn (1998), 'Does EMU Provide Labour-Market Reform?' *Kyklos*, 51(4): 509–36.

Bini Smaghi (1994), 'EMS Discipline: Did it Contribute to Inflation Convergence?', *Banca Nazionale del Lavoro Quarterly Review*, 189: 187–97.

Bishop, G. P. (1998), *Securitising European Savings*, Salomon Smith Barney (Dec. 1998).

—— (1999), 'New Capital Market Opportunities in Euroland', *EIB Papers*, 4(1): 35–45.

Bohn, H., and R. Inman (1996), 'Balanced-budget Rules and Public Deficits: Evidence from the US States', *Carnegie-Rochester Conference Series on Public Policy*, 45: 13–84.

Britton, E., and J. Whitley (1997), 'Comparing the Monetary Transmission Mechanism in France, Germany and the United Kingdom: Some Issues and Results', *Bank of England Quarterly Review*, 37(2).

Brookes, M. (1998), 'The Impact of EMU on Portfolio Management', *EIB Papers*, 4(1): 19–33.

Browne, F., G. Fagan, and J. Henry (1997), 'Money Demand in EU Countries: A Survey', *European Monetary Institute Staff Paper*.

Buiter, W., G. Corsetti, and N. Roubini (1993), 'Excessive Deficits: Sense and Nonsense in the Treaty of Maastricht', *Economic Policy*, 16: 58–90.

Bulmer, S. (1994), 'History and Institutions of the European Union', in M. Artis and N. Lee (eds.), *The Economics of the European Union* (Oxford, Oxford University Press).

Bundesverband Öffentlicher Banken Deutschlands (1997), *Auf dem Weg zur EWWU*, 2.

Burda, M. C. (1999), 'European Labour Markets and the Euro: How Much Flexibility Do We Really Need?' mimeo.

Buti, M., and A. Sapir (eds.) (1998), *Economic Policy in EMU* (Oxford, Clarendon Press).

Calmfors, Lars (1998*a*), 'Macroeconomic Policy, Wage Setting and Employment—What Difference does EMU Make?', *Oxford Review of Economic Policy*, 14: 125–51.

—— (1998*b*), 'Unemployment, Labour-Market Reform and Monetary Union', *IIES Seminar Paper*, 639.

Casella, A. (1999), 'Tradable Deficit Permits', *Economic Policy*, 29: 323–61.

Cecchetti, S. G. (1999), 'Legal Structure, Financial Structure, and the Monetary Policy Transmission Mechanism', *Federal Reserve Bank of New York, Economic Policy Review*, 5/2: 9–28.

Chand, S., and A. Jaeger (1996), 'Ageing Populations and Public Pension Schemes', *IMF Occasional Paper*, 147.

Christodoulakis, N., S. Dimelis, and T. Kollintzas (1995) 'Comparisons of Business Cycles in Greece and the EC: Idiosyncrasies and Regularities', *Economica*, 62: 1–28

Cohen, B. J. (1971), *The Future of Sterling as an International Currency* (London, Macmillan).

—— (1997), 'The Political Economy of Currency Regions', in H. Milner (ed.), *The Political Economy of Regionalism* (New York, Columbia University Press).

Cohen, D., and C. Wyplosz (1989), 'The European Monetary Union: An Agnostic Evaluation', in R. C. Bryant, *et al.* (eds.), *Macroeconomic Policies in an Interdependent World* (Washington, DC, Brookings Institution).

Collins, S. M. (1988), 'Inflation and the European Monetary System', in F. Giavazzi, *et al.* (eds.), *The European Monetary System* (Cambridge, Cambridge University Press).

Courchene, T. (1993), 'Reflections on Canadian Federalism: Are There Implications for European Economic and Monetary Union?', in The Economics of Community Public Finance, *European Economy*, 5.

Cukierman, A. (1992), *Central Bank Strategy, Credibility, and Independence* (Cambridge, Mass, MIT Press).

—— (1995), 'Towards a Systematic Comparison Between Inflation Targets and Monetary Targets', in L. Leiderman and L. E. O. Svensson (eds.), *Inflation Targets* (London, CEPR).

Davis, E. P. (1999), 'Pension Fund Reform and European Financial Markets—A Reappraisal of Potential Effects in the Wake of EMU', in S. C. W. Eijffinger, K. Koedijk, M. Pagano, and R. Portes (eds.), *The Changing European Financial Landscape*, CEPR/ESI conference 1998 (London, Centre for Economic Policy Research).

Debelle, G., and S. Fischer (1995), 'How Independent Should a Central Bank Be?',

in J. C. Fuhrer (ed.), *Goals, Guidelines and Constraints Facing Monetary Policymakers*, Federal Reserve Bank of Boston, Conference Series, 38.

Decressin, J., and A. Fatás (1995), 'Regional Labor Market Dynamics in Europe' *European Economic Review*, 39: 1627–55.

De Grauwe, P. (1996), 'The Economics of Convergence: Towards Monetary Union in Europe', *Weltwirtschaftliches Archiv*, 132: 1–27.

—— (1997), *The Economics of Monetary Integration* (Oxford, Oxford University Press).

—— and W. Vanhaverbeke (1993), 'Is Europe an Optimal Currency Area? Evidence from Regional Data', in P. Masson and M. Taylor (eds.), *Policy Issues in the Operation of Currency Unions* (Cambridge, Cambridge University Press).

De Haan, J., F. Amtenbrink, and S. C. W. Eijffinger (1999), 'Accountability of Central Banks: Aspects and Quantification', *Banca Nazionale del Lavaro Quarterly Review*, 209, 169–93.

—— and J.-E. Sturm (1999), 'Do Financial Markets and the Maastricht Treaty Discipline Governments? New Evidence', *Applied Financial Economics* (forthcoming).

Deutsche Bundesbank (1996), *Annual Report 1995* (Frankfurt-am-Main).

Dominguez, K. M., and J. A. Frankel (1993), *Does Foreign Exchange Intervention Work?* (Washington, DC, Institute for International Economics).

Dornbusch, R., C. Favero, and F. Giavazzi (1998), 'Immediate Challenges for the ECB: Issues in Formulating a Single Monetary Policy', *Economic Policy*, 26: 15–64.

Duisenberg, W. F. (1998), 'Die internationale Rolle des Euros', Vortrag bei der Konrad-Adenauer Stiftung, 22 Oct. 1998, Berlin.

Edison, H. J. (1993), 'The Effectiveness of Central-Bank Intervention: A Survey of the Literature after 1982', *Princeton Special Papers in International Economics*, 18.

Eichengreen, B. (1991), 'Is Europe an Optimal Currency Area?', *NBER Working Paper*, 3579.

—— (1998), 'European Monetary Unification: A Tour d'Horizon', *Oxford Review of Economic Policy*, 14(3): 24–40.

—— and J. von Hagen (1995), 'Fiscal Policy and Monetary Union: Federalism, Fiscal Restrictions and the No-bailout Rule', *CEPR Discussion Paper*, 1247.

—— and C. Wyplosz (1993), 'The Unstable EMS', *Brookings Papers on Economic Activity*, 1: 51–124.

—— and C. Wyplosz (1998), 'The Stability Pact: More than a Nuisance?', *Economic Policy*, 26: 65–113.

Eijffinger, S. C. W. (1996), *Future European Monetary Policy*, Inaugural Lecture at the Humboldt University of Berlin.

—— (ed.) (1999), *Foreign Exchange Intervention: Objectives and Effectiveness* (Cheltenham, Edward Elgar Publishing Ltd).

—— and J. de Haan (1996), 'The Political Economy of Central-Bank Independence', *Princeton Special Papers in International Economics*, 19.

—— and M. M. Hoeberichts (1998), 'The Trade Off between Central Bank Independence and Conservativeness', *Oxford Economic Papers*, 50: 397–411.

—— and E. Schaling (1993), 'Central Bank Independence in Twelve Industrial Countries', *Banca Nazionale del Lavoro Quarterly Review*, 184, 1–41.

Egebo, T., and A. S. Englander (1992), 'Institutional Commitments and Policy Credibility: A Critical Survey and Empirical Evidence from the ERM', *OECD Economic Studies*, 18, 45–84.

Emerson, M., D. Gros, A. Italianer, J. Pisani-Ferry, and H. Reichenbach (1992), *One Market, One Money* (Oxford, Oxford University Press).

Epstein, G. A., and J. B. Schor (1992), 'Structural Determinants and Economic Effects of Capital Controls in OECD Countries', in T. Banuri and J. B. Schor (eds.), *Financial Openness and National Autonomy, Opportunities and Constraints* (Oxford, Clarendon Press).

European Central Bank (1998), *The Single Monetary Policy in Stage Three: General Documentation on ESCB Monetary Policy Instruments and Procedures*, Frankfurt-am-Main (Sept. 1998).

—— (1999), *Possible Effects of EMU on the EU Banking Systems in the Medium to Long Run* (Frankfurt-am-Main).

European Commission, (1993), Stable Money—Sound Finances, *European Economy*, 53.

—— (1995), 'The Impact of Exchange-rate Movements on Trade within the Single Market', *European Economy—Reports and Studies 4.*

—— (1996), 'Economic Evaluation of the Internal Market', *European Economy—Reports and Studies*, 4.

—— (1997), *Agenda 2000 For a Stronger and Wider Union*, Bulletin of the European Union, suppl. 5/97.

—— (1998a), 'European Public Finance' (Begrotingsvademecum).

—— (1998b), 'Financing the European Union'. Commission Report on the Operation of the Own Resources System.

European Federation for Retirement Provision (1996), 'European Pension Funds, their Impact on Capital Markets and Competitiveness' (Brussels, European Federation for Retirement Provision).

European Monetary Institute (1997), *The Single Monetary Policy in Stage Three: General Documentation on ESCB Monetary Policy Instruments and Procedures* (Frankfurt-am-Main).

Fatás, A. (1997), 'EMU: Countries or Regions? Lessons from the EMS Experience', *European Economic Review* 41: 743–51.

—— (1998), 'Does EMU Need a Fiscal Federation?', *Economic Policy*, 26: 165–203.

Feldstein, M. (1997), 'EMU and International Conflict', *Foreign Affairs*, 76(6).

—— (1999), *Costs and Benefits of Price Stability* (Chicago, University of Chicago Press).

—— and C. Horioka (1980), 'Domestic Savings and International Capital Flows', *Economic Journal*, 90: 314–29.

Folkerts-Landau, D., and P. Garber (1992), 'The ECB: A Bank or a Monetary Policy Rule?', in M. B. Canzoneri, V. Grilli, and P. R. Masson (eds.), *Establishing a Central Bank: Issues in Europe and Lessons from the US* (Cambridge, Cambridge University Press).

Forder, J. (1996), 'On the Assessment and Implementation of "Institutional" Remedies', *Oxford Economic Papers*, 48: 39–51.

Frankel, J. A. (1989), 'Quantifying International Capital Mobility in the 1980s', *NBER Working Paper*, 2856.

—— and A. T. MacArthur (1988), 'Political vs Currency Premia in International Real Interest Differentials: A Study of Forward Rates for 24 Countries', *European Economic Review*, 32: 1083–121.

—— S. Phillips, and M. Chinn (1993), 'Financial and Currency Integration in the European Monetary System, the Statistical Record', in F. Torres and F. Giavazzi (eds.), *Adjustment and Growth in the European Monetary Union* (Cambridge, Cambridge University Press).

—— and A. R. Rose (1996), 'The Endogeneity of the Optimum Currency Criteria', *NBER Working Paper*, 5700.

Fratianni, M., and J. von Hagen (1992), *The European Monetary System and European Monetary Union* (Boulder, Colo., Westview).

Freedman, C. (1994), 'Formal Targets for Inflation Reduction: The Canadian Experience', in J. A. H. de Beaufort Wijnholds, S. C. W. Eijffinger, and L. H. Hoogduin (eds.), *A Framework for Monetary Stability* (Dordrecht, Boston, and London, Kluwer Academic Publishers).

Frey, B. S. (1998), 'The Case for Tax Competition in the EU', in Austrian Federal Ministry of Finance, Conference Proceedings, *Tax Competition and Co-ordination of Tax Policy in the European Union* (Vienna, Austrian Institute of Economic Research).

—— and R. Eichenberger (1996), 'To Harmonize or to Compete? That's Not the Question', *Journal of Public Economics*, 60: 335–49.

Gerlach, S., and F. Smets (1995), 'The Monetary Transmission: Evidence from G-7 Countries', *CEPR Discussion Paper*, 1219.

Giavazzi, F., and M. Pagano (1988), 'The Advantage of Tying One's Hands', *European Economic Review*, 32: 1055–75.

—— and —— (1990), 'Can Severe Fiscal Adjustments be Expansionary?', *NBER Macroeconomics Annual* (Cambridge, Mass, MIT Press).

—— and L. Spaventa (1990), 'The "New" EMS', in P. de Grauwe and L. Papademos (eds.), *The European Monetary System in the 1990s* (London, Longman).

Goodhart, C., and D. Schoenmaker (1995), 'Should the Functions of Monetary Policy and Banking Supervision be Separated?', *Oxford Economic Papers*, 47: 539–60.

Goodman, S. F. (1996), *The European Union* (London, Macmillan).

Grilli, V., D. Masciandaro, and G. Tabellini (1991), 'Political and Monetary Institutions and Public Financial Policies in the Industrial Countries', *Economic Policy*, 13: 341–92.

—— and G. M. Milesi-Ferretti (1995), 'Economic Effects and Structural Determinants of Capital Controls', *IMF Staff Papers*, 42(3): 517–51.

Gros, D., and N. Thygesen (1998), *European Monetary Integration* (London, Longman).

Gwartney, J., R. Lawson, and W. Block (1996). *Economic Freedom in the World, 1975–1995* (Vancouver, Fraser Institute).

Hartmann, P. (1998), *Currency Competition and Foreign Exchange Markets* (Cambridge, Cambridge University Press).

Helg, R., P. Manasse, T. Monacelli, and R. Rovelli (1995), 'How Much (A)symmetry in Europe? Evidence from Industrial Sectors', *European Economic Review*, 39: 1017–41.

Hochreiter, E., and G. Winckler (1995), 'The Advantage of Tying Austria's Hands: The Success of the Hard Currency Strategy', *European Journal of Political Economy*, 11: 83–111.

Hoeller, P., M.-O. Louppe, and P. Vergriete (1996), 'Fiscal Relations within the European Union', *OECD Economics Department, Working Paper*, 163.

Holmes, K. R., B. T. Johnson, and M. Kirkpatrick (1998), *1998 Index of Economic Freedom* (Washington, DC and New York, Heritage Foundation and Wall Street Journal).

Houben, A. C. F. J. (1999) 'The Evolution of Monetary Strategies in Europe', Ph.D. thesis, University of Groningen.

Huizinga, H. P., and S. B. Nielsen (1997), 'The Taxation of Interest in Europe: A Minimum Withholding Tax?', in S. C. W. Eijffinger and K. Koedijk (eds.), *The German Economy and the European Union* (Berlin, European Summer Institute).

Hurst, C., E. Perée, and M. Fischbach (1999), 'On the Road to Wonderland? Bank Restructuring after EMU', *EIB Papers*, 4(1): 83–103.

Inman, R. P. (1996) 'Do Balanced Budget Rules Work? U.S. Experience and Possible Lessons for the EMU', *NBER Working Paper*, 5838.

Issing, O. (1994), 'Monetary Policy Strategy in the EMU', in J. A. H. de Beaufort Wijnholds, S. C. W. Eijffinger, and L. H. Hoogduin (eds.), *A Framework for Monetary Stability* (Dordrecht, Boston and London, Kluwer Academic Publishers), 135–48.

Italianer, A., and M. Vanheukelen (1993), 'Proposals for Community Stabilization Mechanism: Some Historical Applications', in The Economics of Community Public Finance, *European Economy*, 5.

Jensen, H. (1997), 'Credibility of Optimal Monetary Delegation', *American Economic Review*, 87(5): 911–20.

Keen, M., and S. Smith (1996), 'The Future of Value Added Tax in the European Union', *Economic Policy*, 23: 375–420.

Kenen, P. (1969), 'The Theory of Optimum Currency Areas: An Eclectic View', in R. Mundell and A. Swoboda (eds.), *Monetary Problems of the International Economy* (Chicago, University of Chicago Press).

—— (1995), *Economic and Monetary Union in Europe* (Cambridge, Cambridge University Press).

Kiyotaki, N., and J. Moore (1997), 'Credit Cycles', *Journal of Political Economy*, 105: 211–48.

Koedijk, K., and J. J. M. Kremers (1996), 'Market Opening, Regulation and Growth in Europe', *Economic Policy*, 23: 443–67.

Krugman, P. (1989), *Exchange Rate Instability* (Cambridge, Mass., MIT Press).

—— (1991), *Geography and Trade* (Cambridge, Mass., MIT Press).

Kuhlmann, M. J. (1993), 'Community Loan and Loan Related Instruments', in The Economics of Community Public Finance, *European Economy*, 5.

Kydland, F. W., and E. C. Prescott (1977), 'Rules Rather than Discretion: The Inconsistency of the Optimal Plans', *Journal of Political Economy*, 85: 473–91.

Laffan, B. (1998), *The Finances of the European Union* (London, MacMillan Press).

Lannoo, K. (1999), 'Financial Supervision in EMU', CEPS.

La Porta, R., F. Lopez-de-Silanes, A. Shleifer, and R. Vishny (1997), 'Legal Determinants of External Finance', *Journal of Finance*, 52: 1131–50.

—— —— —— and —— (1998), 'Law and Finance', *Journal of Political Economy*, 106: 1113–55.

Lemmen, J. J. G. (1998a), 'Is there life after the Stability Pact?', *FT Single Currency in Practice (Dec.)*, 10–13.

—— (1998b), *Integrating Financial Markets in the European Union* (Cheltenham, Edward Elgar Publishing).

—— and S. C. W. Eijffinger (1996), 'The Fundamental Determinants of Financial Integration in the European Union', *Weltwirtschaftliches Archiv*, 132: 432–56.

Lohmann, S. (1992), 'Optimal Commitment in Monetary Policy: Credibility versus Flexibility', *American Economic Review*, 82: 273–86.

Loopesko, B. E. (1984), 'Relationships among Exchange Rates, Intervention and Interest Rates: An Empirical Investigation', *Journal of International Money and Finance*, 3: 257–77.

McCallum, B. T. (1995), 'Two Fallacies Concerning Central-Bank Independence', *American Economic Review*, Papers and Proceedings, 85: 207–11.

McCauley, R. N., and R. W. White (1997), 'The Euro and European Financial Markets', in P. R. Masson, T. H. Krueger, and B. G. Turtelboom (eds.), *EMU and the International Financial System* (Washington, DC, IMF).

McKinnon, R. (1963), 'Optimum Currency Areas', *American Economic Review*, 53: 717–25.

Mayer, C. (1999), European Capital Markets: Competition between Systems', *EIB Papers*, 4(1), 47–57.

Miles, D., and A. Timmermann (1999), 'Risk Sharing and Transition Costs in the Reform of Pension Systems in Europe', *Economic Policy*, 29: 253–86.

Milesi-Ferretti, G. M. (1998), 'Why Capital Controls?: Theory and Evidence', in S. C. W. Eijffinger and H. P. Huizinga (eds.), *Positive Political Economy: Theory and Evidence* (Cambridge, Cambridge University Press).

Mishkin, F. S. (1996), 'The Channels of Monetary Transmission: Lessons for Monetary Policy', *NBER Working Paper*, 5464.

Molle, W. (1994), *The Economics of European Integration* (Aldershot, Dartmouth).

Monti, M. (1998), 'Future Developments in Taxation Systems in the EU', in Austrian Federal Ministry of Finance, Conference Proceedings, *Tax Competition and Co-ordination of Tax Policy in the European Union* (Vienna, Austrian Institute of Economic Research).

Mundell, R. (1961), 'A Theory of Optimal Currency Areas', *American Economic Review*, 51: 657–75.

Oates, W. E. (1972), *Fiscal Federalism* (New York, Harcourt Brace Jovanovich).

Obstfeld, M. (1986), 'Capital Mobility in the World Economy, Theory and Measurement', *Carnegie-Rochester Conference Series on Public Policy*, 24: 55–104.

OECD (1990), *Employment Outlook* (Paris, OECD).

—— (1998a), *Economic Outlook* (Paris, OECD).

—— (1998b), *Employment Outlook* (Paris, OECD).

—— (1999), *EMU Facts, Challenges and Policies* (Paris, OECD).

Ozkan, F. G., and A. Sutherland (1994), 'A Model of the ERM Crisis', *CEPR Discussion Paper*, 879.

Padoa-Schioppa, T. (1999), 'EMU and Banking Supervision', lecture at LSE, 24 Feb. 1999 (http://www.ecb.int.key/sp99024.htm).

Persson, T., and G. Tabellini (1993), 'Designing Institutions for Monetary Stability', *Carnegie-Rochester Conference Series on Public Policy*, 39: 53–84.

Portes, R., and H. Rey (1998), 'The Emergence of the Euro as an International Currency', *Economic Policy*, 26: 307–43.

Poterba, J. (1996), 'Budget Institutions and Fiscal Policy in the U.S. States', *American Economic Review, Papers and Proceedings*, 86: 395–400.

Prast, H., and A. C. J. Stokman (1997), 'Kosten en baten van de EMU: een tussenbalans', *ESB*, 82: 356–8.

Rabobank (1998), *Rabobank's Guide to ECB Watchers* (London)

Reuters (1997), *EMU Explained* (London, Kogan Page).

Rogoff, K. (1985), 'The Optimal Degree of Commitment to an Intermediate Monetary Target', *Quarterly Journal of Economics*, 110: 1169–90.

Sala-i-Martin, X., and J. Sachs (1992), 'Fiscal Federalism and Optimum Currency Areas: Evidence for Europe from the United States', in M. B. Canzoneri, V. Grilli, and P. R. Masson (eds.), *Establishing a Central Bank: Issues in Europe and Lessons from the US* (Cambridge, Cambridge University Press).

Schinasi, G. J., and R. T. Smith (1998), 'Fixed-income Markets in the United States, Europe, and Japan: Some Lessons for Emerging Markets', *IMF Working Paper*, 98/173.

Scobie, H. M. (1997), *The Cost and Timescale for the Switchover to the European Single Currency for the International Securities Market* (Zurich, International Securities Market Association).

Sibert A., and A. Sutherland (1997), 'Monetary Regimens and Labour Market Institutions', *CEPR Discussion Paper* 1731.

Sinn, H.-W. (1990), 'Tax Harmonisation and Tax Competition in Europe', *European Economic Review*, 34: 489–504.

—— (1997), 'The Selection Principle and Market Failure in Systems Competition', *Journal of Public Economics*, 66: 247–74.

—— and H. Feist (1997), 'Eurowinners and Eurolosers: The Distribution of Seigniorage Wealth in EMU', *European Journal of Political Economy*, 13: 665–89.

Stokman, A. C. J. (1995), 'Effects of Exchange Rate Risk on Intra-EC Trade', *De Economist*, 143: 41–54.

Szász, A. (1999), *The Road to European Monetary Union* (London, Macmillan).

Tanzi, V., and H. Z. Zee (1998), 'Consequences of the Economic and Monetary Union: Lessons from the US Experience', in Austrian Federal Ministry of Finance, Conference Proceedings, *Tax Competition and Co-ordination of Tax Policy in the European Union* (Vienna, Austrian Institute of Economic Research).

Tavlas, G. S. (1991), 'On the International Use of Currencies: The Case of the Deutsche Mark', *Princeton Essays in International Finance*, 181.

—— and Ozeki, Y. (1992), 'The Internationalization of Currencies: An Appraisal of the Japanese Yen', *IMF Occasional Paper* 90.

Tiebout, C. M. (1956), 'A Pure Theory of Local Expenditures', *Journal of Political Economy*, 64: 416–24.

Tracy, M. (1989), *Government and Agriculture in Western Europe, 1880–1988* (New York, Harvester Wheatsheaf).

Triffin, R. (1963), 'The Latent Crisis of the Reserve Currencies', *The Banker* (Aug.).

Tsoukalis, L. (1997), *The New European Economy Revisited* (Oxford, Oxford University Press).

Ungerer, H., J. Houvonen, A. Lopez-Claros, and T. Mayer (1990), 'The European Monetary System: Developments and Perspectives', *IMF Occassional Paper*, 73.

Vander Vennet, R. (1999), 'Causes and Consequences of EU Bank Take-overs', in S. C. W. Eijffinger, K. Koedijk, M. Pagano, and R. Portes (eds.), *The Changing European Financial Landscape*, CEPR/ESI conference 1998 (London, Centre for Economic Policy Research).

Viñals, J., and J. F. Jimeno (1996), 'Monetary Union and European Unemployment', *CEPR Discussion Paper*, 1485.

von Hagen, J. (1991), 'A Note on the Empirical Effectiveness of Formal Fiscal Restraints', *Journal of Public Economics*, 44: 199–210.

—— (1992), 'Fiscal Arrangements in a Monetary Union: Evidence from the US', in D. Fair and C. de Boissieux (eds.), *Fiscal Policy, Taxes, and the Financial System in an Increasingly Integrated Europe* (Dordrecht, Kluwer).

—— (1995), 'Inflation and Monetary Targeting in Germany', in L. Leiderman and L. E. O. Svensson (eds.), *Inflation Targets* (London, CEPR).

—— (1999), 'A Fiscal Insurance for the EMU?', paper prepared for the workshop Tools for Regional Stabilisation, The Hague, 12 Feb. 1999.

Wagenvoort, R., and P. Schurer (1999), 'Who are Europe's Efficient Bankers?', *EIB Papers*, 4(1): 105–26.

Walsh, C. E. (1995), 'Optimal Contracts for Central Bankers', *American Economic Review*, 85: 150–67.

Walter, I. (1999), 'Financial Service Strategies in the Euro-zone', *EIB Papers*, 4(1): 145–68.

Watson Wyatt (1997), *Benefits Report Europe USA Canada 1997* (Brussels, Watson Wyatt Data Services Europe).

Weber, A. A. (1991), 'EMU and Asymmetries and Adjustment Problems in the EMS: Some Empirical Evidence', *European Economy*, spec. edn., 1: 187–207.

Williamson, J. (ed.) (1994), *Estimating Equilibrium Exchange Rates* (Washington, DC, Institute for International Economics).

Wilson, J. D. (1999), 'Theories of Tax Competition', *National Tax Journal*, 20: 269–304.

Winston, C. (1993), 'Economic Deregulation: Days of Reckoning for Microeconomists', *Journal of Economic Literature*, 31(3): 1263–89.

Index